Developing Timeshare and Vacation-Ownership Properties

Principal Author
Diane R. Suchman

Contributing Authors
Richard L. Ragatz
Edward D. Stone, Jr.
William B. Renner, Jr.
Robert Koch
Pamela Temples McMullen
Pura Rojas
George Leposky
Kurt P. Gruber
Andrew T. Marcus
Jeffrey A. Owings
Mike Sheridan
Terry J. Lassar
Lloyd Bookout

Foreword by
Christel DeHaan

Urban Land Institute

About ULI–the Urban Land Institute

ULI–the Urban Land Institute is a non-profit education and research institute that is supported and directed by its members. Its mission is to provide responsible leadership in the use of land to enhance the total environment.

ULI sponsors educational programs and forums to encourage an open international exchange of ideas and sharing of experience; initiates research that anticipates emerging land use trends and issues and proposes creative solutions based on that research; provides advisory services; and publishes a wide variety of materials to disseminate information on land use and development.

Established in 1936, the Institute today has more than 15,000 members andassociates from 50 countries representing the entire spectrum of the land use and development disciplines. They include developers, builders, property owners, investors, architects, public officials, planners, real estate brokers, appraisers, attorneys, engineers, financiers, academics, students, and librarians. ULI members contribute to higher standards of land use by sharing their knowledge and experience. The Institute has long been recognized as one of the country's most respected and widely quoted sources of objective information on urban planning, growth, and development.

Richard M. Rosan
President

Project Staff

Rachelle L. Levitt
Senior Vice President, Policy and Practice
Publisher

Gayle Berens
Vice President, Real Estate Development
  Practice

Dean Schwanke
Senior Director, Real Estate Development
  Practice
Project Director

Diane R. Suchman
Project Director and Principal Author

Nancy H. Stewart
Director, Book Program

Carol E. Soble
Manuscript Editor

Helene Redmond/HYR Graphics
Book Design/Layout

Meg Batdorff
Cover Design

Maria-Rose Cain
Word Processor

Diann-Stanley Austin
Associate Director of Publishing
  Operations

Recommended bibliographic listing:
Suchman, Diane R., et al. *Developing Timeshare and Vacation-Ownership Properties.* Washington, D.C.: ULI–the Urban Land Institute, 1999.

ULI Catalog Number: DC2
International Standard Book Number: 0-87420-874-2
Library of Congress Catalog Card Number: 99-63906

Copyright 1999 by ULI–the Urban Land Institute
1025 Thomas Jefferson Street, N.W.
Suite 500 West
Washington, D.C. 20007-5201

Sponsors

This book was made possible through the generous support of the following organizations:

CHRISTEL HOUSE

INTERVAL INTERNATIONAL®

WORLD CLASS VACATION EXCHANGE

RCI®

The World's Premier Exchange Company℠

A Cendant Company

Advisory Committee

About the Authors

Principal Author

Diane R. Suchman is an independent writer and consultant on real estate development, specializing in housing, community development, and revitalization strategies for low-income neighborhoods. She recently served as special assistant to HUD's assistant secretary for policy development and research and previously was director of housing and community development research for the Urban Land Institute. She has also worked as a real estate market analyst. The author of numerous books, articles, and case studies, Suchman has a master's degree in planning from the University of Virginia.

Contributing Authors

Richard L. Ragatz, PhD, is executive vice president of RCI Consulting. A leading market researcher in the resort industry, he specializes in market feasibility analysis, consumer and product research, economic impact analysis, and project evaluation. He has published more than 50 articles on vacation housing and is a frequent speaker at resort industry conferences. Ragatz has a BA in geography and a master of city planning from the University of California, Berkeley, and a PhD from Cornell.

Edward D. Stone, Jr., FASLA, is chair and founder of E D S A, one of the leading planning and landscape architecture practices in the United States, with expertise in planning and design for resort and community development. Stone began his 36 years of professional practice in Ft. Lauderdale, Florida, founding E D S A in 1960. He graduated from Yale University with a degree in architectural design and has a master's degree from Harvard University's Graduate School of Design. As a respected authority on resort and tourism planning and leisure community planning, Stone lectures widely to international audiences. He is a fellow of the American Society of Landscape Architects (ASLA) and was awarded the 1994 ASLA Medal—the highest honor bestowed by the society. Stone also received the 1997 Evelyn Bartlett Award from the Ft. Lauderdale Chapter of the American Institute of Architects.

William B. Renner, Jr., AICP, is an associate principal of E D S A/Edward D. Stone, Jr., and Associates, an international planning and landscape architecture firm based in Ft. Lauderdale, Florida. An expert in urban and community planning, Renner has been responsible for the master planning of large-scale new communities and resort communities in the United States, South America, the Caribbean, Europe, and Asia. Before joining E D S A in 1986, he was a project manager for Westinghouse Communities. Renner received a master's degree in landscape architecture from Harvard University.

Robert Koch is president of Fugleberg Koch, a full-service architecture, interior design, planning, and imaging firm that specializes in the hospitality and residential industries. Koch directs the business development of the firm and oversees design of all the firm's projects. Professional acknowledgments include numerous design awards from the American Institute of Architects, ARDA, and home builder associations. He is a frequent speaker at national seminars on design trends and has written numerous articles for national publications.

Pamela Temples McMullen is the president and founder of Pamela Temples Interiors, Inc., in Orlando, Florida, an award-winning firm that specializes in interior designs for the hospitality industry, including hotels, resorts, and timeshare, as well as the health care industry. McMullen has

more than 20 years of experience in interior design. She is a member of the American Society of Interior Design and has been recognized in *Who's Who in Interior Design.* A frequent speaker at industry conferences, McMullen has taught design at the University of South Carolina and written numerous articles for trade and development magazines.

Pura Rojas is an independent consultant and project manager for Pamela Temples Interiors. She has collaborated with PTI in various design projects and articles since 1989. Rojas is a graduate of Barnard College, Columbia University, with a BA in art history and architecture, and has taken postgraduate courses in art and design at Pratt Institute, the University of Colorado at Boulder, and the University of South Florida.

George Leposky is editor of *Vacation Industry Review,* a bimonthly trade magazine published by Interval International, and is Interval International's director of communications. He coauthored the *AEI Resource Manual,* a study guide published by the American Resort Development Association for the ARDA Education Institute; has written extensively for hospitality-industry trade magazines and newspaper travel sections; and has taught college courses in timeshare management and English composition. Leposky earned bachelor of arts and master of arts degrees in political science from Washington University in St. Louis, Missouri. He attended the Graduate School of Journalism at Columbia University in New York as a fellow in the Advanced Science Writing Program.

Kurt P. Gruber practices real estate law in the Orlando office of Baker & Hostetler, LLP, with special concentration in the resort and leisure industry, which includes resort condominiums, vacation ownership, hotels and motels, membership campgrounds, the exchange industry, and the travel industry. In addition, Gruber assists clients with other real estate issues, such as licensing, title insurance, land acquisition, and development. He received both his undergraduate and law degrees from the University of Texas and is an active member of ARDA.

Andrew T. Marcus is a partner in the national law firm of Baker & Hostetler, LLP, Orlando office. He practices in the area of real estate and related business law, with an emphasis on timeshare and resort industries. Marcus has extensive experience representing condominium, hotel, and timeshare clients in a broad range of development, management, regulatory, association, and ad valorem tax matters. In addition to being an active member of ARDA, Marcus serves as general counsel to the Florida Vacation Rental Managers Association and is a member of the American Hotel & Motel Association's Condominium and Vacation Ownership Committee. He received his bachelor's degree from the State University of New York at Binghamton and his law degree with honors from the University of Florida. He is a member of the Florida Bar and the American and Orange County Bar associations.

Jeffrey A. Owings is senior vice president of FINOVA Capital Corporation's Resort Finance Division, a group he has managed since 1991. Through this division, FINOVA, a financial services company headquartered in Phoenix, Arizona, provides one-stop shopping to resort developers through its acquisition, construction, working capital, equity, and receivables financing. Owings holds a BS degree with a specialty in finance from Arizona State University's College of Business Administration.

Mike Sheridan, a full-time journalist based in Houston, Texas, has spent more than three decades as a professional writer. Sheridan, who has written articles for a number of national magazines and international periodicals, spent a year in Japan as a Fulbright Scholar. He is a graduate of Columbia University in New York City as well as of the University of Hawaii in Honolulu. Sheridan specializes in real estate–related topics and in corporate financial journalism.

Terry Jill Lassar, an independent communications consultant, provides public relations, writing, and research services to developers, planners, architects, and public sector clients. Lassar was on the research staff of the Urban Land Institute for five years. She is the author or contributing author of five books on planning and development subjects and has published extensively in *Urban Land* magazine. She earned an undergraduate degree from Boston University and graduate degrees from the University of Virginia and Washington University.

Lloyd Bookout, ULI's vice president for programs, joined the ULI staff in 1987 and has held several senior staff positions with the Institute. He also has worked as a development consultant and a public planner. The author of numerous books and articles on real estate issues, Bookout has a BA from the University of California, Santa Barbara, and a master's in urban planning from the California State Polytechnic University.

Acknowledgments

This book represents the cooperative efforts of many talented people. I had the pleasure of working with an outstanding advisory committee, whose members offered suggestions, answered questions, provided information, and reviewed the manuscript. The chapter and case study authors were all highly professional industry experts whose contributions reflect what they have learned from their many years of practical experience in timeshare development. The great organizations that underpin the timeshare and vacation-ownership industry—American Resort Development Association, Interval International, and Resort Condominiums International—generously provided up-to-date information and examples.

In addition, I am grateful to the many industry leaders who took time to talk with me and share their insights, including Ed McMullen, Robert A. Miller, Richard Ragatz, Don Harill, Steve Miller, Jan Wyatt, George Donovan, Jeff Jackard, David Matheson, Bob Howeth, and all of the developers of the projects featured as case studies in Chapter 9. ULI's Rachelle Levitt, Gayle Berens, and Dean Schwanke gave me good advice and unstinting support in developing the manuscript, and Joan Campbell helped ferret out current timeshare research. On behalf of all the authors, I would also like to thank ULI's production team, led by Nancy Stewart and including Carol Soble, Helene Redmond, Meg Batdorff, and Kim Rusch, for transforming the raw manuscript into an attractive book.

Diane R. Suchman

Foreword

Who would have dreamed 25 years ago that timesharing, also called vacation ownership, would redefine the way people vacation? When we founded Resort Condominiums International, Inc. (RCI) in 1974, our business was vacation exchange—which we pioneered. After achieving limited success in Europe (where there was no exchange component), timesharing was just on the American horizon. The variety and flexibility offered through vacation exchange—trading a timeshare week for different resort locations and/or different vacation times—proved to be the "missing link" needed to gain consumer acceptance of timesharing.

It is hard to believe that our pioneering efforts, and those of the exchange companies that followed RCI, would become the catalyst in transforming a cottage industry into a global phenomenon—and the fastest-growing sector of the leisure travel industry. In 1998, 2 million American families took a timeshare vacation, representing more than 7 million people of all ages. To put that figure in perspective, just 5.5 million Americans took a cruise vacation last year. Timesharing is truly becoming "mainstream."

For the last 20 years, timeshare-owner studies have consistently shown that the primary motivations for purchasing include "exchange opportunity with other resorts," "sav[ing] money on future vacation costs," and the "certainty of having quality accommodations." The most recent YP&B/Yankelovich Partners National Leisure Travel MONITOR® study, which tracks U.S. consumer lifestyle preferences, reveals that 75 percent of today's leisure travelers are aware of timesharing and that 15 percent are interested in purchasing. In addition, 58 percent say they have an interest in vacationing in a resort condominium sometime in the next two years, suggesting enormous potential for increasing the penetration rate of U.S. timeshare owners. International leisure research points to similar conclusions.

The expansion into timesharing by brands such as Hilton, Marriott, Westin, Hyatt, Embassy, Radisson, and Ramada has elevated industry awareness and credibility. Wall Street's acceptance of timesharing could not have been envisioned ten years ago. A handful of successful public offerings—including Intrawest, Signature (now Sunterra), Silverleaf, Trendwest, and Vistana—have made their appearance in the last few years. Timesharing is here—and for the long term.

Fueled by a quarter-century of impressive growth, timesharing is experiencing the most dramatic changes in its history. The movement toward vacation clubs, point-based use programs, and value-added owner services will redefine timesharing in the years ahead and make timeshare purchases more appealing to a wider audience. In ten years, it is projected that 20 percent of all U.S. households with incomes of $50,000 or more will be timeshare owners, up dramatically from today's 6 percent penetration rate.

While the timeshare industry has proved to be a solid financial performer—with an annual compounded sales growth rate of 16 percent over the last decade—it also has proved to be one of the most complex and challenging businesses. Timesharing involves multiple disciplines—real estate, finance, hospitality, and travel—all rolled into one. It has to be promoted, sold, and serviced for a lifetime. The rewards of timesharing can be outstanding, but success requires mastery of all its disciplines.

The purpose of this book is to identify the opportunities and challenges associated with timesharing. If you are considering entry into the timeshare industry, if you are new to the business, or if you need to become more broadly informed, *Developing Timeshare and Vacation-Ownership Properties* is an essential reference.

This long-awaited book is the Institute's third timeshare title and first update in 17 years. ULI's first timeshare-focused publication, *Timesharing,* was released in 1977, when only 50 U.S. timeshare projects had been in existence for longer than 12 months. *Developing Timeshare and Vacation-Ownership Properties* should be required reading for all students of the timeshare industry—from novices to veterans.

Christel DeHaan
President and Founder
Christel House Inc.

Contents

Developing Timeshare and Vacation-Ownership Properties

Chapter 1
Introduction

Diane R. Suchman

T imeshare and vacation ownership is the most rapidly growing and creatively evolving segment of the resort development industry. As shown in Figure 1, between 1980 and 1997 the annual volume of total timeshare sales increased from $490 million to $6 billion—a compounded worldwide annual growth rate (CAGR) of 16 percent. Significantly, industry expansion continued even during economic and/or real estate recessions, such as the 1990–1991 recession in the United States.

With the business and its buyers becoming increasingly sophisticated, timesharing is rapidly moving out from under the shadow cast by its history of questionable industry practices. At the same time, the business is growing more diverse, complicated, and competitive.

What Is Timeshare?

While similar in many respects to resort hotels and condominiums, timeshare developments can be distinguished from other types of real estate development in many ways—particularly, as described later, by their target market, project and unit design, purchase and use arrangements, project financing, legal structure, marketing approach, and operations.

Timeshare and vacation-ownership resorts provide a type of shared ownership through which a buyer purchases access to use a furnished dwelling unit for a specific length of time (usually a week) each year. The purchase may be for a set period of years or

Figure 1-1 Growth in the Worldwide Timeshare Industry: 1980–1997

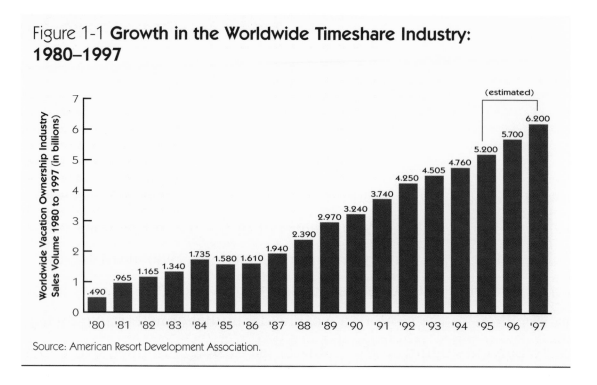

Source: American Resort Development Association.

in perpetuity and may involve fee-simple ownership or a right to use the accommodation. It is generally regulated as a form of real estate ownership. Timeshare developments vary widely in location, design, and associated amenities and services. They may be conversions from other uses or "purpose-built" freestanding projects or part of a larger, multiple-use resort. Timeshare developers may be local or international, private or public companies. Given that timeshare is an unsought good and that potential buyers are widely dispersed, marketing and sales of timeshare intervals is particularly challenging and expensive. And, because purchasers are making a long-term commitment to the use and exchange value of the product, management is critical to a project's—and a developer's—success.

To reflect the variety of timeshare product types and to underscore the idea that a timeshare purchase is the purchase of a lifetime of vacation experiences, the term "timeshare" is often used interchangeably with "interval ownership" or, increasingly, "vacation ownership." The latter term is used especially to refer to membership in

vacation clubs, in which buyers purchase a bundle of vacation rights (typically specified at the time of purchase as a certain number of points) rather than the traditional timeshare product of yearly access to a specific unit at a specific time. Preference for the term "vacation ownership" also reflects the industry's determination to recast its public image.

For the purchaser, the primary advantage of owning a timeshare versus a traditional second home is affordability. Prices for new timeshare intervals range from $5,000 to more than $100,000 per unit/week; most hover in the $10,000 price range. In addition, buyers pay a yearly fee to cover resort operations and management.

Another major advantage of timeshare ownership is flexibility. Through affiliation with an international exchange company, such as Resort Condominiums International (RCI) or Interval International (II), timeshare owners can, for a nominal fee, exchange their own interval for a similarly valued interval elsewhere in the world. In 1997, according to the American Resort Development Association (ARDA),

42 percent of U.S. timeshare owners chose to exchange their intervals. Recently, use of a timeshare purchase has become even more flexible with the introduction of new product types, such as point systems and vacation clubs (described in chapter 3), which enable buyers to use their timeshare purchase to gain access to a wide variety of vacation experiences and travel-related services.

History

Timeshare is a general term that originated in the computer industry; it referred to shared use of computer facilities. In the mid-1970s, the term came to be used in connection with shared use of lodging accommodations.

The history of timeshare and vacation ownership began in the 1960s at a ski resort in the French Alps. The first developments in the United States were located in Florida during the late 1960s. Overbuilding had created a number of underperforming or unsold condominium apartments, hotels, and motels. By converting these properties to timeshare developments through legal subdivision of "whole" units into 52-week intervals, developers found that they could respond to market demand for much more affordable prices while realizing significantly greater profits. A major concern was market resistance to vacationing at the same place and time each year, which was addressed with the formation of the two primary timeshare exchange companies in the mid-1970s. In the early 1980s, timesharing was reintroduced to Europe and began its expansion to a worldwide market.

Because early U.S. timeshare developments were too often poorly constructed and relied on high-pressure and unethical sales practices, the industry as a whole earned a measure of disrepute. Despite increasing regulation of the industry, especially at the state level, and self-policing efforts led by the ARDA, the industry still

The clubhouse at Disney's Old Key West Resort in Orlando, Florida, viewed here from the lagoon, has won awards for architectural design.

A forest of palms shades the walkways that wind between the thatch-roofed villas at Club Cascadas de Baja in Cabo San Lucas, Mexico.

struggles to shed its tainted image. The recent entry of national and international brand-name hospitality companies has helped reinvigorate and reshape the industry by making it more competitive, quality-conscious, and creative. In addition, brand participation has helped spur greater consumer confidence and interest in the timeshare concept.

As noted, the expansion of the timeshare industry is taking place not only in the United States but also on a worldwide basis. The trend is evident in the increasing number and locational variety of resorts as well as in the emerging global nature of development companies, the growth of international development partnerships and franchises, and the formation of networks of affiliations for the exchange of timeshare accommodations and other vacation products and travel services.

Snapshot of the Industry

Today, the industry accounts for approximately 5,000 timeshare and vacation-ownership resorts in 81 countries, with global annual sales estimated at approximately $6 billion. More than 3 million households in 174 countries own timeshares. The largest proportion—almost half—of timeshare resorts is located in North America. Europe is the second most popular vacation-ownership des-

◆ The American Resort Development Association (ARDA)

The American Resort Development Association, based in Washington, D.C., is a not-for-profit trade association established in 1969 to provide its members with leadership and information about the resort and vacation-ownership industry. The organization works closely with state and federal officials, both proactively and reactively, on issues affecting the resort and vacation-ownership business and has taken the lead in helping shape the industry's professional standards. In particular, ARDA's Code of Standards and Ethics, to which all members must agree to adhere, outlines detailed professional guidelines for all facets of industry practice, from real estate development to marketing to hospitality management. The code has helped transform both the image and reality of the vacation-ownership industry's relationship with its customers.

ARDA's approximately 1,000 member companies, which represent more than 4,000 resorts, come from all facets of the international resort development industry, including timeshare and second-home resorts, community development properties, vacation-ownership resorts, and fractional interests. Types of member companies range from privately held single-site developers to global corporations.

ARDA's stated mission is to foster and promote the growth of the industry and to serve its members through

- ethics enforcement;
- education;
- legislative advocacy;
- membership development; and
- public relations.

ARDA fulfills its mission through meetings and networking opportunities, legislative advocacy, education programs, research on industry performance, communication of industry information and issues within and outside the organization, and volunteer leadership opportunities for its members.

ARDA created two organizations to serve specific needs.

1. The ARDA Resort Owners' Coalition (ARDA-ROC) is a separate legal entity established in 1989 to represent directly the needs and concerns of vacation owners through legislative and regulatory advocacy and research. The voluntary contributions of individual owners fund ARDA-ROC.

2. The ARDA Education Institute (AEI) creates learning and professional advancement opportunities for professionals currently working in the vacation-ownership industry and professionals seeking to enter the industry. AEI offers educational sessions, seminars, publications, tests, and professional designations (Associate Resort Professional—ARP; Registered Resort Professional—RRP).

In addition, the ARDA International Foundation, a 501(c)(3) nonprofit organization, was formed to support, conduct, and disseminate research and technical studies and to develop expanded educational resources for industry professionals and the public.

Source: American Resort Development Association.

Timeshare owners enjoy a beautiful setting amid mountain and sea at Sunterra Corporation's Royal Palm Resort in St. Maarten.

tination, with more than 1,000 timeshare resorts.

As of 1996, the U.S. timeshare industry[1] included 1,204 resorts and an estimated 64,300 timeshare units. Three hundred, or 25 percent of all U.S. timeshare resorts, were in active sales. In 1996, the number of weeks sold totaled 218,000 at an average price of $10,000 per week, resulting in a total dollar sales volume of $2.18 billion. The industry has seen an average increase in timeshare sales volume of approximately 13.8 percent per year. The average occupancy rate for U.S. timeshare resorts is 87.5 percent.

As of 1997, a total of 1.77 million households, or 1.95 percent of the population, owned timeshare intervals in the United States. By 1998, the total number of U.S. timeshare owners exceeded 1.9 million and the total dollar value of U.S. timeshare sales approached $3 billion.

As described in detail in chapter 2, the typical vacation owner is an upper-middle-income, middle-aged, well-educated couple. The home region of purchasers has become increasingly diverse, with demand spread throughout the country.

As of 1997, the industry directly employed more than 50,000 people, although direct and indirect employees together generated close to 270,000 jobs. The timeshare industry contributed $18 billion to the U.S. economy through employment, consumer and business expenditures, and taxes.[2] Clearly, the industry has a positive economic impact on a variety of sectors, including service and retail; manufacturing; finance, insurance, and real estate; and transportation and public facilities.

Hilton Grand Vacations Club Sea World in Orlando, Florida, offers a comfortable family setting, with units that feature a large kitchen and spacious living area furnished in a brightly colored summer cottage theme.

Marriott Vacation Club International's Desert Springs Villas II reflects the terrain and colors of its location in both the interior treatment of the villas and the resort's architectural design.

◆ Glossary of Timeshare Terms

Exchange—Trading the use of all or part of an owner's time in a timeshare accommodation. The trade may be for either the use of the same or a different unit within the same resort at a different time or for the use of a comparable accommodation at another resort at the same or a different time. Systems that allow split weeks or use of points enable many combinations and variations of exchange.

Exchange Company—An organization that provides services, such as reservations and information, to timeshare owners and developers to effect and facilitate the exchange process. The two primary exchange companies in the United States are Resort Condominiums International and Interval International.

Fee-Simple Ownership—Deeded ownership (in a timeshare, of a particular unit during a specific period of time) in perpetuity.

Fixed Time—Ownership of a timeshare unit during a specific time—typically, a specific week—of the year.

Floating Time—Ownership of a timeshare unit for a period of time—typically, a week—that may vary at the owner's discretion, usually within a given season.

Fractional—A timeshare product offered for periods of time greater than one week per year—typically, between one-fifteenth and one-quarter interest.

Leasehold Product—A timeshare product in which a purchaser's property rights exist for a specified period of years (for example, 30 years), after which the rights revert to the resort's owner.

Lockoff—A portion of a timeshare unit that is designed to be occupied separately from the rest of the unit, enabling owners to maximize opportunities for use and exchange.

Minivacation—A discounted or free short visit to a timeshare resort used in many marketing programs to permit prospective purchasers to sample the product.

Nondisturbance Clause—A clause in the sales contract that assures the timeshare owner of his or her accommodation rights, even if the developer defaults.

Point System—A system through which timeshare purchasers obtain a number of "points" or symbolic values that can be used to obtain various vacation accommodations and services. Timeshare purchasers who buy points may or may not obtain deeded ownership to a specific unit/week.

Rescission—The decision to change one's mind about a (timeshare) purchase, made within the statutory cooling-off period (that period under federal or state law when the purchaser can rescind his or her purchase decision without penalty and receive a refund on any deposit).

Right-to-Use—The purchase of access to an accommodation for a specific time period, with no ownership of the underlying real estate.

Split Week—Division of use of a week's time in a vacation-ownership property into two or more segments used at different times. Through exchange, the times may also be used in different locations.

Undivided Interest—A form of unsubdivided property ownership that typically provides for tenancy in common, with bylaws stipulating the owner's rights and obligations.

Unit/Week—The use of a unit for a week—the traditional timeshare purchase.

Vacation Club—A timeshare product that involves a system of multiple, geographically diverse resorts under the management of a single entity. The club format allows access to any of the club's accommodations and related travel and leisure services.

Purpose, Audience, and Organization of the Book

This book is intended to provide information on the nature of today's timeshare development industry and the current state of the art in timeshare development. The information is oriented to real estate developers, public officials, members of the financial community, providers of development services, academicians, and others with a basic understanding of the real estate development process.

The remainder of the book begins with an exploration of the universe of prospective buyers of timeshare intervals—their demographic, economic, and psychographic profiles, why they buy, how they

Resort Properties's
Hollywood Mirage
resort in Tenerife,
Canary Islands.

Courtesy of RCI Europe

feel about their purchase, and the likely depth of the market. The next chapter provides an overview of the range of timeshare products on the market today and how they are evolving. Subsequent chapters highlight the most important considerations in project planning and design, marketing, and financing and the legal and regulatory framework that governs timeshare development practices. A chapter on the timeshare development business outlines the most important ways the business differs from other types of real estate development. Chapter 9 presents ten case studies that offer examples of today's range and variety of timeshare development activity. Together, the case studies represent different product types, different purchase arrangements and legal

structures, different locations and target markets, and the work of different types of developers. The final chapter describes the ways in which the industry is changing and evolving in response to consumer demand, increasing and sophisticated competition, technological advances, and shifts in the larger economic environment.

The information in this book is based on the professional knowledge and experience of the various authors, supplemented by recently published information and interviews with timeshare developers and other industry participants. Information in the case studies was derived from site visits, interviews with project developers, and printed materials provided by the developers. Though the authors believe that the material in the book is timely, correct, and useful, they have made no attempt to verify independently the accuracy of the information.

Notes

1. This and the following two paragraphs were excerpted from an undated ARDA fact sheet, "The Vacation Ownership Industry in the U.S." The data are based on a 1996 survey by KPMG Peat Marwick LLP and Stephen Miner Research and Appraisal, the updated results of which were published by ARDA and the Alliance for Timeshare Excellence in *The Resort Timeshare Industry in the United States: Overview and Economic Analysis 1997 (Washington, D.C.: ARDA, 1997)*; 1998 data are from RCI Consulting.

2. ARDA and the Alliance for Timeshare Excellence, *The Resort Timeshare Industry in the United States: Overview and Economic Impact Analysis 1997*, p.3.

Chapter 2

Resort Timeshare Owners

Richard L. Ragatz, PhD, RCI Consulting

Timeshare developers seeking to understand the market for timeshare resorts need to look first to the nature, characteristics, and reported experiences of consumers who have purchased the timeshare product in the past, especially in the recent past. This chapter describes the buyers of resort timeshares, including their demographics, the purchasing process, and various aspects of consumer satisfaction. It concludes with a brief look at existing and potential market demand for resort timeshares.

Most information in the chapter is derived from a series of ten consumer surveys of resort timeshare owners conducted over the past 20 years by RCI Consulting (formerly Ragatz Associates).[1] The surveys were based on random samples of resort timeshare owners residing throughout the United States irrespective of the date or characteristics of their purchase. Collectively, almost 50,000 timeshare owners responded to the surveys.

Notable changes have occurred in the resort timeshare industry during the period covered by the surveys. The industry has expanded tremendously. Annual sales volume in U.S. timeshare resorts grew from less than $300 million in 1978 to almost $3 billion in 1998. The number of U.S. timeshare resorts has increased from 240 to over 1,200. The number of U.S. households owning timeshare has grown from less than 100,000 to over 1.9 million.

Major changes also have occurred in the types of companies involved in the timeshare industry. Participating companies have

Figure 2-1 **Median Income (All Timeshare Owners versus U.S. Population)**

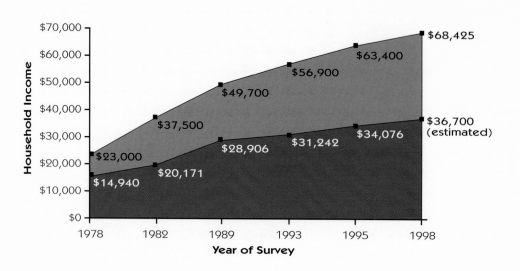

Source: Richard Ragatz, *Timeshare Purchasers: Who They Are, Why They Buy* (Eugene, Oregon: RCI Consulting, 1998).

evolved from small to medium-sized firms to major hotel companies and corporations worth hundreds of millions of dollars. Likewise, the product has improved, new concepts have emerged, and the entire industry has gained in stature and credibility. This chapter documents the effects of these changes from a consumer perspective.

Characteristics of Timeshare Owners

As described below, the typical timeshare consumer is an upper-middle-income, middle- to upper-aged, well-educated couple. Of course, this is simply an aggregate profile. Increasingly important segments of the market include high-income households, singles, older owners, and those with a higher education. In other words, as prices for timeshare intervals increase, as the product improves, and as the concept continues to gain stature and credibility, the consumer profile tends to move up the socioeconomic ladder.

Household Income

As shown in Figure 2-1, the median household income of timeshare owners has increased dramatically since the first national survey, from $23,000 in 1978 to $68,425 in 1998, for a 197.5 percent increase over 20 years. Owners' median income increased by 7.9 percent in just the past three years. And, over time, the median income of timeshare owners has increased more than the median income of all U.S. households (which has grown by only 145.6 percent since 1978).

As shown in Figure 2-2, timeshare-owning households have considerably higher median incomes than U.S. households in general—$68,425 compared with $36,700. Some 73 percent of timeshare owners have incomes over $50,000 while only 34.3 percent of all U.S. households can claim the same. Recent timeshare owners—those who purchased in 1996 and 1997—are even more affluent than previous owners, with a median income of $70,050. The proportion of higher-income timeshare buyers has also grown. In 1978,

Figure 2-2 Resort Timeshare Owners and Recent Purchasers Compared with All Households in the United States

Characteristic	Percentage of Resort Timeshare-Owning Households		All U.S. Households[1]
	All Owners	Recent Purchasers (1996 and 1997)	
Household Income			
Under $50,000	27.0%	24.1%	65.6%
$50,000 to $74,999	31.2%	32.3%	18.0%
$75,000 to $99,999	20.2%	20.6%	8.1%
$100,000 and over	21.5%	23.1%	8.2%
Total	100.0%	100.0%	100.0%
Approximate median	$68,425	$70,050	$36,700[2]
Age of Household Head			
Under 35	4.9%	8.9%	24.2%
35 to 44	19.7%	20.5%	23.6%
45 to 54	29.0%	29.0%	18.7%
55 to 64	23.3%	22.5%	12.3%
65 and over	23.1%	19.1%	21.2%
Total	100.0%	100.0%	100.0%
Average	54	52	46
Household Type			
Single female	8.7%	8.0%	29.3%
Single male	4.1%	4.1%	16.9%
Couple	87.2%	87.9%	53.8%
Total	100.0%	100.0%	100.0%
Educational Attainment of Household Head			
High school or less	21.1%	20.8%	51.7%
Bachelor's degree (at least)	57.4%	57.1%	24.5%[2]
Graduate degree	27.1%	25.9%	7.8%

[1]Source: *Current Population Survey* (Washington, D.C.: Bureau of the Census, 1997); and Richard Ragatz, *Timeshare Purchasers: Who They Are, Why They Buy* (Eugene, Oregon: RCI Consulting, 1998), p. 6.

[2]Estimated.

only 9.3 percent of purchasers had incomes over $50,000 compared with 72.9 percent in 1998. Today, almost a quarter have incomes over $100,000.

Reasons for the dramatic increase in the income of timeshare owners include general income inflation in the United States over the past 20 years as well as the increasing income of earlier timeshare buyers over time, the increasing cost of timeshare intervals, and the increasing attractiveness of the timeshare concept to higher-income households (due to improving product, market entry of more brand-name development companies, and so forth).

A bubbling spa within the main pool at the clubhouse complex delights vacationers at Marriott Vacation Club International's Cypress Harbour Resort in Orlando, Florida.

Age of Household Head

The average age of the head of all time-share-owning households has increased significantly since 1978, from 46 to 54 years in 1998. In 1978, 24.2 percent of timeshare household heads were under 30 years of age, and only 3.2 percent were 65 or over. In 1998, the proportions for all owners were only 1.2 percent and 23.1 percent, respectively. This trend does not suggest, however, that older households now tend to be more frequent purchasers of time-share; rather, it simply reflects the aging of a large base of earlier purchasers.

In fact, most recent purchasers are younger than all current owners. For example, of those buying in 1996 or 1997, nearly one in ten (8.9 percent) was under 35 compared with only one in 20 (4.9 percent) of all owners. Nonetheless, the large share of the overall timeshare-owning population (both existing and most recent purchasers) is between 40 and 60 years of age (52.5 percent).

On the whole, timeshare ownership continues to appeal primarily to age groups that tend to enjoy a significant level of discretionary income—persons age 35 or older. Before age 35, most Americans cannot readily afford a discretionary purchase of the magnitude of a timeshare, and many are not even settled enough to want a timeshare. At the other end of the spectrum, the upper age limits of purchasers is not as readily apparent. Even though census data indicate that discretionary income tends to decline significantly after age 60, nearly one-third (30.2 percent) of all timeshare purchasers in 1996 or 1997 were 60 or older, and nearly one-fifth (19.1 percent) were 65 or older. The data are counterintuitive; it would seem that most older Americans need to conserve resources during their retirement years and, with children no longer living at home, would not need/desire family vacations. Nonetheless, strong evidence suggests that an affluent senior population has both the ability and willingness to purchase timeshare intervals.

Heads of households that own timeshares are more frequently represented in the middle- to upper-age categories of 35 to 64 than are heads of all U.S. households. In fact, 71.9 percent of the former group and only 53.8 percent of the latter group are in the middle- to upper-age categories.

Household Type

The vast majority (87.2 percent) of time-share owners are couples while 12.8 percent are either single males (4.1 percent) or single females (8.7 percent). These figures have changed somewhat since the first survey in 1978 when 92.6 percent of owners were couples, 3.8 percent single males, and 3.6 percent single females. A plausible explanation for the changes is that a growing proportion of earlier purchasers are now single through divorce or the death of a spouse. By comparison, single individuals head a much larger proportion of all U.S. households (46.2 percent compared with only 12.8 percent of all timeshare-owning households). Among the most recent (1996 or 1997) purchasers,

87.9 percent are couples. The remaining 12.1 percent are either single males (4.1 percent) or single females (8 percent).

Nearly two-thirds—65.2 percent—of owners have no children under 18 years of age living at home. That this figure is up considerably from 1978's 39.4 percent is not surprising given that 46.4 percent of all current owners are 55 years of age or older. The high childless component also reflects the growing proportion of single households in the United States as well as the share of couples who choose not to have children. As might be expected, their higher representation in the younger age categories makes the most recent (1996 or 1997) purchasers more likely than all timeshare owners to have children under 18 living at home (36.4 percent compared with 34.8 percent).

Educational Attainment

The high level of educational attainment among timeshare owners continues to be an important distinguishing characteristic. For example, 57.4 percent of all timeshare owners and 57.1 percent of the most recent (1996 or 1997) purchasers reported that their head of household had at least a bachelor's degree. This figure compares with only 24.5 percent of all household heads nationwide.

Making the Timeshare Purchase

Motivations for Purchasing

Figure 2-3 charts trends in the factors motivating consumer purchase of timeshare intervals. The figure shows that the ranking among motivating factors has remained largely the same, although more recent buyers evidence some change in their motivations.

As in all past national timeshare owner surveys, the 1998 survey revealed "exchange opportunity with other resorts" as the most frequently cited motivation for purchasing a timeshare. Over four-fifths (84.2 percent) of all timeshare owners and

Timeshare buyers often vacation in family groups, and children find much to do at Hampton Vacation Resorts's Oak Plantation in Orlando, Florida.

Figure 2-3 **Most Important Motivations for Purchasing Timeshare (All Timeshare Owners and Most Recent Purchasers)**

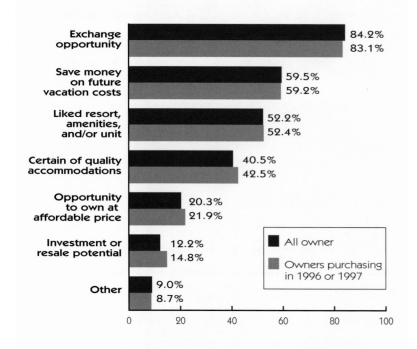

Source: Richard Ragatz, *Timeshare Purchasers: Who They Are, Why They Buy* (Eugene, Oregon: RCI Consulting, 1998), p.23.

checked reasons were "liked the resort, amenities and/or unit" and "certainty of having quality accommodations." The most infrequently checked motivations were "opportunity to own at affordable price" and "investment or resale potential."

It is interesting that 38 percent checked "investment or resale potential" in the 1978 survey. This proportion has declined in each successive survey: 37.3 percent in 1982, 27 percent in 1989, 18.2 percent in 1993, 14.7 percent in 1995, and only 12.2 percent in 1998. One reason for the decline is that, in recent years, salespersons have correctly placed little, if any, emphasis on the investment/resale issue during sales presentations. The decline also indicates that responsible developers, industry associations, and consumer protection agencies have succeeded in their efforts to oppose the selling of timeshare as an investment. It also may reflect recognition among owners that timeshare intervals often can be difficult to resell at a profit.

Reasons for Hesitating Before Purchase

The surveys asked respondents to indicate which of several reasons caused them to hesitate before buying their timeshare. In the 1998 survey, the most frequently checked response was "dislike the idea of an annual maintenance fee" (43.6 percent). About one-third or more of all owners in the 1998 survey checked only three other items: "was not sure would make enough use of it" (39.7 percent), "concept was new or unfamiliar" (35.7 percent), and "cost too much" (32.4 percent).

The proportion checking "concept was new or unfamiliar" has remained fairly constant since the early surveys. As the concept of timesharing becomes more widely understood, however, lack of familiarity is emerging as less of a factor among recent purchasers (26 percent marked the item compared with 35.7 percent of all owners). Hesitation because of "had heard

83.1 percent of all recent (1996 or 1997) purchasers checked "exchange opportunity" as one of the three most important reasons for their purchase. Exchange opportunity has increased in importance since 1978, when only 75.3 percent of owners checked it. Obviously, the flexibility of use in resort locations, which is made possible by affiliation with an exchange company at relatively little additional cost to the timeshare owner, continues to be a major factor in the timeshare-buying decision.

The next most frequently checked purchase motivation in the 1998 survey was, as in most previous surveys, to "save money on future vacation costs." Nearly three-fifths (59.5 percent) of all 1998 owners and 59.2 percent of those purchasing in 1996 or 1997 checked this item. For both sets of owners, the next most frequently

or read something negative about time-sharing" remained about the same among all owners in 1998 as in past surveys (31.5 percent). It was, however, lower among recent purchasers at 28.1 percent, indicating that the timeshare industry's public relations effort is succeeding.

"Was not sure would make enough use of it" was the second item checked by more than one-third (39.7 percent) of all 1998 respondents and 40.3 percent purchasing in 1996 or 1997. This figure has grown significantly since earlier surveys, perhaps suggesting that owners either have less discretionary time or now have a greater number and variety of choices in how they use their leisure time.

With the exception of "dislike the idea of annual maintenance fee," most other reasons for hesitation have remained fairly constant when comparing all owners in the 1998 survey against all owners in pre-vious surveys. In 1982, only one in three (32.2 percent) timeshare owners indicated that maintenance fees were a reason for hesitation. In the current survey, 43.6 percent checked this item as an issue.

Certain variations in responses between 1996 and 1997 purchasers and all owners reflect changes unfolding in the timeshare industry. For example,

◆ improving sales techniques are apparent in that only 22.2 percent of recent purchasers checked "sales presentation was too high-pressured" compared with 27.2 percent of all owners; and

◆ the increasing complexity of the industry's new products and concepts is evident in that 10.8 percent of recent purchasers checked "concept was complicated to understand" compared with only 7.7 percent of all owners. In all previous surveys, the proportion was well under 10 percent.

Designed to appeal especially to golf aficionados, Marriott's Grande Vista Resort in Orlando, Florida, is located adjacent to the Faldo Golf Institute, which includes a nine-hole golf course, 27-hole championship putting course, computer and video instruction studio, and practice areas.

How Purchasers First Heard About Resort

The two most frequent means by which all owners first heard of their timeshare resort are direct mail (30.1 percent) and an off-premises contact (OPC, described in chapter 4) (21.7 percent). The decreasing use of direct mail in the timeshare industry is illustrated by the fact that only 21.2 percent of recent purchasers first learned of their resort through the mail. On the other hand, contact through telemarketing grew from 5.3 percent of all owners before 1982 to 11.8 percent of those purchasing in 1996 and 1997, for an increase of 122.6 percent.

Referrals from a friend or relative decreased from a high of 22.2 percent in the 1982 survey to 15.5 percent among those purchasing in 1996 or 1997. Other methods have remained fairly constant over time. It appears that few buyers were attracted to their timeshare through print or media advertising, probably reflecting the industry's limited reliance on these communication channels.

Source from Which Timeshare Was Acquired

The vast majority (80.6 percent) of all owners purchased their interval from a salesperson at the resort where they own. However, of those buying in 1996 or 1997, only 77.7 percent purchased their interval from a salesperson at their resort. The difference may represent an increase in both resales and intervals acquired through auctions or as a gift or inheritance. The proportion of all owners who purchased at resale increased from 1.8 percent in 1989 to 9.5 percent in 1998. The proportion of resales among most recent purchasers is even higher, at 12.4 percent—more than one in ten new purchases. The proportion of owners who acquired their interval via an auction, gift, or inheritance grew from 0.5 percent in 1989 to 2.1 percent in 1998.

Shopping for Timeshare

Most industry observers believe that timeshare sales prospects are increasingly knowledgeable about timesharing. Survey results bear out this observation. Only 16

Timeshare units are designed to be a "home away from home" for vacationing families or friends. As seen in this view from the kitchen of a villa at Vistana Resort in Orlando, occupants can eat at the kitchen bar, the dining room table, or a table on the balcony or patio, or they can enjoy a night out in a local restaurant.

Courtesy of Vistana, Inc.

percent of respondents—about one in six —purchased during the first sales presentation they attended. Nearly one-third (29.9 percent) attended one other sales presentation while over half (54.1 percent) attended two or more other sales presentations in addition to the one during which they decided to buy.

On average, respondents report that they attended 3.3 presentations before becoming timeshare owners, including an average of 1.1 sales presentations at the resort where they purchased (including the presentation during which they purchased) and an average of 2.2 presentations at other resorts.

A comparison of the results of the 1992 and 1998 surveys reveals a significant trend toward increased shopping for a resort timeshare before the actual purchase. The proportion of respondents attending more than one sales presentation at the resort where they most recently purchased an interval increased from 6.1 percent in 1992 to 12.1 percent in 1998. The proportion of respondents attending a sales presentation at another resort before purchasing their most recent timeshare increased from 34.1 percent in 1992 to 84 percent in 1998.

Satisfaction with the Timeshare Purchase

General Satisfaction

As shown in Figure 2-4, an extremely high 81.1 percent of respondents expressed satisfaction with their timeshare purchase, including 52.8 percent who are very satisfied. The combined satisfaction rates are up from 75.3 percent in 1995; only 6.8 percent of respondents expressed any dissatisfaction with their purchase.

How Closely Timeshare Ownership Experiences Match Expectations

Another measure of owner satisfaction is the degree to which the experiences of ownership have matched owners' expecta-

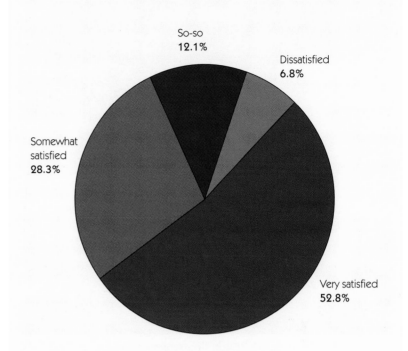

Figure 2-4 **Satisfaction with Timeshare Purchase**

So-so 12.1%

Dissatisfied 6.8%

Somewhat satisfied 28.3%

Very satisfied 52.8%

Source: Richard Ragatz, *The Benefits of Owning Resort Timesharing* (Eugene, Oregon: RCI Consulting, 1998), p. 34.

tions at the time of purchase. In a strongly positive result, 74.6 percent of owners say that ownership has at least matched their expectations. A similar proportion report that they are very satisfied or satisfied with their purchase. The average score of 5.7 (on a scale where "matched" is a 5 and "exceeded" is a 9) suggests that owners are finding the ownership experience more positive than expected, though by only a moderate margin. Perhaps the content of sales presentations raises expectations so high that exceeding them by a significant margin is difficult.

Those who have owned timeshare longer, those who own multiple weeks and/or in multiple locations, those who own larger units, couples, respondents without children living at home, older respondents, and more affluent respondents are the most likely to report that the ownership experience has exceeded their expectations.

Courtesy of Deer Valley Club

Luxury features, such as spa tubs in the master bathrooms at Deer Valley Club in Park City, Utah, make timeshare vacationers feel pampered.

How Timeshare Ownership Has Affected Owners' Lives

Among owners surveyed about how timeshare ownership has affected their lives, a remarkable 66.6 percent of respondents point to a very positive or positive impact. About one in four (23.2 percent) report no impact either positive or negative, and just 10.3 percent claim that the impact has been negative. When examined by category of respondent, the results generally mirror the findings previously cited regarding owner satisfaction. In other words, couples as well as those who have owned longer, own more weeks, own in multiple locations, and own larger units are more likely than the average respondent to say that timesharing has had a positive impact on their lives.

Recommendation of Timesharing To Others

Three-quarters (75.2 percent) of timeshare owners recommend timesharing to others. Not coincidentally, the proportion is about the same for those who say that they are very satisfied or somewhat satisfied with their timeshare purchase, that they would definitely or possibly purchase again, or that their expectations of timesharing at time of purchase have at least been met. More than one in five respondents (21.5 percent) report that they frequently recommend timesharing to others, and 54.9 percent sometimes recommend timesharing. Only 24.8 percent do not recommend timesharing.

Number of Weeks Owned

Perhaps the clearest expression of consumer satisfaction and perceived value is the purchase of additional timeshare intervals after experiencing ownership. The average survey respondent owns 1.8 weeks of timeshare while 43.6 percent of respondents own two weeks or more, including 26.4 percent who own two weeks, 8.5 percent who own three weeks, and 8.7 percent who own four weeks or more.

Those who have owned timeshare longest are most likely to own multiple weeks. Respondents who made their first timeshare purchase within the past five years own an average of 1.4 weeks compared with an average of two weeks for those who first purchased eight or more years ago. More than half (51.2 percent) of those who purchased eight or more years ago own two or more weeks.

The high rates of additional purchases are especially significant when considering that

- timeshare units do not wear out and thus do not require replacement;
- most households have limited vacation time and therefore have little need for additional weeks;
- the flexibility offered by exchange affiliation means that the purchase of an additional interval is not necessary to change vacation locations; and
- timeshare units are relatively expensive items and require maintenance fees for each interval owned.

Multiple-week ownership is highest among

- couples;
- households without children at home, probably because many households first bought before their children had left home;
- older respondents, probably because they have owned longer and thus have had more opportunity to repurchase;
- more educated households, probably because they have higher incomes; and
- highest-income and, surprisingly, lowest-income households, perhaps because many of the earliest owners are now in retirement.

Number of Resorts Where Timeshares Are Owned

More than a quarter (26.4 percent) of respondents own a timeshare at more than one timeshare resort. The longer a household has owned a timeshare, the more likely it is to purchase intervals at additional locations. Respondents who made their first timeshare purchase within the past five years own in an average of 1.1 resorts; however, the number of purchases

jumps to an average of 1.5 resorts among respondents who have owned for eight years or longer. These statistics provide some of the most direct evidence that timeshare owners find value in the product they have purchased.

Increased Vacationing with Timeshare Ownership

Timeshare ownership seems to increase overall vacation time spent in resort areas. Respondents vacationed away from home an average of 11.8 days annually before becoming timeshare owners, not counting time spent at the homes of friends or relatives. Time away from home jumped to an annual average of 16.1 days once respondents became timeshare owners. Some of the increase may be attributable to additional vacation time away from home, and some may be a redirection of time previously spent with friends or relatives.

Timeshare owners who own multiple weeks and/or multiple locations dramatically increase the amount of time they devote to vacations compared with the period during which they did not own a

To enable vacationers to obtain whatever they need within the resort complex, Royal Resorts in Cancun, Mexico, operates a minigrocery store and a number of other shops and services.

Diane R. Suchman

timeshare. Those owning multiple weeks say the average time they spend on resort vacations has jumped from 12.4 to 19.6 nights per year. Those owning timeshare intervals in multiple locations have lengthened their vacations from 11.8 nights on average to 20.4 nights. Clearly, more timeshare ownership encourages more time spent enjoying resort vacations

Unique Benefits of Timeshare Ownership

The vast majority of timeshare owners say that ownership makes their vacations less expensive and/or allows them to obtain more value for the dollar. A high 70.8 percent agree that ownership has permitted them to stay in higher-quality resorts. More than half (51.6 percent) concur that they have stayed in higher-quality overnight accommodations as a result of owning timeshare. Some 64.8 percent believe they have saved money on vacation accommodations. These findings are encouraging because a core concept of timesharing is that it allows consumers the opportunity to prepurchase their vacation accommodations in today's dollars rather than paying what the market will bear in future years. According to consumers, the concept works.

The timeshare concept was originally developed as a way to save money on vacations. The first enhancement of the concept was the exchange opportunity, which provides flexibility in vacation location. Consumers are highly likely to agree that the enhancement works; in fact, 71.5 percent agree that they have enjoyed a wider range of vacation experiences since

©Tim Stahl

Resorts such as Grand Pacific Palisades Resort and Hotel in Carlsbad, California, offer two-bedroom units to accommodate older baby boomers and their children or grandchildren.

they purchased an interval. Similarly, 72.5 percent have experienced more vacation destinations. More than four in ten (41.4 percent) say that they have expanded their personal horizons by taking up new sports and activities and/or partaking of other educational/experiential pursuits while on vacation.

As shown in Figure 2-5, more than seven in ten timeshare owners (73.1 percent) agree that they derive greater enjoyment from their vacations since purchasing time-share. Two-thirds (65.9 percent) have enjoyed more restful and revitalizing family vacations through timeshare ownership, and more than half (59.6 percent) agree that they have experienced more fun and excitement on their vacations.

Most trend watchers say that a signifi-cant problem for the middle and upper-middle class is a shortage of leisure time, which leads to the desire for hassle-free solutions to household and personal needs. Timesharing seems to respond to the need for straightforward and predictable vacation arrangements. The majority (59.5 percent) of respondents agree that timesharing per-mits greater peace of mind when planning vacations. Similarly, nearly two-thirds (64.5 percent) of respondents find that they have a greater sense of confidence that they can vacation without worry.

Timesharing seems to make owners want to vacation more—hardly a surprising finding if timeshare vacations are easier to arrange, more enjoyable, and less expen-sive. Almost seven out of ten timeshare owners (66.8 percent) say that they have taken more vacations away from home than they did before interval ownership.

Although timeshare ownership is pri-marily about vacation enjoyment, many owners appreciate the property ownership benefits. More than half (58.6 percent) of respondents have pride and a sense of ownership in their resort property. Some 44.4 percent take comfort in the knowl-edge that they have vacation property to pass on to their children.

Figure 2-5 Impact of Timeshare Ownership on Various Aspects of Life

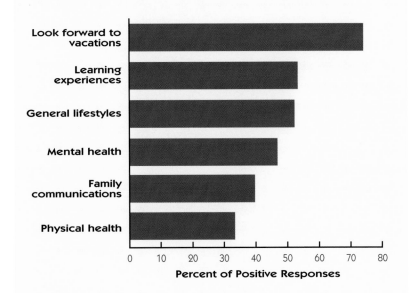

Source: Richard Ragatz, *The Benefits of Owning Resort Timesharing* (Eugene, Oregon: RCI Consulting, 1998), p. 52.

Part of the enhanced dollar value of timeshare vacations may come from the fact that owners are treated as individuals rather than as part of the masses, a bene-fit experienced by 53.9 percent of time-share owners. Since purchasing timeshares, nearly half (49.9 percent) reported an en-hanced sense of status and exclusivity while on vacation. Some 40.2 percent indicate they have been waited on and pampered during their vacations.

Family and interpersonal relationships are enhanced through timeshare owner-ship, say many owners. Almost two-thirds (61.2 percent) agree that they have more opportunity to spend time with family dur-ing vacations. About half (49.9 percent) have been better able to communicate with their spouses or children during vacations. More than one-third (38.4 percent) report that enhanced communication persists after vacations come to an end. Even re-lationships with strangers take on a new dimension, perhaps because timeshare

Figure 2-6 Timeshare Penetration Rates by State

States with Highest Penetration Rates among All Households		States with Lowest Penetration Rates among All Households	
Colorado	3.55%	Mississippi	0.59%
Arizona	3.51	North Dakota	0.60
Nevada	3.25	Arkansas	0.80
Virginia	3.21	Louisiana	0.86
Connecticut	3.10	Texas	0.92
Rhode Island	3.09	Alabama	0.94
Massachusetts	3.07	Hawaii	0.99
New Hampshire	3.06	Wyoming	1.04
Washington	2.68	Oklahoma	1.06
Maine	2.65	Kansas	1.16
California	2.63	Illinois	1.27
Vermont	2.55	Michigan	1.28
New Jersey	2.45	Kentucky	1.30
Utah	2.41	Oregon	1.37
Florida	2.30	Iowa	1.38

Source: Richard Ragatz, *Timeshare Purchasers: Who They Are, Why They Buy* (Eugene, Oregon: RCI Consulting, 1998), p. 47.

owners have more in common than most resort hotel guests. One-third say that, since becoming timeshare owners, they have made more friends during their vacations. The net result is that about two-thirds (66.3 percent) of timeshare owners believe that their purchase has positively affected their lives.

Impact of Timeshare Ownership on Specific Aspects of Life

As shown in Figure 2-5, when asked to indicate the impact of timeshare ownership on specific aspects of their lives, three out of four timeshare owners (76 percent) agree that, more than anything else, timesharing has made them look forward to vacations. In addition, more than half of all timeshare owners indicate that ownership has increased their learning experiences—perhaps because of travel to more locations.

Given that vacations contribute to a positive attitude, about half of timeshare

owners agree that ownership has had a positive impact on their mental health. Nearly one-third (35.2 percent) even believe that timeshare ownership has benefited their physical health, and 39 percent agree that family relationships tend to be enhanced through timeshare vacations. With these results, it is not surprising that 55.8 percent of respondents agree that timesharing has produced a very positive or positive impact on their general lifestyle. Few respondents report any level of negative impact—fewer than 5 percent for any individual item.

Remaining Market Potential

Existing Penetration Rates and Remaining Market Demand

As noted, 1.9 million households in the United States, or about 1.95 percent of all households in the country, own resort timeshare intervals. As shown in Figure 2-6, penetration rates range from 0.59 percent in Mississippi to 3.55 percent in Colorado.

On a regional basis, the penetration rate is higher in the New England region (3.02 percent), the Mountain region (2.98 percent), and the West (2.48 percent). It is lower in the South Central (1.04 percent) and North Central regions (1.48 percent).

As shown in Figure 2-7, penetration rates rise with household income. They stand at about 0.38 percent for households with incomes under $35,000, 1.84 percent for households with incomes between $35,000 and $50,000, 4.42 percent for households with incomes between $50,000 and $100,000, and 5.93 percent for households with incomes of $100,000 and over. As noted earlier, more than half of all timeshare-owning households report incomes between $50,000 and $100,000.

Assuming that income eligibility for resort timeshare purchases now begins at $50,000, it is possible to estimate the size of the remaining untapped market. Subtracting the 1.4 million households with incomes over $50,000 that already own timeshare from all 29.1 million households with such incomes indicates that the United States accounts for about 27.7 million income-eligible households.

Assuming that the current penetration rate of 4.8 percent for the $50,000-and-over income segment can be increased to 10 percent, even in the absence of growth in the number of households, the remaining market potential for timeshare ownership is about 1.5 million households. The penetration rate could rise as high as 20 percent; if so, the remaining market totals about 4.4 million households. Under the first scenario, about 55 percent of the potential market has been absorbed; under the second, about 30 percent.

Figure 2-8 shows the ten states with the highest remaining market demand potential based on a penetration rate of 20 percent of households with incomes over $50,000.

Current timeshare owners have purchased an average of 1.8 weeks while the average price in timeshare resorts with active marketing and sales programs is currently about $10,325. Without accounting for future inflation or new household formations, the potential timeshare market could generate a sales volume of between $28 and $82 billion, as shown in Figure 2-9.

Analyzing the Market for a Timeshare Development Project

While the size and composition of the potential aggregate market for timeshare development can be demonstrated with some precision, estimating the size and nature of the market for a specific timeshare development is somewhat more problematic. As with other market analyses, consideration of the market for a timeshare development involves evaluation of demand and supply and an estimate of the amount of residual demand a proposed project can capture. Therefore, it is wise to enlist the aid of an experienced market analyst before commencing a new pur-

pose-built vacation-ownership project or conversion.

Demand

In the case of timeshare developments, demand is determined from the following sources:

- The local tourism industry. The market analyst looks at the magnitude of the

Figure 2-7 Estimated Penetration of U.S. Resort Timeshare Ownership by Income: 1998

Income Category	United States
Under $35,000	
Total households	51,480,600
Households owning timeshare	196,750
Percent of total households	52.10%
Percent of total households owning timeshare	10.20%
Penetration rate	0.38%
$35,000 to $49,999	
Total households	18,020,400
Households owning timeshare	332,050
Percent of total households	18.30%
Percent of total households owning timeshare	17.30%
Penetration rate	1.84%
$50,000 to $99,999	
Total households	22,171,000
Households owning timeshare	979,900
Percent of total households	22.50%
Percent of total households owning timeshare	51.00%
Penetration rate	4.42%
$100,000 and Over	
Total households	6,963,500
Households owning timeshare	413,200
Percent of total households	7.10%
Percent of total households owning timeshare	21.50%
Penetration rate	5.93%
Total	
Total households	98,635,500
Households owning timeshare	1,921,900
Penetration rate	1.95%

Source: Richard Ragatz, *Timeshare Purchasers: Who They Are, Why They Buy* (Eugene, Oregon: RCI Consulting, 1998), p. 49.

Figure 2-8 U.S. Timeshare Market Potential by State

State	Number of Households
Texas	300,950
California	276,500
Illinois	229,500
New York	214,900
Michigan	158,600
Ohio	154,350
Florida	150,100
New Jersey	143,000
Pennsylvania	135,050
Maryland	78,500

(Number of households with incomes over $50,000 that have not purchased timeshare intervals based on an assumed 20 percent potential penetration rate.)

Source: Richard Ragatz, *Timeshare Purchasers: Who They Are, Why They Buy* (Eugene, Oregon: RCI Consulting, 1998), p. 53.

tourist flow and how it has changed over both the long term and recent past. In addition, the composition of the tourist flow is important, particularly with regard to demographics—household income, family composition, age, marital status, and so forth. The local chamber of commerce, city department of tourism, or a university may collect such information through intercept surveys. Patterns of visitation and length of stay are also major considerations because repeat visitors and those who stay longer are better prospects for timeshare sales. The types of activities tourists pursue, such as visiting the beach, golfing, or skiing, may suggest amenities or linkages for the new development. Taken together, all the information can help determine the extent of the total market for timeshare development within the tourist market.

♦ Overall market area. The market analyst also evaluates the resident market—people who live in the areas surrounding the proposed timeshare development. Generally, the local market falls within a 250-mile radius of the proposed project. The population includes people who are not yet necessarily tourists. Of particular importance is the number of households with income over $50,000. Regardless of development experience, a new timeshare development company or any company entering an untested market is well advised to conduct primary research (surveys and focus groups) and

Figure 2-9 Potential Timeshare Sales Volume

	Penetration Rate	
	10%	20%
Households with incomes over $50,000	29,134,500	29,134,500
Potential market at penetration rate	2,913,450	5,826,900
Households with incomes over $50,000 already owning timeshare	1,393,100	1,393,100
Remaining market (households)	1,520,350	4,433,800
Times average purchase of 1.8 weeks (weeks)	2,736,650	7,980,850
Times average price of $10,325 per week	$28 billion	$82 billion

(Based on an assumed 1.8 weeks of purchase at $10,325 per week by each of the 20 percent of households with incomes over $50,000 that have not yet purchased timeshare intervals.)

Source: Richard Ragatz.

thus obtain the best possible quantitative and qualitative market data. Surveys should focus on incoming tourists (based on hotel guest lists or the like) and residents in the primary market area.

Supply

The supply, or competition for the proposed timeshare development, is determined through an evaluation of the local hotel industry and other recreational properties in the area.

- Local hotel industry. The analyst needs to note the number, location, and characteristics of local hotels and consider month-by-month occupancy and rack rates for a minimum of 24 months. Higher occupancy rates and higher rack rates point to a greater market potential for timeshare development, especially if rates were sustained for at least 12 months.
- Other area recreational properties. Sales prices and the sales pace for other recreational properties, such as second homes or resort condominiums, are other measures that indicate the potential and positioning of a proposed timeshare development.

The analyst must then evaluate the market demand and supply for timeshare development in a particular area, relying on long-time experience and educated judgment to estimate the potential remaining market demand and the amount of the remaining demand that could be captured by the proposed development.

The analyst next estimates the number of sales that could be made to new purchasers, timeshare exchangers, owners purchasing additional timeshare intervals, and renters. Several factors contribute to the analyst's estimates. For example, some people buy for exchange purposes, adding market value to "hot" destinations such as Orlando. The exchange value can be determined by looking at the prices of and the percent of owner-occupancy in existing timeshare properties. Other factors include the quality of the resort (higher-quality resorts tend to have more "reloads," or additional purchases by existing owners), whether demand is high year-round or seasonally, and the level of customer satisfaction with the quality of resort management.

Note

1. One series of comparable surveys conducted in 1978, 1980, 1982, 1983, 1989, 1993, and 1998 resulted in seven editions of *Timeshare Purchasers: Who They Are, Why They Buy.* A second series of comparable surveys conducted in 1992, 1995, and 1998 resulted in three editions of *The Benefits of Owning Resort Timesharing.*

Chapter 3

Timeshare and Vacation-Ownership Products

Diane R. Suchman

As the industry has evolved over time, the term "timeshare" or "vacation ownership" has come to encompass a wide range of product choices. Timeshare products can be differentiated in a number of ways, including by location, project and unit size and design, type of original use, legal structure for ownership, and subdivision of time. Developments may range from small-scale individual buildings to multiple-resort complexes. They may be conversions from hotels, condominiums, or apartments, or they may be purpose-built. They may be located on a beach, in the mountains, or in the center of some of the world's most exciting cities. Purchasers may buy a week's time in the same unit every year or access to all offerings within a worldwide system of diverse resort properties and travel services. Units range in size from studios to four-bedroom products in a variety of architectural styles. Any number of legal structures may be used to consummate the timeshare purchase.

All timeshare products have in common shared use of resort accommodations and facilities, a legal structure that enables purchasers to own or occupy a unit for a certain period of time, a range of amenities and services, provision for management of the resort(s), and an administration/reservation system. Described below are the most important attributes that characterize and differentiate the various timeshare and vacation-ownership product types available today.

Though this chapter focuses primarily on timeshare products within the United States, the timeshare industry is evolving and

Figure 3-1 Geographic Location of Resorts

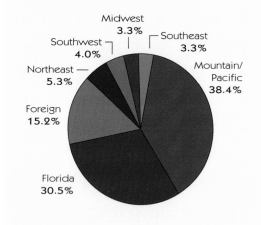

Region	States Included
Northeast	CT, DC, DE, MA, MD, ME, NH, NJ, NY, PA, RI, VA, VT, WV
Southeast	AL, AR, GA, LA, MS, NX, SC, TN
Southwest	AZ, CO, NM, OK, TX
Midwest	IA, IL, IN, KS, KY, MI, MN, MO, ND, NE, OH, SD, WI
Mountain/ Pacific	AK, CA, HI, ID, MT, NV, OR, UT, WA, WY
Foreign	Puerto Rico, U.S. Virgin Islands, Canada, Mexico, and other foreign countries

Source: American Resort Development Association, *Financial Performance Digest 1997: A Survey of Time-share and Vacation Ownership Resort Developers* (Washington, D.C.: ARDA, 1997), p. 2.

Photo on page 30:
Swimming pool at Bali Desa, in Bali, Indonesia, a boutique property with 28 three-bedroom "supervillas" set in a 3.7-acre tropical garden. Bali Desa is part of a Jakarta-based vacation club, Klub Awani.

George Leposky, Interval International

share purchasers—and thus developers—prefer established resort locations near a population base. Established locations offer visitors places to go and things to do.

With the emergence of theme parks (such as Disney World) as powerful tourist attractions, timeshare developments have followed the tourists. In fact, in 1996, Florida (especially because of the Orlando area) represented one-fourth of all time-share sales in the United States.

Urban timeshare development began more than a decade ago in New Orleans and San Francisco and has recently spread to other U.S. cities, including New York, Miami, Washington, D.C., and Boston. Urban timeshare appeals to the many visitors who seek the excitement, shopping, entertainment, and cultural offerings associated with cities. One of this book's case studies, Hotel de l'Eau Vive, a small time-share development in downtown New Orleans, is a good example of an urban timeshare development.

So-called regional resorts such as Myrtle Beach, South Carolina, or the Ozarks attract a market from within a reasonable driving radius. Destination resorts, such as Las Vegas or the ski resorts in Colorado, draw from throughout the United States. Others, such as Orlando or anywhere in Hawaii, appeal to a worldwide market.

Obviously, year-round resorts are more valuable and desired timeshare locations than seasonal resorts. In year-round resorts, there is no need to lower the purchase price based on seasons, and occupancy tends to remain consistently high throughout the year.

According to recent surveys conducted for ARDA,[1] timeshare resorts evidence regional differences. The most active time-share market is Florida, in part because the state's desirable climate and easy access draw vacationers from a broad market. This, coupled with the tourism value of Orlando's theme parks, gives buyers excellent exchange currency. In the Northeast, the ski resorts of New England, the beaches

expanding throughout the world. The following feature box describes the status of and recent developments in the global industry. In addition, three of the resort case studies featured in this book are located outside the United States.

Location, Location, Location

Successful timeshare resorts are located in places that people like to visit. Traditionally, this has meant resort locations that feature an amenity such as a beach or lake or mountains. Generally, time-

◆ International Timeshare Development

RCI Consulting reports that 1998 (the most recent year for which data are available) saw 4.25 million timeshare owners world-wide, or about 12.75 million vacationers, residing in more than 200 countries. There were more than 5,000 timeshare resorts around the world.

As seen in the tables below, the industry has shown impressive growth since 1980. Both the number of resorts and the number of owners have increased markedly, and timesharing has expanded into markets such as Latin America and Asia. New markets—most recently, India and Eastern Europe—continue to emerge as industry growth continues apace.

Global Timeshare Projects

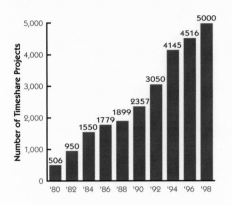

Global Timeshare Intervals

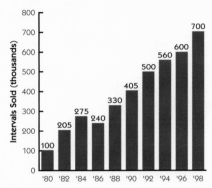

Global Timeshare Owners

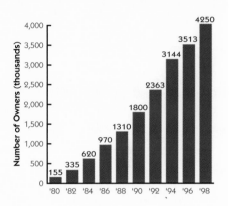

As of 1997, the distribution of timeshare resorts and timeshare owners around the world was as follows:

Timeshare Projects by Area of the World: Percent of Total

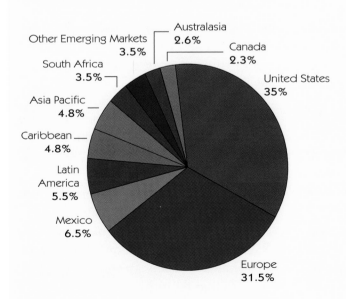

Timeshare Owners by Area of the World: Percent of Total

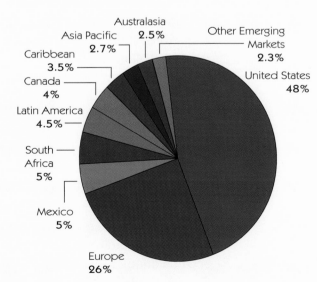

continued next page

◆ International Timeshare Development (continued)

The following table gives a snapshot of activity in the timeshare industry in selected locations in Europe:

European Timeshare Industry: Selected Statistics

Location	Number of Resorts	Number of Units	Number of Owners	Average Price per Unit/Week[1]	Estimated Total Sales Volume (new weeks)
United Kingdom/Ireland	121	3,500	70,000–75,000	$7,200	$72 million
Canary Islands	161	13,000	290,000–300,000	$8,500	$345 million
France	130	6,000	20,000	$10,000	$25–28.5 million
Italy	178	11,000	70,000–75,000	$10,500	$110 million
Portugal and Madeira	108	7,130	90,000	$6,400–29,000	$90 million
Germany, Austria, and Switzerland	98	4,000	70,000	$10,000	$68 million
Spain and Balearic Islands	239	10,500	225,000	$8,500	$345 million

1. Prices in U.S. dollar equivalents.

Sources: RCI Consulting, *Timeshare Industry Overview 1998* (Kettering, Northamptonshire, U.K.: author, 1998), pp. 14–15; and Chris Moule, RCI Consulting Europe, 1997 series of unpublished reports on the resort timeshare markets in the above countries.

of Cape Cod, the resorts of the Pocono Mountains, and, more recently, New York City and Boston are the dominant timeshare markets; they tend to attract regional visitors. In the Southeast, regional markets are drawn to beach and mountain resorts. The strongest timeshare destination in this region is Hilton Head, which attracts golfers and family groups. Myrtle Beach, the location of one of the chapter 9 case studies (Shore Crest Vacation Villas) is another magnet for golfers and beach lovers in the Southeast. The central United States accounts for fewer timeshare resorts, and those that exist—such as in the Wisconsin Dells—tend to be regional. As a rule, they center around lakes, golf courses, or ski areas, but, according to ARDA, casinos may become another focal point for timeshare developments in the central United States as gaming generally continues to gain popularity. In the Mountain region, ski resorts and desert resorts predominate. However,

many are seasonal and are often located in areas that are remote from buyers' homes. The Pacific region is the fastest-growing timeshare location in the United States. Growth is especially strong in those parts of the far West such as Hawaii, southern California, and parts of Nevada that boast warm climates year-round and unique locational attributes.

Timeshare resorts in different types of locations tend to offer different amenities, different types of units, and different use plans. For example, in Florida, and especially in Orlando, timeshare developments generally attract large numbers of family groups and international visitors. Thus, larger unit sizes and a wide range of family-oriented amenities predominate. Urban timeshares typically attract older, affluent couples that require less unit space but expect hotel-style services such as a 24-hour front desk, maid service, and concierge services.

◆ Urban Timesharing: A Different Product

Urban timesharing is a specialized product that can thrive in certain cities if developers and marketers understand its quirks and complexities.

First and foremost, urban timesharing is not necessarily a week-by-week product. Instead, it is distinguished by demand for stays as short as a single day, a characteristic that carries significant implications for the product's physical design and cost structure. Second, an urban timeshare relies on the city itself as the primary amenity. Urban timesharing can succeed only where strong business, arts, cultural, and sporting activities make a city attractive throughout the year both to residents of the city and its suburbs and to international visitors. Third, urban timesharing provides an alternative form of the pied-à-terre for people who occupy a primary residence elsewhere in the surrounding region but might otherwise own a home or apartment in the heart of the city for overnight stays.

The urban timeshare market segment consists primarily of older, more affluent empty nesters whose psychographics differ from those of the typical timeshare owner. They are willing to pay more than the typical timeshare owner for the product, maintenance fees, and taxes. They purchase multiple weeks, take advantage of bonus time, and provide more and better-qualified referrals. They tend to use the accommodations they have purchased more often than they exchange them.

Attributes of the urban timeshare product typically include

- daily maid service, a necessity with single-day occupancies;
- a reservation system designed to accommodate the relatively high level of activity generated by single-day occupancies;
- a knowledgeable concierge to assist in meeting the amenity and recreational requirements of a discerning and demanding clientele;
- a 24-hour front desk;
- high-level security throughout the property;
- other intensive guest services (bell service, valet service, and so forth);
- relatively small unit sizes, reflecting higher product costs per square foot of space;
- small kitchens (most occupants dine out most of the time);
- design for noise control;
- meeting/function space to facilitate use by a corporate clientele; and
- a mixed-use property, renting vacant units to transient-stay hotel guests.

Industry experts disagree on the added value of a point system for urban timeshares. Proponents claim that significant benefits accrue from attributing a use-demand value to a timeshare product marketed through a point system. Critics of point programs for urban timesharing complain that too many variables drive the demand for timeshare accommodations to permit the successful quantification of point values.

Because of the year-round amenity values offered by cities, the exchange companies have rated urban timeshare projects for high seasonality throughout the year. Interval International recently surveyed its consumer members to determine their most desired exchange vacations. Ten of the top 100 places mentioned by respondents were urban destinations.

Source: Paul W. Rishell, chief operating officer of Interval International, adapted from *Urban Land* Timeshare Supplement, August 1997, pp. 13–14.

Types of Resorts

During the 1970s, most timeshare projects took the form of conversions of hotels, motels, apartments, and, especially, condominiums that did not sell as full ownership. Today, almost 60 percent of all timeshare resorts were partly or entirely purpose-built for timesharing; the remainder are conversions. In many cases, timeshare resorts are part of a larger development that encompasses other related uses. More than 40 percent of timeshare developments include some condominiums. Almost a quarter include hotel rooms; about 12 percent include single-family homes or lots and another 12 percent rental apartments.[2] A small percentage share their site with campsites or recreational vehicle space. Some resorts offer more than one other use along with the timeshare component. For example, a large master-planned resort community might include single-family homes, condominiums, a hotel, and timeshare units. An urban mixed-use development, such as the Manhattan Club in New York City, might accommodate both hotel and timeshare uses.

Mixing uses has a number of advantages as well as some disadvantages. On the positive side, mixed-use developments permit developers to diversify risk, spread fixed costs, and realize some efficiencies in administration, procurement, use of facilities and amenities, and deployment of human resources. For example, given that most hotels cater to business travelers, they experience their lowest occupancies on weekends—when timeshare projects are bursting at the seams. At the same time, business from timeshare owners increases the revenues of a colocated hotel's food and beverage services. And, with the year-round demand for timeshare developments from owners and participants in exchange programs, the timeshare component helps even out the seasonal fluctuations experienced by many hotel operations.

The potential for cross-marketing is another advantage, particularly where a hotel and timeshare development coexist. Hotel guests indicate by their presence at a property their interest in traveling to a particular location and thus are a natural source of leads for timeshare sales. (The case study of Hilton Grand Vacation Club Las Vegas Hilton in chapter 9 offers a good example of cross-marketing.) In large resorts, timeshare owners help achieve the critical mass necessary to justify the costs of constructing and maintaining infrastructure and amenities such as a country club or golf course or health spa. Because developers of large mixed-use resorts control the uses that surround the timeshare resort, they can also ensure compatibility in land use and architectural quality and design.

The primary disadvantages of multiple uses, as discussed in chapter 7, are the additional challenges associated with planning and permitting, more complicated project administration and management, and the complexity of the legal structure that enables timeshare owners to use the facilities and amenities of the colocated hotel or resort.

Like many timeshare resorts, Pacific Shores Nature Resort in British Columbia, Canada, was originally built as a condominium development.

Unit Types and Amenities

Units, which are often called "villas" in newer upscale resorts, vary in size from studios to four bedrooms. Two-bedroom units are the most common, especially in purpose-built resorts, and account for

Dramatic features enhance the lounge of Sunterra Corporation's Villa Mirage Resort, a regional resort in Scottsdale, Arizona.

about half of all timeshare resort units in the United States today. (Most remaining units, especially in older resorts, include only one bedroom.) A typical modern two-bedroom unit sleeps six (it includes a sleeper-sofa) and has a full kitchen, two baths, eating space, a television, and perhaps a small balcony. It is fitted and furnished to be homelike and comfortable.

The industry trend is toward building larger units, particularly, as noted, in areas that attract family groups. In Florida, for example, more than four-fifths of units contain two or three bedrooms.[3] At the same time, in keeping with the trend toward offering timeshare buyers increased flexibility, lockoff units are becoming more common. A lockoff unit is, as its name suggests, a portion of a two-bedroom or larger timeshare unit that can be locked off and used as a separate unit. An owner may choose to occupy the entire unit, the master suite, or perhaps the lockoff. Lockoffs typically consist of one bedroom and one bath and sometimes limited kitchen facilities; they have a separate entrance. The units provide timeshare owners with more flexibility by enabling them—as an alternative to using their entire unit for their assigned time—either to occupy only a portion of their unit and exchange the other portion for an equivalent value in a different resort or to exchange both portions of their unit separately. Today, about 6 percent of all timeshare units include lockoffs, though the proportion is larger in newer resorts.

All timeshare resorts contain some common facilities and/or amenities for owners' use. In urban locations, amenities tend to be minimal because it is the city itself that draws visitors. In resort timeshare developments, the most common amenities, in order of frequency, include a swimming pool, whirlpool tub, tennis courts, and an on-site beach. Other common facilities include a clubhouse, exercise facilities, and playgrounds. Less commonly, timeshare resorts might offer a restaurant or bar,

Courtesy of RCI

Hotel Plaza Las Glorias in Manzanillo, Colima, Mexico.

boating or fishing, golf, or convenience stores or other retail uses. Comparatively few offer skiing, a health spa, or gaming.

Use Arrangements

Timeshare products also differ according to their use plans or the arrangements for buyers to occupy the accommodations they have purchased. (See Figure 3-2 on page 41.)

One-Week and Split-Week Intervals

Most commonly, time use is sold in one-week intervals that provide the buyer

38

Fairfield Communities's 18,000-acre Pagosa Springs Resort in Colorado features individual cabins with stunning panoramic views. Among others, activities at this resort include trout fishing, trail rides, white-water rafting, golf, tennis, skiing, boating, and hot air balloon rides.

Courtesy of Fairfield Communities, Inc.

with the use of resort accommodations for a single week each year. The oldest and most common timeshare is the fixed week. Today, almost 94 percent of all U.S. timeshare resorts sell timeshare interests in increments of one week of use per year or as points. Studies show, however, that vacationers increasingly prefer shorter, more frequent vacations. As a result, many timeshare developers permit buyers to use their time in split-week vacations of three or four days at a time during two separate visits to the home resort or elsewhere. Some urban timeshare developments even accept reservations for periods as short as a single day.

Biennials

Another popular form of interval is the biennial purchase, which provides the buyer with use for one week every other year and thus offers an affordable alterna-

tive to annual ownership. Biennial sales are especially common in Hawaii, where costs and travel distances are an issue in timeshare ownership. Some buyers choose biennial purchases not only because it is a more affordable alternative but also because the arrangement gives them access to "bonus time" and other owner benefits. From the developer's standpoint, biennials generate less income but impose the same administrative burden as an annual unit/week purchase. Some observers believe that as point systems (described below) become more popular and enable buyers to buy greater or fewer points, purchases of biennial interests may become a thing of the past.

Fractional Interests

Fractional interests provide use intervals that are longer than one week, typically for one-quarter use (12 weeks), one-fifth use (ten weeks), or one-twelfth use (three weeks every other year; four weeks in the alternate years). Generally, owners use multiple weeks at various times of the year according to a fixed or rotating schedule. Fractional vacation ownership appeals to people who like the idea of owning a second home in a beach or ski resort but are unable or unwilling to assume the full expense or responsibility of ownership. Fractionals are more expensive than other forms of timeshare and can be more difficult to exchange.

Undivided-Interest Programs[4]

An undivided-interest (UDI) timeshare creates a membership structure wherein each member shares equal rights to lodging and amenities. UDIs offer high-quality lodging opportunities and amenities in a private club setting. Instead of owning a specific unit, members are deeded a fraction of the entire project. For instance, a member of the Melrose Club in South Carolina becomes a 1/1,550 owner of the club's facilities (the maximum number of memberships at the club is 1,550). The member is granted a specific number of days of lodging in a rotation that depends on the competition for the reservation. Unlike a vacation club strategy (where members' rights are limited by the length of stay purchased through points), UDI members also have the opportunity to stay—for a nominal fee—at either the 52-room Melrose Inn or one of the UDI cottage units. Typically, UDIs offer amenities such as tennis and croquet and other "software" amenities for free while activities such as golf and boat charters might involve a nominal fee.

◆ Fractional Ownership—An Upscale Owner's Option

The trend toward greater use options and the desire to attract a more upscale market have resulted in the proliferation of so-called fractional-ownership resorts in which purchasers can buy more than a single week of occupancy per year in some of the world's poshest resorts. Purchasers can acquire a fractional-ownership interest for a small percentage of the cost of a comparable "whole" ownership but are entitled to virtually all the benefits of whole ownership.

For example, the original Owners Club project was developed at Indigo Run Plantation on Hilton Head Island, South Carolina, by a joint venture of the Melrose Company, a local developer, and the Dallas-based Club Corporation of America, the nation's largest owner and operator of private clubs. For between $40,000 and $50,000, Owners Club purchasers receive a deed to a one-thirteenth undivided-fee interest in a freestanding three-bedroom cottage

on a separate lot as well as up to 27 days and nights of occupancy each year, with additional "bonus" occupancy available at a relatively nominal cost on a first-come, first-served, space-available basis.

Occupancy periods at the Owners Club can last for as few as three and as many as 11 consecutive days and nights as long as owners do not exceed the aggregate annual maximum of 27 days and nights. As additional Owners Clubs are developed around the country (a dozen or more are planned), members will be permitted to divide their use and occupancy among the various locations, each of which is to provide similar accommodations. The primary lure of membership in the Owners Club is the opportunity to play golf on some of America's best courses. Benefits include the right to reserve tee times well in advance of the desired date and eligibility for discounts on green fees and cart rentals. Purchase prices of ownership

interests at future Owners Club locations will vary based at least in part on the price of comparable whole vacation homes in the same resort market.

Another prominent fractional-ownership resort is the Franz Klammer Lodge in Telluride, Colorado. Purchasers of fractional-ownership interests in this high-end project receive a recorded deed to a one-tenth undivided-fee interest in a two- or three-bedroom condominium unit, along with the right to occupy and use the resort's accommodations for up to five weeks per year. The project's developer has targeted primarily prosperous individuals who can easily afford to pay $1 million or more for whole ownership of a vacation home but instead choose to purchase a fractional interest for as much as $200,000.

Source: Mel Weinberger, "Sharing Time in Vacation Ownership," *Urban Land* Timeshare Supplement, August 1997, pp. 20–21.

Similar in many ways to a country club, UDIs are most successful if they are readily accessible to their market, thereby ensuring frequent patronage.

At one time, UDIs were thought to be the new wave of vacation ownership, but many have struggled. The market has tended to favor vacation clubs (see discussion below), which offer members greater flexibility in tailoring a vacation to their particular needs and preferences. Still, UDIs have established a place for themselves in affluent niche markets. For instance, Deer Valley Club at Deer Valley, Utah, uses a UDI strategy to offer purchasers a 1/195 ownership interest in club accommodations and facilities combined with the high-quality service and personal attention a country club might offer. (Chapter 9 presents a case study of Deer Valley Club.)

Even though many members of UDIs targeted to niche markets might be able to buy a second home or a three-bedroom condominium for $600,000, they would rather pay $150,000 for a one-sixth share of a unit and still enjoy the benefits of software amenities, such as tuned skis, and the luxury of a high-quality resort. Many resort developers are currently looking to the UDI concept as a strategy to remedy lackluster hotel and condominium projects.

Point Systems

Because of their flexibility, point systems have become an increasingly popular method of providing buyers with access to resort accommodations. Timeshare developers sell points in number amounts that symbolize the value of the purchase.

Holiday Club Katenkulta in Finland.

Courtesy of RCI Europe

The purchaser can use the points as currency to obtain access to timeshare accommodations or, in some cases, other travel services. The concept is similar to other types of reward systems that have become familiar to many consumers.

Many resorts that are based on a point system sell points in increments equivalent to one unit/week of use. The number of points needed to gain access to a particular resort unit or to a certain travel service varies over time according to overall member demand. Moreover, points may be revalued periodically as properties enter or leave the system. Points are commonly used as the basis for exchange in vacation clubs (described below).

Point systems, though increasingly popular, are still evolving as a basis for timeshare use and exchange. Clearly, points provide consumers with a number of benefits, primarily maximum flexibility to design their own vacations. In addition, most systems allow buyers to purchase additional points, "bank" unused points, and borrow from the next year's allotment to accumulate the number of points needed for a desired vacation. Especially in systems that also make available other types of accommodations and travel services, consumers can use their points in countless combinations to vacation according to the place, time, and manner of their choosing. At the same time, point systems are complicated and expensive to establish, operate, and explain to potential purchasers. And balancing demand and inventory can pose a challenge. Periodic revaluation is necessary as additional buyers and properties join the system. Based on what has been learned by the various companies using points, the industry can expect to see refinements to the point concept within the next several years.

Floating Time and Floating Units

Timeshare resorts differ in the degree of flexibility accorded to buyers in the use of the time purchased. Traditionally, time-

Summer Bay resort in Orlando, Florida, offers timeshare in single-family-home units that have won awards for architectural excellence.

share resorts sold fixed-week/fixed-unit intervals such that the owner returned to the same resort and the same unit each year. While that arrangement is still popular owing to ease of administration and buyer certainty of a predictable vacation, consumer demand for greater flexibility

Figure 3-2 **Purchase Arrangements: 1996**

Timeshare Use Plans

Fixed time	60.8%
Floating within a season	21.1%
Floating year-round	20.3%
Points	5.9%
Other	8.8%

Types of Intervals

One-week or points	93.7%
Biennials	12.1%
Fractions or multiweeks	8.8%
Undivided interests	6.7%

Source: American Resort Development Association, *The Resort Timeshare Industry in the United States: Overview and Economic Impact Analysis 1997* (Washington, D.C.: ARDA, 1997), p. 24.

has spawned a number of variations on the single-week purchase. Some resorts sell "floating" weeks, which means that the buyer purchases a week of accommodations at a particular resort and returns to the same resort each year but can request a particular week. With some floating time arrangements, that week might fall during a designated season; with others, it might fall at any time during the year. In some resorts, the units float; buyers return each year to the same resort at the same week but are assigned to units on an availability basis. Some resorts offer both floating time and floating units.

◆ Resort Condominiums International, LLC (RCI)

RCI, celebrating its 25th anniversary in 1999, is the world's leading time-share exchange company. It represents more than 3,400 affiliated resorts in more than 90 countries. In 1997, RCI booked over 1.8 million exchanges, sending more than 6.5 million people on vacation. As a single-source provider of integrated timeshare solutions, the company's services include feasibility analyses, market research, technological support, and lead-generation strategies along with club development and operations. RCI is a subsidiary of Cendant Corp. (NYSE: CD), one of the world's foremost providers of consumer and business services.

Source: Resort Condominiums International, LLC.

◆ Interval International

Founded in 1976, Interval International is a global member services company providing innovative travel and leisure products and programs to vacation-owners as well as operational, consulting, and program design services to resort developers. Interval's leading service is vacation exchange. Offered through its World-Class Vacation Exchange Network, the company has attracted leading independent and brand-name developers to its network, which now includes over 1,700 resorts in more than 65 countries. These resort affiliations have resulted in a product of unparalleled quality and a balanced resort system comprising national and international destinations. Interval serves nearly 1 million member families worldwide through more than 31 offices in 25 countries.

Through Interval's longstanding relationships with other travel providers, including leading airlines, cruise lines, and hotels, consumer members enjoy a full complement of travel and leisure services. Interval offers its developer-members a wide range of ancillary services such as consulting, sales, and marketing support; customized program design; and backroom services, including reservations and financial and purchasing services.

Source: Interval International.

Exchange

Timeshare's popularity is due, in large part, to the opportunity for exchange provided by exchange companies. Because most people would not choose to vacation at the same place and time every year, timeshare owners typically pay an annual membership fee to affiliate with an exchange company that will, on request, arrange an exchange of time purchased at their "home resort" for time at a different resort. As discussed in chapters 2 and 5, surveys indicate that, other than the resort itself, exchange is the primary reason that vacation-owners buy timeshares.

An exchange company enables a buyer to exchange a time interval internally— within the same resort or system of resorts —or externally—for a time interval of similar value at a different resort, within the inventory of the exchange company or vacation club. To effect an external exchange for a nominal fee, an owner can place an interval into the exchange company's pool of available resorts and select a comparable different resort/interval from the pool on a first-come, first-served basis.

Most resorts affiliate with an international exchange company, and owners may decide individually to join that same company for an annual membership fee. The two major timeshare exchange companies are Interval International (II) and Resort Condominiums International, LLC (RCI). Smaller exchange companies operate in the United States and abroad, but they have much less impact on the industry.

According to ARDA, in 1997, 42 percent of all U.S. timeshare intervals were used

◆ Club Sunterra

In September 1998, Sunterra Corporation launched Club Sunterra. Sunterra is the largest timeshare owner and operator in the United States devoted exclusively to vacation-ownership operations, with 87 properties located throughout the world and more than 240,000 owner-families. The purpose of the point-based Club Sunterra, according to Sunterra CEO Steve Miller, is to provide owners with more flexibility in the use of time and with greater variety in the way they vacation. Club members purchase a deeded timeshare interest and receive an allotment of "Sun Options" each year. Points can be carried over to or borrowed from the next year. U.S. members pay an annual fee of $139, which includes membership in RCI.

Currently in the process of shifting from a traditional interval-based system, the company plans to sell only club memberships and points within the United States. (It already operates a club system in Europe.) The existing product is the traditional week, with either fixed or floating time depending on the system that was in place when Sunterra acquired various properties. Existing owners will be invited to convert to the club system on a voluntary basis.

According to Miller, the issues associated with conversion to a club system require Sunterra to ensure that

◆ growth in company strength keeps pace with growth in size;
◆ the company recruits and retains superior, well-trained management and staff;
◆ the technical infrastructure (such as a call center, training, information technology, and predictive modeling) is in place to manage the conversion process; and
◆ the sales force understands the new product and its value and is trained to sell it.

"Operating a club system," says Miller, "means you have to do many things well at the same time." As a result, it is important not only to develop people within the company but also to acquire outside talent when needed. Miller believes that the club system is the wave of the future and that it makes sense for developers to establish a long-lived (beyond the sales transaction) affinity relationship with the customer. Furthermore, a club system enables the company to consolidate different functions that are important to the customer, such as sales, hospitality, vacation planning, and reservations; and it moves the industry away from a transaction orientation to a customer service orientation.

Orlando-based Sunterra Corporation, established as Signature Resorts in 1992, is a public company traded on the New York Stock Exchange (NYSE: OWN).

---

for exchange compared with 39 percent that were occupied by their owners; in addition, 81 percent of all U.S. timeshare owners have taken at least one exchange vacation.

Moreover, the exchange companies have been a source of stability, industry information, and political advocacy. They have enforced standards of quality within the industry through their affiliation requirements, resort rating systems, and threat of suspension for those who fail to meet their quality standards. In cases where resorts failed financially, the exchange companies have helped operators recover from their problems by maintaining their exchange activity, advising the receivers and owners' associations, and sometimes even helping identify potential purchasers for the troubled development.[5]

Vacation Clubs

Some timeshare developers offer buyers the opportunity to exchange time within their own system of multiple resorts through an arrangement known in the industry as a vacation club. "Vacation club" is a term generally applied to a system of multiple, geographically diverse resorts under the management of a single entity that sells access to the club's accommodations and related travel and leisure services. Sales can take the form of an ownership interest tied to a particular home resort but, more typically, take the form of points. Depending on the club, the purchaser may obtain either a deeded interest or a right-to-use interest for a specific period of time. In many clubs, buyers receive priority when making reservations

◆ Fairfield Communities's FairShare Plus Vacation Program

Fairfield Communities, Inc., was a pioneer in developing a point system for vacation ownership. Its goal was to provide resort owners with flexibility in designing their own vacations. One of the industry's largest developers and operators, Fairfield is a publicly traded company that operates 26 properties in various regional and destination resort locations. In addition, it is affiliated with three other resorts and Carnival Cruise Line.

In the Fairfield points program known as FairShare Plus, each real estate interest is assigned a certain number of symbolic points based on resort location, unit size, and the season associated with the purchase. For example, a high-season week in a two-bedroom unit at a typical Fairfield resort would be worth 154,000 points. FairShare Plus members have several options for using their points. They can, for example,

- vacation for a week in a two-bedroom unit at a FairShare Plus resort;
- vacation in a resort of different value or in a different season within the FairShare Plus resort network;
- take two or more vacations in Fair-Share Plus resorts by dividing one week into shorter stays, occupying a smaller unit, or both;

- reserve vacations at Associate Locations, which include affiliated international destinations and cruises; and
- exchange for a vacation at one of their exchange companies' participating resorts worldwide. Most Fairfield resorts are affiliated with RCI, but several recent additions to Fairfield's inventory are in Interval International's exchange network.

In this way, members specify where, when, for how long, and in what types of accommodations they would like to vacation each year. From the company's standpoint, a point-based system makes it possible to realize marketing efficiencies through mass marketing, off-site urban sales centers, and other sophisticated sales techniques. In addition, a point system provides Fairfield with a range of options in the use of various resort accommodations.

Fairfield sells both fixed-week and UDI deeded ownership. Owners of fixed-week intervals may elect to assign the use rights to their interval week to the FairShare Plus program in exchange for a point allocation. UDI owners are allocated a certain number of annual points at the time of purchase based on the value of the use rights they acquire. Fixed-week or UDI owners can assign their title

or use rights in perpetuity to the FairShare Plus Vacation Club in exchange for the use of a certain number of annual renewable points. Club members receive priority in making reservations in any club-affiliated resort. All FairShare Plus members may borrow or rent points from future years or purchase additional points to augment their allocation.

The FairShare Plus Board of Directors oversees the management of the Fair-Share Vacation Owners' Association. FairShare Plus members pay an annual fee to fund program operations and to cover the underlying property owners' association maintenance fee.

The FairShare Plus Program was marketed to Fairfield's existing owner base as well as to new purchasers. Not all owners of Fairfield resorts are FairShare Plus members. Owners who predate the program or chose not to participate at the time of their purchase must pay a $1,500 to $2,000 fee to convert to the point system. Approximately 15 to 20 percent of Fairfield's existing fixed-week owners have converted to FairShare Plus.

Source: Fairfield Communities, Inc.

at their home resort. Some developers have created vacation clubs that consist of timeshare properties they have developed or purchased. In other cases, a vacation club may be composed of an affiliated group of timeshare resorts developed by independent operators, regional resort developers, or others. All offer ease of access to properties and services within the club, though each club operates somewhat differently in terms of its offerings and arrangements.

For example, Cypress Harbour Resort, featured in chapter 9, is part of the Marriott Vacation Club. Through the Marriott system, owners can take advantage of a number of exchange options. They can exchange a week of time for a week in the same season at a different Marriott resort; exchange their unit/time through Interval International's exchange system; partake of the menu of options under the Marriott Rewards Program (SM), which offers lodging in Marriott hotels worldwide,

Exchange Options Example

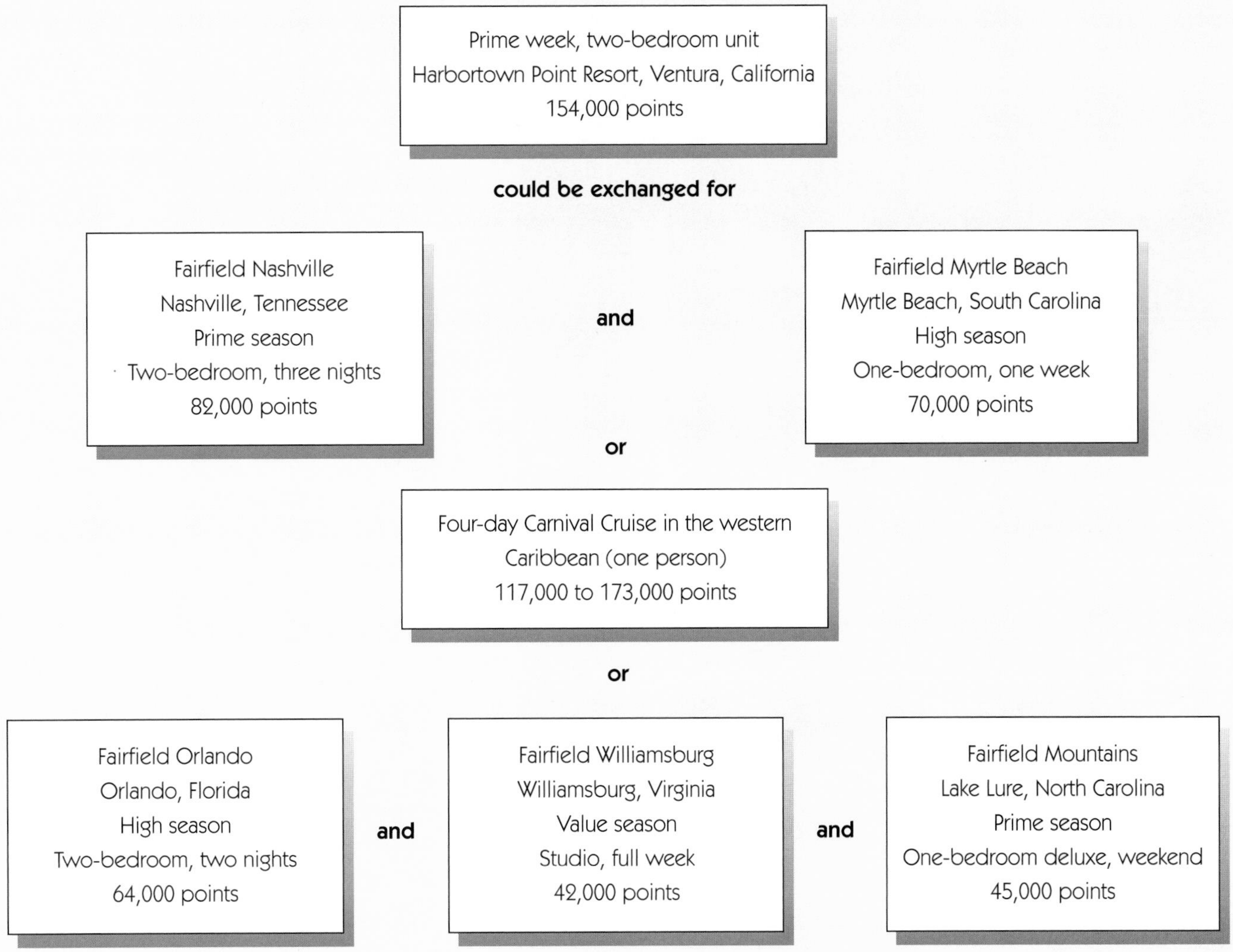

Prime week, two-bedroom unit
Harbortown Point Resort, Ventura, California
154,000 points

could be exchanged for

Fairfield Nashville
Nashville, Tennessee
Prime season
Two-bedroom, three nights
82,000 points

and

Fairfield Myrtle Beach
Myrtle Beach, South Carolina
High season
One-bedroom, one week
70,000 points

or

Four-day Carnival Cruise in the western
Caribbean (one person)
117,000 to 173,000 points

or

Fairfield Orlando
Orlando, Florida
High season
Two-bedroom, two nights
64,000 points

and

Fairfield Williamsburg
Williamsburg, Virginia
Value season
Studio, full week
42,000 points

and

Fairfield Mountains
Lake Lure, North Carolina
Prime season
One-bedroom deluxe, weekend
45,000 points

and, through affiliated partners, air travel, cruises, car rentals, and more; or exchange within the Florida Club, an arrangement whereby owners of Marriott resorts in Orlando, Ft. Lauderdale, Palm Beach, and any future Marriott vacation-ownership resort in Florida can exchange time (weeks or split weeks) among themselves. Procedures and fees vary among the various options.

Many timeshare vacation clubs are based on point systems. Two examples featured here are Fairfield Communities's FairShare Plus and Sunterra Corporation's Club Sunterra. Use of a point system in a vacation club makes it possible for consumers to design their own vacations based on a wide range of choices in time, duration, place, and type and size of accommodation. And, typically, choices extend to other travel opportunities and services offered through the vacation club and its affiliated exchange company.

While they provide the consumer with maximum flexibility, point systems are—

The Marbella Beach Resort in Marbella, Spain, is Marriott Vacation Club International's first timeshare venture outside the United States. The resort, including the villa interiors, has a distinct Spanish flavor.

from a developer's standpoint—complicated, time-consuming, and document-intensive to establish. Moreover, they require sophisticated computer systems and personnel. And it can be difficult to achieve high levels of member satisfaction while realizing desired occupancy rates in all club properties.

Legal Structures

Fee Simple

A timeshare purchase may be in the form of fee-simple ownership, which is similar to ownership of any other form of real estate in that the buyer receives a deed of trust for a fixed week in a specific unit at a specific resort. As with a home mortgage, the owner can sell, transfer, or bequeath fee-simple timeshare ownership and obtain certain tax benefits.

Right to Use

Alternatively, the purchase may take the form of a right to use the timeshare property through a vacation lease, vacation license, or membership in a vacation club. The purchaser obtains the right to use the accommodations for a designated period of time—typically ten to 50 years—while the developer (or club or other owner) retains legal title to the property. At the end of the use period, the occupancy rights revert to the owner. Right-to-use arrangements are often preferred in single-building condominium conversions when a mix of uses is contemplated or where local laws (as in Ireland or along the coast of Mexico) prohibit foreigners from owning property. Right-to-use arrangements also help avoid the heavy administrative and legal burdens associated with the conversion of a large number of apartments to timeshares.[6]

Figure 3-2 shows that the proportions of households purchasing timeshares through fee-simple ownership or point systems have increased while the percentage pur-

Figure 3-2 **Legal Format of Timeshare Interest(s)**

	All Owners 1995	All Owners 1998	Purchasers 1996 or 1997
Fee simple or undivided interest	78.5%	89.6%	89.7%
Right-to-use	21.6%	14.1%	16.3%
Ownership of points	1.9%	4.8%	9.1%
Other	1.5%	1.7%	2.2%

Source: Richard Ragatz, *Timeshare Purchasers: Who They Are, Why They Buy* (Eugene, Oregon: RCI Consulting, 1998), p. 16.

chasing right-to-use or "other" forms of ownership has declined.

Any of the above types of use arrangement, whether fixed, floating, or points, may be sold as either a deeded interest in real estate or a form of right-to-use accommodations and travel services. Chapter 7 discusses the legal implications of the various ownership structures.

Notes

1. The following information on regional variations in timeshare developments and locations was reported by ARDA and the Alliance for Timeshare Excellence in *The Resort Timeshare Industry in the United States: Overview and Economic Impact Analysis 1997* (Washington, D.C.: ARDA, 1997), which is an excellent resource on timeshare products and purchasers. Unless otherwise noted, the statistics in this chapter come from that publication.

2. ARDA and the Alliance for Timeshare Excellence, *The Resort Timeshare Industry in the United States: Overview and Economic Impact Analysis 1997,* p. 19.

3. *The Timeshare Industry in the United States 1997* (Indianapolis: RCI Consulting, 1998).

4. Discussion of UDIs is taken from Dean Schwanke et al., *Resort Development Handbook* (Washington, D.C.: ULI–the Urban Land Institute, 1997), pp. 195–196.

5. World Tourism Organization, *Timeshare: The New Force in Tourism* (WTO: Madrid, Spain, 1996), p. 36.

6. Keith Trowbridge, *Resort Timesharing* (New York: Simon and Schuster), p. 34.

Chapter 4

Planning and Design
of Timeshare Resorts

Edward D. Stone, Jr., and William Renner, E D S A;
Robert Koch, Fugleberg Koch Architects;
and Pamela Temples McMullen, ASID,
and Pura Rojas, Pamela Temples Interiors, Inc.

For two reasons, timeshare design and development is one of the most creative sectors of the real estate industry. The first reason lies in the flexibility of ownership and use arrangements; the second, in the competition for sites and the continuing advances in design. Recent years have seen a renaissance in the planning and design of timeshare resorts as characterized by an increasing emphasis on the creation of high-quality projects. As with other consumer-oriented businesses, the timeshare business has responded to heightened consumer quality-consciousness by providing greater perceived value in design and operations, especially in the more visible aspects of design such as amenities, architecture, interiors, and landscaping.

Several other trends have also emerged. First, tourism has come to be recognized as entertainment while resort life in particular is considered a series of stage sets wherein the visitor enjoys memorable experiences in environments substantially different from home (and other resorts). The stages can be both natural and created. Second, timeshare developers have begun to respond to the market's interest in experiencing the natural environment and in the concomitant demand for resort developments that preserve and respect nature. As a result, natural areas have become valuable amenities, and developers have discovered the economic benefits of building with environmentally sensitive materials.

The Design Process

The Design Team

As in the case of other real estate projects, the design process for a successful time-share resort requires collaboration among the developer, planner, architect, interior designer, landscape architect, engineer, and other specialty disciplines.

To enable the best use of the available land and budget, the interior designer and the architect should participate with the project manager and land planner throughout the planning stages of the development. The purpose of planning is to integrate appeal and function in every detail of the product, beginning with the building footprint. Space planning, market appeal, budgets, and the scheduled completion date influence both the design process and the product. In addition to buildings, the resort complex includes the amenities and activities desired and expected by the potential buyer according to climate and geographic location. Ideally, the physical layout of the complex should provide for a careful balance between attractive public areas that encourage community feeling and private areas that are sanctuaries of peace and quiet. It is, however, the unit layout that most directly affects potential clients. In individual timeshare units, as in all dwelling units, the foremost design principle is the maximum use of available square footage. Critical, too, are the nuances that characterize successful spaces, such as a sense of arrival, fluid traffic patterns, flexible use opportunities, and the most elusive: a sense of comfort.

Complicating the need for physical creature comforts is the issue of market appeal. The target market may, for example, consist of families or couples, or people within a particular age group, or households with a given income range or education level. Obviously, the market segment helps determine design features. Design decisions are also a function of the development's location. Areas such as Walt Disney World and Miami Beach, for example, appeal to predetermined potential market segments.

To optimize the use of project funds, all members of the design team should understand and remain aware of the developer's budget limitations. These limitations influence construction options, the choice of design details and frills, and the options for unit layouts. In addition, the design team can assist in streamlining the construction schedule by coordinating construction details and participating directly in the specification, purchasing, and installation of furniture, fixtures, and equipment (FF&E).

Phasing Issues

Few timeshare resorts are built in a single phase. If they are constructed as one-phase projects, they typically involve an interim use—usually a hotel-type operation—at the outset. Single-phase development is often best suited to property conversions, small resorts, urban settings, or other situations in which the demand for accommodation is so great that short-term use will readily support the carry through the sales phase. In any event, a hotel-type interim use sparks the interest of future owners in a timeshare resort but adds concerns associated with prebookings, levels of service, and operational ramp-up. Other issues include wear and tear and evolving demand on support services as rental guests, who are usually more service-dependent than owners, are eventually replaced with owners, who generally expect to be self-catering.

Responsible cash-flow management suggests that the entire common area cannot be built in one step. The development must begin with a critical mass of amenities as well as with modest but adequate facilities for all indoor needs. In what is a difficult but important task for containing development costs, the common and support areas must be programmed to expand to meet the growing demands of the resort during development.

Photo on page 48:

Architecture, landscaping, and site design work together to create a second-home environment at Disney's Vero Beach Resort in Vero Beach, Florida.

Courtesy of E D S A

Accommodating changes along the way will be disruptive, and sensitive forethought must anticipate each step with a plan to mitigate the hardships and inconvenience.

Project Design

The overall timeshare project is designed on two levels. The first level addresses basic issues such as infrastructure, zoning, and building codes. The second level addresses design issues that differentiate one project from another, such as the design theme and entertainment-related design amenities. All timeshare project designers must deal with first-level issues and, in the most successful projects, with both first- and second-level issues.

Project Design Issues

Figure 4-1 provides a checklist of first-level planning and design issues. They range from identification of environmental factors such as wetlands to the availability of

The Hyatt Regency Cerromar in Dorado, Puerto Rico, blends amenities with the natural environment. A naturalistic freshwater pool winds throughout the site for 1,776 feet. The watercourse connects five pools with waterfalls, a subterranean whirlpool, water slides, a swim-up bar, water volleyball, and a children's pool.

Courtesy of E D S A

Courtesy of E D S A

Figure 4-1 A Checklist of First-Level Planning and Design Issues for Timeshare Project Development

Environmental
Endangered species
Flora/fauna
Wetlands/uplands
Hazardous waste
Riverine or coastal systems
Flooding

Water Supply and Quality
Potable water
Irrigation
Grey water

Climate
Prevailing direction and intensity
    of wind
Rain days and amount
Sun angles
Hazardous storms

Soils
Drainage
Bearing for foundations
Suitability and availability for planting
Subsurface conditions

Vegetation
Existing
Available plant material
Transplantability

Topography
Suitability of steep slopes for construction
Views

Archeological/Historical/Cultural Features
Archeological sites
Cultural and historical influences
    on design

Visual Quality/Views
On site
Off site
Special features

Infrastructure
Roads
Sanitary sewer
Potable water
Structured drainage
Electricity
Telephone and cable
Natural gas

Services
Police
Fire
Medical

Access/Location
Proximity to related facilities
    (same "flag")
Arrival sequence
Surrounding land use
Commercial support
Transit
Distance from workplace
Distance from airport

Political Environment
Pro- or antidevelopment
Government stability/elections
Development incentives/disincentives
Tax incentives

Legal Requirements
Zoning
Land use
Environmental
Permitting process
Bureaucratic system

Landownership/Control
Land cost
Sale versus lease
Financing
Surrounding development and
    development potential

Construction Constraints
Budgets
Imports
Taxes
Available workforce

Demand
Market
◆ Marketability
◆ Competition
Sales restrictions
Operations
◆ Availability of skilled labor
◆ Operation as "hotel" during sales
    or low seasons
◆ Reservation systems
◆ Maintenance

Source: E D S A/Edward D. Stone, Jr., and Associates, Ft. Lauderdale, Florida.

building materials. While these issues are fundamental, their resolution offers the designer many opportunities to generate value for a client.

Figure 4-2 lists some potential second-level design issues, ranging from food outlets to design themes. As is discussed throughout the remainder of this chapter, it is in addressing these second-level issues that designers do in fact generate value.

Project Design Process

The project design process typically begins with *site selection,* followed by *analysis and*

Figure 4-2 **A Checklist of Second-Level Planning and Design Issues**

Site Amenities

Natural areas—beaches, ocean, bays, marshes, mountains, and so forth

Master-planned community features—golf course, trails, and so forth

Neighboring attractions—theme parks, retail, and so forth

Theme

Telling a story

Architecture

Interior design

Landscape architecture

Graphic design and signage

Employee approach and uniforms

Restaurants and menus

Entertainment

Food outlets

Shows

Recreational facilities

Special events

Off-site venues

Cultural offerings

Environmental

Other "Software"

"Basecamping"—connections to off-site activities, amenities, and entertainment

Conferences and meetings

Educational activities

Source: E D S A/Edward D. Stone, Jr., and Associates, Ft. Lauderdale, Florida.

preliminary programming to understand the project's development opportunities and constraints. Figure 4-3 provides a general list of the types of elements that may be considered for a specific project during the analysis and programming stage. Each of these elements may be described in both quantitative and qualitative terms. For example, the quantitative description of the pool area may be ten square feet per unit, with deck area for one chair per room. The qualitative description may indicate tropical landscaping and pool structures with a particular theme. *Site planning* follows and addresses building location, massing, circulation, and infrastructure and, during the conceptual design stage, focuses on the more creative, second-level issues of "scripting" and thematic development.

Conceptual design offers the first opportunity for value engineering—a reality check to see if the project is on budget. During the *design development* phase, contract documents are drafted to specify materials, construction details, and design elements. A second cost estimate initiates another round of value engineering. Bids are obtained from contractors, selections are made, and construction begins. During *construction,* designers make periodic site visits on behalf of the developer to ensure

that construction is proceeding in accordance with project design.

Design Theme

The several tasks described above represent the academic side of the design process. By contrast, the creative side of the process calls for developing project themes that will differentiate the resort from the competition and provide guests with an entertaining and memorable environment. The design theme might evoke a specific type of vacation experience. For example, at Disney's Florida Beach Resort in Vero Beach, the "storyline" was a nostalgic visit to an old beachfront hotel. The architecture is reminiscent of earlier days. As for the landscape, the design theme translated into the preservation of old oak trees to reinforce the site's maturity. In a subtle way, the script evokes memories and provides activities for both adults and children.

Alternatively, the design theme might be derived from a project's location. Though vacationers continue to seek amenities such as a beach, mountains, or entertainment, they increasingly want exposure to the area or culture they are visiting. In Florida, the design theme may be a low-key tropical retreat designed in the style of Key West or an old Florida beach house. In the mountains, a project might be designed as a rustic ski lodge, a Victorian mansion, or a hunting lodge.

Setting

As discussed in chapter 3, timeshare resorts are built today in a wide range of locations throughout the world. Regardless of location, a timeshare resort's site or setting is crucial to project success. Most resort settings are distinguished by unusual and attractive natural features. Mountain ranges, shorelines, virgin wilderness, the animal kingdom, and desirable weather frequently combine in some way to inspire a location's appeal. The timeshare development should respect these features by seeking to incorporate elements of nature into the resort. Pacific Shores Nature Resort and Club Asia, two of the case studies featured in chapter 9, base much of their appeal on the preservation and enjoyment of the natural beauty of their respective settings.

Figure 4-3 **Planning and Design Program Considerations**

Design Theme

Responding to an entertainment-oriented "script" for a visit

Unique or fantasy design theme for a particular location

Local vernacular theme

Units

Mix and amenities
- Studio
- One, two, or three bedroom
- Lockoffs
- Kitchen/dining
- Hot tubs

Density in response to
- Economic targets
- Building height and lot coverage constraints

Preservation of and views to natural areas or amenities

Common Areas

Entrance, lobby, and reception area and services

Food and beverage
- Three-meal restaurant
- Specialty restaurants
- Cafeteria
- Snack bars
- Convenience stores
- Kitchens

Club- and activity rooms

Locker rooms

Storage

Security stations

Site

Parking

Drop-off

Guard stations

Utility easements and areas

Landscape/hardscape

Maintenance and storage

Service access

Exterior function areas

Amenities

Central facilities building
- Porte-cochère
- Conference rooms
- Business center
- Community room
- Clubroom
- Health spa/exercise area
- Game rooms

Interiors
- Differentiated or themed design
- In-room hot tubs
- Artwork

Site
- Beach club
- Multiple-pool areas
- Areas for special events
- Water park features
- Spa
- Water features
- Golf—full course and miniature
- Connections to skiing
- Walking trails
- Marina
- Lake or natural area
- Equestrian center
- Tennis

Other
- Concierge services
- Programmed activities for adults and children
- Special events

Operations

Back of house

Deliveries

Maintenance

Maid stations

Internal transportation

Bellman

Developer Facilities

Sales center

Remote (off-property) sales center

Offices

Source: E D S A/Edward D. Stone, Jr., and Associates, Ft. Lauderdale, Florida.

Concept story boards were used to help Disney create a nostalgically themed "1920s Atlantic Seaboard Resort" called Disney's Vero Beach Resort.

Design for Flexibility

Flexibility is an issue in both initial project planning and designing for use. Whether a project is part of a planned resort community or a standalone development, the interaction and tensions among permitting constraints, environmental assets, and the development program require the planning team to create alternative approaches to site planning. At the same time, public or common areas within the site plan and within the architectural plan must accommodate multiple uses.

Flexibility in land planning can be achieved by first considering alternative approaches to the placement and design of major program elements such as site access, internal vehicular service and pedestrian circulation systems, parking amenities, environmentally important areas such as nature preserves and views, development to ensure compatibility with adjacent land uses (both desirable and undesirable), and building configuration. Typically, the project team generates two or three alternative site plans and reaches consensus on the best approach or combination of approaches. The team must consider a number of plan variations

so that the developer is prepared to respond to challenges during the site plan approval process.

Flexibility in design is also critical to satisfying the needs of different facility users and the different ways that facilities are used. Differences in users and uses can lead to tensions that need to be resolved according to the target market, the development program, site conditions, and the project theme. Disney's Old Key West Resort in Lake Buena Vista, Florida, provides an instructive solution to accommodating the need for flexible public spaces while respecting the development's overall design theme. Though the timeshare's restaurant is somewhat modest in size for a 499-unit resort, its food service function is supplemented by additional outdoor seating and an outdoor snack bar with access from the main pool area. Together, the resort's three pool amenity areas accommodate a large number of people and still offer varying degrees of activity, privacy, and proximity to the timeshare units.

Increasingly, some timeshare projects —obviously those not adjacent to a flagship hotel—need to function in part as hotels. The reason for the projects' dual

Hilton Grand Vacations Club Sea World International Center, Orlando, Florida, is a vacation-ownership resort that reflects the historic ambience of a Bermuda seaside village. It features a 4,000-square-foot formal pool and a 3,800-square-foot grotto pool with a rock escarpment emulating the Bermuda shoreline.

function is the growing number of mini-vacations associated with sales; market demand for shorter, more flexible vacation schedules; and the lack of an established influx of potential buyers in locations that are unique or otherwise offer opportunities for adventure. From a design standpoint, shared use with a hotel translates into demand for more common areas (especially restaurants) and a stronger amenity program.

Landscape Design and Signage

Site design, which includes landscaping, hardscaping (paved areas), pools, parking, circulation, site furnishings, fountains, and other amenities, is influenced by several factors, most notably program requirements and budgets. (As a rule of thumb, budgets for site work range from 15 to 20 percent of total project budget.) Landscaping should also reflect and reinforce the project design theme.

The existing vegetation in any environment is usually pivotal to conveying an image of project success and maturity.

Depending on the project budget, other plant material may be available for transplant. In fact, use of native plants reduces irrigation needs, which is always a consideration in project development. Soil conditions (acidity, available nutrients, stability, and so forth) and climate are other controlling factors that dictate plant selection. Clearly, the choice of plant material is largely site-specific and highly variable, though not always apparent from natural conditions. For example, in rainfall-deficient Aruba, the soil can be extraordinarily productive when irrigated.

Because it is visible, signage is another critical design consideration. It guides circulation and use and is one of the most useful ways to communicate design quality and theme. Site signage generally encompasses the following:

- entrance, boundary, and off-site signs, which are prospects' first encounter with the development and therefore should be of particularly high quality;
- sales and construction signs, which are temporary but can convey a sense

of project completion early in the sales cycle;

- vehicular direction and control signs, which should be highly functional;
- signs indicating pedestrian circulation to units, facilities, and amenities; and
- signs that announce amenities or provide instructions.

All signage types must be coordinated with project logos, themes, color schemes, and other recurrent design elements. They must also be hierarchical in structure, size, and placement. The signage for amenity areas can be less substantial than that for other uses and purposes but should nonetheless incorporate lettering and colors similar to that of other project signage.

Signage is created by a capable graphic designer and should provide a consistent and entertaining project accent and a seamless guide to visitors—all without cluttering the environment. The graphic designer should coordinate the design of the exterior signage with the landscape architect and the design of the interior signage with the interior designer and architect and serve as the liaison between the two.

Amenities

Programming amenities is one of the most difficult issues facing a developer. On the one hand, amenities (such as whirlpool tubs, swimming pools, other sports facilities, or even the level of security) represent much of a project's marginal cost. On the other hand, these amenities are usually what distinguishes a project from the competition. Several factors influence the programming of amenities, including the level and nature of market demand, amenities provided or planned by competitive projects, budget considerations, project location and natural features (for example, mountains or beach), and project phasing plans.

Outdoor Amenities

Figure 4-2 provides examples of typical design amenities. The list expands every

year as creative developers and their consultants find new ways to attract buyers. At the same time, it is important to remember that an amenity is more than a specific feature; its value lies in its execution. The difference between a basic pool and deck and a themed pool with unique character, attractive features, and dramatic expanse can be monumental. For most timeshare developers, the goal is to provide a few first-rate amenities rather than a long list of forgettable features. Current trends in timeshare amenities point to the following:

- In more traditional market areas, resorts will demonstrate a stronger residential character.
- Pool areas will continue to be a day-time and evening social focus and may become activity centers for all age groups.
- Health and fitness programs, tennis instruction, nature tours, golf training programs, and learning activities will increase, with appropriate areas needed to stage these activities.
- Security, to some extent an amenity, will probably become more of a design factor and will include guard stations and unit security systems.
- Site planning will increasingly incorporate subtle environmental features that

Disney's Vero Beach Resort creatively integrates function and ambience to announce amenity areas, using an archway to the pool area.

Disney's Old Key West Resort offers amenities for both children and adults.

require the retention or construction of more natural areas.

As the palette of design amenities expands, the entertainment value of resorts will likely grow. At the same time, the thematic elements in building, interior, and site design will incorporate more fantasy and indigenous styles. As a result, timeshare developments will offer increasingly exciting and competitive resort environments.

Indoor Amenities

Even the most benign of environments needs sheltered activities. The choice of indoor activities varies with a resort's market position. Family resorts emphasize a broad range of indoor activities; adult resorts focus on night-time activities and opportunities for pampering and relaxation.

As in the case of outdoor amenities, a critical mass of essential indoor activities must be in place at the outset of project operations, with elective choices added later. Expansion, even of the initial offerings, should be anticipated.

Designing facilities to grow with the least disruption to continued use is a challenge. The best course of action is to construct complete structures that accommodate multiple activities and then relocate selected activities to subsequently completed facilities, thereby allowing the early activities to expand. This approach keeps heavy construction away from guests and guest activities.

Such flexibility requires development to be executed at low to moderate densities and presents challenges associated with construction sequencing, staging, and renovation, particularly with respect to capital and operating budgets. These potentially critical matters can affect both guest impressions and the resort's profitable performance.

Desirable indoor amenities would likely include the following:

◆ Fitness center. A fitness center is an essential initial component. Many vacationers wish to maintain their ongoing fitness regimen while on holiday. Basic apparatus should include aerobic equipment such as treadmills, stair-step equipment, and stationary cycles. Weight machines and free weights are secondary offerings. A floor area for exercise classes (shown on videotape) is the third element in a broadly appealing package.

◆ Kids' club. Facilities and staff that offer children fun-filled activities appeal to parents seeking to enjoy their own activities guiltlessly. Interior activities should be age-segregated for toddlers, juveniles, and teens. The youngest group should usually receive the highest priority in the phasing process. Equipment and design features should reflect the targeted age groups. An indoor playground, video arcade, movie theater, and craft area are a sampling of uses that should be considered.

◆ Food and beverage. Guests may intend to prepare and eat meals within their units, but experience shows that vacationers obtain many meals through home delivery or from outside vendors or on-site food outlets. An area's offerings heavily influence the scale and operating hours of a timeshare resort's food and beverage facilities. The accurate sizing of a food operation is important to keeping it a "self-funding" enterprise. Food and beverage operations are usually not profitable at timeshare resorts because operations costs typically outpace guest demand.

◆ Adult facilities. Many resorts provide clublike facilities intended for the mature guest. Facilities might include a clubroom with lounge, a billiards room, television, live entertainment, and other leisure pursuits.

◆ Departure lounge. Timeshare resorts experience the highest guest turnover during the weekend. On these days, checkout may be required before departure while incoming guests may arrive before units are available. Providing owners with facilities for changing clothes and storing their personal belongings permits them to enjoy the first and last hours of their holiday with minimum inconvenience.

◆ Retail. The most popular vacation activity is shopping, which typically centers around area offerings. Within a self-catering property, however, a convenience retail outlet serves owners' daily needs. It may be characterized as a general store that offers packaged food products, souvenirs, logo apparel, and toiletries and serves other minor needs. It may take the form of a small shop

A pool and its amenities at Port de Plaisance Resort on St. Maarten in the Netherlands Antilles are fashioned from the natural contours of the site and entertain guests day and night.

The units at Summer Bay Resort in Orlando, Florida, are both striking and comfortable.

near the front desk managed by front desk personnel, or it may be an independent outlet leased to a vendor from outside the resort.

◆ Concierge services. Concierge services fulfill timeshare owners' occasional needs for information or assistance, especially information on the surrounding area, tour packages, ticket sales, car rentals, and other services that must be readily available.

Common Facilities

As described below, the design of timeshare developments must also consider common areas and facilities.

Central Facilities Building

The central facilities building typically accommodates the reception area, resort operations, and sales activities. As with hotels, the timeshare guest's initial contact with the property takes place in the reception area. However, given that most timeshare guests check in or out on the same day, the lobby of a timeshare development must accommodate a large number of people at once. Usually located in

the central facilities building, the lobby serves not only as a reception area for owners, but it also establishes the resort's personality and theme either subliminally or exuberantly and reinforces the wisdom of the purchase decision. Most important, it should maximize the use of space to enable all functions to flow easily, reflecting efficiency in operations and a commitment to the satisfaction and comfort of guests. Unique to the timeshare industry, sales activities require the sales office to be separated from the guest registration and check-in area yet integrated into the lobby. Some central facilities buildings also include uses such as an activity room, a restaurant or lounge, and a convenience store.

Operations Areas

Guests and owners form impressions of the resort from the people and activities they observe. From the reservation telephone to the front desk, resort employees and support areas are integral to conveying an impression of quality.

The operations staff functions 24 hours a day every day of the year, even though guests arrive and depart during only a few days of the week. Certain days see more intense use than others, and the demands placed on common areas change as the development of the resort proceeds. To avoid the wastefulness of oversizing or the inconvenience of undersizing, staged expansion should be planned.

The front desk functions symbolize the arrival experience. From the front door of the lobby to the door of the unit, the timeshare resort should greet the senses with visual drama, appealing fragrances, high-touch surfaces, pleasant sounds, and even tempting treats for snacking. The attention to detail during arrival should be of the highest order.

At the same time, certain staff needs can be housed beyond the view of guests. Reservations staff, security, bell storage, the switchboard, and front desk management can all be positioned for easy access while still permitting expansion with little exposure to guests.

The activities that involve the guest should be carefully orchestrated to allow growth without major disruption. Front desk, concierge, and guest services must convey a sense of permanence during all phases of development, minimizing the impression of change or inconvenience.

Sales Centers

Sales are the lifeline of the timeshare industry. The sales staff is critical to the process, but the sales facility shares a great responsibility as well. The architecture of the sales center needs to respond to the needs of the sales process. Spaces must convey a sense of delight, welcome, and comfort. Traffic flows should provide easy movement, minimize conflict between prospects, and offer a variety of presentation paths designed to meet the weather, volume, and prospect variables.

The sequence of the sales process is usually developed by the project sponsor in a manner that best serves the sales operation. Several steps typically characterize the process, including the following:

♦ The welcome. The sales staff expects the prospect for a scheduled appointment and awaits the prospect's arrival. The path to the welcome desk should be obvious; the prospect should wait no more than a few minutes before a host arrives to begin the tour.

♦ Addressing family needs. The sales staff offers facilities for the needs of the family. Restrooms and child care are available for those who need them. Facilities that appeal to the child also appeal to the parent. Children should be nearby but out of sight, yet parents should feel free to check on their children when they wish.

♦ The warm-up. The host becomes acquainted with the prospect and offers

The parlor/morning room in the central facilities building of Hilton Grand Vacations Club Sea World in Orlando, Florida, is a place for leisure activity.

©Sargent, courtesy of Pamela Temples Interiors, Inc.

snacks and beverages. Settings that convey a sense of energy and vitality keep the interest high.

- The show. A standardized presentation usually follows. It could be a live interactive presentation, a media presentation, or both. It seeks to relax, impress, entertain, and bring a smile (if not a laugh) to the prospect.

- The tour. A walking tour usually highlights the product's major elements. It might include a fixed or interactive display that showcases the sponsor, the master plan, exchangeability, and available services and benefits; a survey of major amenities; and a visit to a sample unit (predetermined during the warm-up) that best reflects the prospect's holiday needs.

- The close. A comfortable setting allows a formal presentation of the offering on an individual basis.

- The thank you. A gift is usually more than a reward for visiting the resort or purchasing a timeshare. For the non-purchaser, the presentation of a gift represents a final chance to offer an exit purchase. For the buyer, it could mean a clubroom setting and complimentary celebration (nonalcoholic champagne) to welcome the "new owners" into the membership of fellow resort owners.

The personalized process adopted by various companies' sales groups differs greatly and affects the design of sales centers as well as their size, flexibility, and features.

Back of the House

The invisible "back-of-the-house" service functions should be organized to ensure a high-quality, unobtrusive resort experience. The goal of the back-of-the-house staff is to keep the resort meticulously groomed each day. Operational facilities for housekeeping, grounds, engineering, storage, maintenance, transportation, and waste management, as well as utilities and staff housing, must be located on the resort site. In more urban settings, many of these services can be outsourced. In larger resorts, they may be outsourced until a critical mass allows the efficient delivery of the services by resort personnel. Plans for the

The location theme dominates the design vocabulary in the clubhouse lounge of the Paradise Village resort in Nuevo Vallarta, Mexico.

©Starling Productions/Orlando, FL, courtesy of Pamela Temples Interiors, Inc.

provision of these services determine the size and timing of required facilities. In large, low-density resorts, the delivery of services becomes a major concern in programming and designing needed spaces. Services and materials that must be provided over vast acreage must be planned in terms of the variety and suitability of transportation conveyances and delivery systems.

If any element is likely to be underplanned, it is back-of-the-house operations. Long-term back-of-the-house needs frequently outstrip the land area assigned to them, often necessitating outsourcing or off-site support facilities, which add cost and inconvenience to the operation. Moreover, as resorts succeed, the level of services demanded by guests grows. Over time, new services and facilities never considered during conceptualization of the resort become competitive necessities. They can challenge the most conscientious effort to forecast long-term needs and product necessities.

Accommodations

The unique nature of the timeshare industry has resulted in hybrid and seemingly contradictory guidelines for interior design. The timeshare product straddles the design elements of hotel and home. Like a hotel, the design must generate broad market appeal. But the comforts of home —or of the "ideal" home—must be considered as well. After all, the potential client is making a more considerable investment and staying for longer periods of time than in the case of a hotel. At the same time, the durability standards common to hotel design need to be maintained. In some instances, higher occupancy rates in timeshare complexes dictate even more stringent durability standards.

Unit Configurations

The theme and number and distribution of different types of units are determined

Amenities such as a delicatessen enhance the value and convenience of timeshare ownership. The design of the deli at Hilton Grand Vacations Club Sea World echoes the marine motif of nearby Sea World.

©Sargent, courtesy of Pamela Temples Interiors, Inc.

by factors such as cost per square foot, sleep value versus exchange value, location, and market appeal.

Timeshare units are often represented by the number of persons they can sleep. The minimum head count goal is generally as follows: a studio sleeps four; a one-bedroom unit sleeps four; a two-bedroom unit sleeps six; and a three-bedroom unit sleeps eight. When units are designed as lockoffs, the bed count may be even higher.

Timeshare units typically include a living room, kitchen, dining area, bathrooms, and sleeping accommodations. As noted, units range from studios to two bedrooms plus a lockoff. The latter permits conversion to a three-bedroom unit. In fact, one-bedroom timeshare units are often designed to connect with a lockoff to create a two-bedroom unit. To achieve maximum occupancy and revenue, floor plans need to be flexible and versatile. For example, the smallest studio unit usually sleeps four but exchanges for sleeping two. To the customer, however, the perceived value of the studio is that of a suite. One bay accommodates two use areas: a sleep-

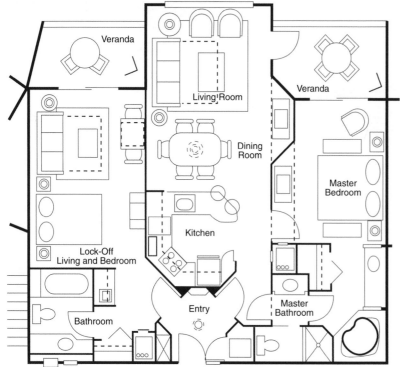

In the Hyatt Hacienda del Mar in Dorado, Puerto Rico, the washer/dryer is located in the vestibule of the two-bedroom lockoff unit, both to maximize living space within the unit and to enable guests occupying both parts of the unit to use the appliances.

Courtesy of Pamela Temples Interiors, Inc.

ing area and a sitting area. The conversion of existing hotel rooms into a timeshare property usually transforms two hotel bays into a one-bedroom unit and three bays into a two-bedroom unit.

The design of timeshare accommodations has been marginally standardized through the influence of international exchange organizations that set minimum standards for unit design and features. At the same time, in competitive marketplaces such as Orlando, Florida, major players stand side by side with their alternative offerings. Styles may vary and unit size and construction may differ, but timeshare units typically share several common characteristics as noted below.

Interior Design and FF&E

The selection of interior design elements and fixtures, furnishings, and equipment (FF&E) depends not only on the overall design theme but also on knowledge of

the project's target market and that market's expectations of luxury and comfort. In addition, consideration of geographic location and type of use are crucial. Clearly, a family at a beach has different requirements than a couple in Las Vegas.

As noted, a timeshare unit is intended to serve as a luxurious "home" for the duration of a vacation. To that end, the following interior design considerations should apply:

- A strong sense of "home away from home." The unit plan must convey a residential rather than a hotel feel. Plan layouts, décor, appointments, and even utensils must suggest a private dwelling. The architectural design program should call for smaller buildings, convenient front-door parking, private entries, private patios and balconies where appropriate, and themes with a residential flair.

- Small but well-featured kitchens. The kitchen signals the primary difference between a hotel suite and a self-catering unit. It implies independence, efficiency, and economy by permitting guests to enjoy a meal or snack without room service. Storage is not an issue, but function is of the utmost concern. Appliances and cabinetry should serve guest needs for a two-week stay. The features should be those found in full-size kitchens. A microwave oven, ice maker, and even dishwasher (in larger units) are almost essential.

- Ample sleeping accommodation. Given that timeshare buyers generally believe that a timeshare unit costs less than multiple hotel rooms for the same group over the desired period, emphasis on bed count is important. A typical two-bedroom unit is frequently outfitted with, at minimum, a queen-size bed in the master suite, two double beds in the second bedroom, a sleeper-sofa in the living room, and enough floor area for a crib or rollaway.

- A complete housewares package. The sleeping population of the unit suggests the needed quantity of plates, cups, and silverware. In addition, frequently used countertop appliances and accessories should be considered. A coffee maker, toaster, teapot, hand blender, and the like permit efficient use of the kitchen.

♦ Ample dressing areas. The group occupying a holiday unit generally arrives and departs in unison. As a result, group members tend to dress and retire at the same time. The design and number of bathrooms and dressing areas should therefore reflect likely concurrent demand. Multiple-bedroom units should contain multiple bathrooms. When practical, bathrooms should be compartmentalized with a sink outside the hygiene facilities. Mirrors are also a premium. Larger or multiple mirrors offer plenty of primping space for all occupants.

♦ A television by every bed. Family members' viewing choices likely vary. Youngsters and some adults find video games a pleasurable pastime. With a television positioned by every bed (including the sleeper-sofa in the living area), most occupants can satisfy their viewing desires without infringing on one another.

♦ Vacation-sized closets and dressers. Unlike the case of the primary or second home, where residents permanently store their possessions, guests occupying a timeshare bring needed articles and possessions with them for the visit. Luggage capacity controls the amount of clothing guests will need to store. The largest demand on the closet is the luggage itself. An extra closet for the sleeper-sofa is desirable.

♦ Blackout curtains. People on holiday usually do not set the alarm clock. Therefore, the curtains in the living areas as well as in the bedrooms should be capable of darkening the unit, even at midday.

♦ Expandable or large dining tables. Since a unit's bed count is normally greater than its bedroom count, the dining area

In the residential units of Bluegreen Mountain Loft in Gatlinburg, Tennessee, the interior design emphasizes physical comfort and relaxation and reflects local traditions in the choice of fabrics, artwork, and furniture styles.

should be sized to accommodate the unit's actual number of occupants. Bar counter seats can be counted as part of the total. A two-bed unit should consider a six-seat table plus two bar seats as minimum dining accommodations.

◆ A standard tub in the common bath. Few occupants prefer baths to showers, but a family often uses the tub to bathe youngsters.

◆ Master bathroom. The master bathroom provides an excellent opportunity for making a statement in a timeshare resort, and the master suite should suggest the ultimate in self-indulgence. Master bathrooms should be large and emphasize all the luxuries that owners and guests do not find at home. (As times change, such features should at least equal those in the home.) Large whirlpool tubs, mirrors, double-vanity areas, double sinks, and shower areas are stan-

dard items in most timeshare baths. A two-person tub, frequently outside the bathroom and on display in the bedroom itself, is a typical feature. Viewing the television from the tub under dim, romantic lighting is a private indulgence often not associated with home.

◆ Exceptional views. Unlike hotel rooms, the holiday unit is lived in, not just slept in. Accordingly, the unit's orientation toward an amenity or natural feature is important to the dwelling's livability.

Color

A unit's color scheme helps convey a sense of arrival and must be presented with dramatic flair. Color is used to move the emotions. The decision to create a sense of home or a surge of vibrant energy depends on a development's market. Whatever the case, the careful choice of color can give a development a competitive edge.

Bright, vibrant colors are best suited for resort destinations that offer constant and varied activities. Yellow is a good wall color; it suggests the warmth of the sun, even on cloudy days. While brightness is an important component, color should also be used for contrasts between shades and tones. If a room is all beige with only minor hints of color, it may not present itself as well as a room with color on the walls and a contrasting color on the ceiling. At Pirates Pension at Bluebeard's Castle in St. Thomas, the yellow walls suggest the area's nearly year-round sunny environment. Moreover, green ceilings contrast with yellow walls and white crown moldings and trim.

While all rooms do not need bright and bold primary colors, they do need color contrast. Further, the exterior environment should influence the interior color palette. For example, because Bluegreen's Mountain Loft resort in Gatlinburg, Tennessee, is nestled in the mountains, designers selected a calm, relaxed color scheme. During sales presentations, the sales staff paints a picture of quiet and solitude, as reflected in the units' interior design. Deep beige walls

Bluebeard's Castle in St. Thomas, Virgin Islands, was converted from a hotel to a timeshare resort. These floor plans show how unit floor plans were reconfigured to accommodate the change in use.

Courtesy of Pamela Temples Interiors, Inc.

provide a neutral backdrop for the red and green of the draperies and furniture. The richness of these colors is mirrored in the trees and their leaves.

Durability and Maintenance

The demands of durability and preventive maintenance dictate the selection of commercial-quality furniture. The development of trevira fabrics, with a better hand and a wide range of patterns, permits design sophistication while satisfying fire codes. Laminated fabrics are essential in areas that come in contact with water or food; similarly, plastic laminate is the best choice for countertops. Upholstery fabrics must have above 30,000 double rubs (a measure of durability) and be able to withstand sun exposure and cleaning without noticeable fading. Due to higher occupancies and longer stays, furniture in a timeshare unit wears harder than in most hotels and residences; therefore, all chairs and tables require reinforcement. Flooring specifications should call for medium to heavy contract standards; at minimum, all carpets should be solution-dyed nylon. Providing for maximum durability reduces maintenance requirements and thus contains costs.

For a timeshare unit to show well for sales, it must exhibit residential qualities as well as commercial durability. Elaborate window treatments and furniture with round, soft edges add to the residential ambience. Round, skirted tables with a glass top—rather than square or rectangular end tables with four legs—enhance the décor. Since most timeshare units are of minimum square footage, a glass-top dining table makes the dining area appear larger.

Image

The overall design of a timeshare resort must respond to several missions, each of which forges a part of the holiday experience. The design approach can shape product identity and inspire the success

In the Bluebeard's Castle resort in St. Thomas, Virgin Islands, the units focus on exterior space, with a wide expanse of windows providing a great ocean view. The Caribbean décor brings the exterior inside: the colored walls and ceilings convey the freshness of the geographic location. The tile floors are typical of the area.

of a development both during its initial stages and throughout ongoing operations. Through careful attention to design, the image of a resort can be molded to achieve the following:

Although the one-bedroom units at Hilton Grand Vacations Ocean Plaza in South Beach, Miami, Florida, are small, the strategic placement of the bathroom allows access from both sleeping areas. Therefore, the unit sleeps four and exchanges four. During the day, the pocket doors are opened and hidden, turning the whole area into one undivided space.

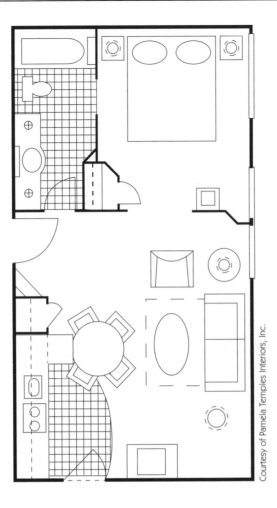

Courtesy of Pamela Temples Interiors, Inc.

◆ Create a theme. As noted earlier, most successful timeshare projects incorporate a theme that is reinforced by the resort's architectural design, signage, sales center, and unit interiors. The theme gives the sales staff a story to tell as they escort potential buyers around the property. An instructive example of an integrated project theme is the first Hampton Vacation Resorts project, called Oak Plantation, which is located in Orlando. Developed by Vistana, the project converted apartments into timeshare units. The overall Southern plantation theme is the product of several coordinated exterior and interior elements: the large expanse of oak trees on the property, the unit architecture that simulates cottages, and the sales facility designed to resemble a large plantation. The reception center's main focus is a fireplace complemented with overstuffed lounge seating and artwork depicting magnolias.

◆ Suggest a second-home environment of the most desirable nature. The architec-

To appeal to urban sophisticates, a neutral color palette and "cutting edge" furniture was selected. Because the building was in a historic district when it was converted from a hotel to timeshare, the exterior facade could not be modified. Unit layout and furniture placement sometimes produced unusual window placements. Consequently, windows were de-emphasized with simple, neutral treatments.

©Michael Lowry Photography, courtesy of Pamela Temples Interiors, Inc.

ture can borrow from a world of design inspiration, but no adaptation should come from forms and materials alien to the underlying residential purpose.

- Inspire a unique setting that promises the fantasy of a perfect holiday. Well-conceived settings are almost-perfect escapes from reality. All aspects of the visual and sensual experience should convince visitors that they have left the "real" world behind.

- Produce memorable and photogenic encounters that prompt visual excitement. Visual delight results from the complete integration of all elements of the resort into a well-orchestrated whole. A nearly perfect photograph of the holiday setting shown to friends at home is almost always accompanied by glowing comments about "how nice the place was." Photographs and memories are the best long-term advertising any development can buy.

- Provide features and landmarks that orient guests in large resorts. In large resorts, new guests or owners can be easily overwhelmed and even lose their way. Architecture represents major reference points within the resort. Stylistic features and important common buildings should orient guests by providing familiar references to the part of the resort they call home.

- Promote the importance of the individual. Architecture and design elements can quickly overpower both the setting and the individual. A project must impress but not intimidate. The scale of buildings and treatment of entries and exterior surfaces should enable individuals to identify their dwelling as exclusively their own.

- Integrate all elements of the resort to create a cohesive image. Buildings, landscaping, signage, amenities, and interior décor as well as printed materials, accessories, and even transport should work in concert to communicate a strong, singular image of the resort.

Cost Issues

Each year the bar is raised on product delivery as unit, décor, amenity, and presentational expectations take aim at creating a better product in tune with market interests and marketing objectives. The result is increases in capital expenditures, maintenance budgets, and operations costs. The consumer responds with ever-stronger demand, an increased willingness to pay incrementally more for the product, and growing respect for the industry.

Decisions about amenities are especially difficult. Amenity costs can easily challenge a project's budget, but the impact of well-executed amenities is central to differentiating a given resort from the competition. Unit amenities communicate private benefits. Whirlpool tubs, a wet bar, a big-screen television, fireplaces, and the like add sizzle to the décor and offer lifestyle opportunities often not available at home. The costs are significant to the overall budget, but the developer incurs the associated expenses with the construction of each unit. In a multiple-building resort, the total dollars spent on development ideally should keep pace with dollars earned.

Project amenities such as swimming pools, golf, and ski facilities; architectural quality and theming; and beautifully landscaped campuses make owners' and guests' holiday experiences exciting and memorable. At the same time, project amenity costs can seldom be expensed over the development period. The developer must provide a significant portion—if not all—of the amenity package during the initial phase. The capital demands are great and the repayment is protracted, stretching over the length of the development and sales cycle. Thus, decisions on the number and nature of project amentites must be carefully evaluated in light of costs, benefits, and project financing.

Chapter 5

Effective Vacation-Ownership Marketing

George Leposky, Interval International

Effective marketing and sales of timeshare and vacation-ownership properties involves generating leads, converting leads into sales, and retaining sales once they are made. In the industry's early years, scattershot marketing and heavy-handed, high-pressure sales tactics earned timesharing a questionable reputation. Recent years, however, have seen a trend toward the use of more sophisticated techniques, such as database management, that target likely prospects. In addition, softer-sell approaches build personal relationships while demonstrating the prospect's need for the product.

At first, timeshare marketing techniques drew heavily from the experience of professionals with a mass-marketing orientation in fields such as land sales, vacation real estate, consumer-product marketing and sales, and finance. In the 1970s, marketing professionals from these backgrounds began to experiment with marketing the concept of shared ownership of vacation property.

Traditional Marketing Techniques

The objective of a marketing program is to generate leads or sales prospects. Recognizing that they were dealing with a new product, the early timeshare promoters assumed that incentives would capture the attention and interest of prospective customers. Incentives included premiums such as clocks, luggage, pots and pans, and vacation certificates promising free or discounted travel to and accommodations at popular destinations. Experience has shown, however,

Recognizing the importance of first impressions, Hilton Grand Vacations Club Sea World in Orlando, Florida, features an elegant, beautifully landscaped entrance to its timeshare resort.

that premiums, especially those not related to the timeshare product, tend to attract people who are more interested in the premium than the timeshare.

Based on their previous marketing and sales experience, the early timeshare promoters drew on and adapted the familiar lead-generation techniques listed below.

- Box programs. Box programs attempt to encourage people to fill out and deposit in a box a slip of paper with their name, address, and telephone number. Boxes are located in high-traffic locations such as hotel and restaurant lobbies, convenience stores, shopping malls, and tourist-oriented rest stops along major highways. Box programs are inexpensive and easy to maintain, but they do not target prospects accurately and thus lead to few closings.

- Direct mail. While direct mail generates a predictable volume of leads on a controllable basis, its cost-effectiveness varies with the quality of the mailing list, the design of the mailing piece or package, the nature of the premium offered, and the response rate.

- Sweepstakes. Sweepstakes are a special type of direct mail that offer recipients who attend a sales presentation a chance to win a high-ticket gift. Because many sweepstakes promotions fail to disclose the minuscule chances of winning, Florida regulators prohibited sweepstakes in the 1980s.

- Telemarketing. The timeshare industry uses telemarketing to identify which respondents to box programs are qualified purchasers and to arrange tours for such prospects. It is also used for cold calling (making telephone calls to con-

Photo on page 70:

Club Intrawest's Tremblant ski resort looks particularly inviting under its mantle of snow.

Courtesy of Club Intrawest

sumers with whom the resort and its representatives have made no previous contact) to generate leads, although new telemarketing laws in many states restrict cold calls.

- ◆ Minivacations (often called mini-vacs). A mini-vac is a short vacation offered to guests at little or no charge. In the early days of the timeshare industry, minivacations typically required participants to attend a timeshare sales presentation during their stay. Today, mini-vacs, in conjunction with a low-key invitation to an optional sales presentation, are gaining popularity. The mini-vac is an extremely successful lead-generation technique. It allows the resort to sell itself by permitting prospective buyers to experience some of the pleasure and enjoyment of ownership. Its use, however, is limited by inventory constraints. Many marketers say they would make more extensive use of mini-vacs if they had more space to house mini-vac guests either on the premises or nearby.

- ◆ Off-premises contact (OPC). Working on a busy street or beach or in a booth in a high-traffic location such as a convenience store, shopping mall, or hotel or restaurant lobby, OPC representatives try to initiate contact with passersby and offer an incentive to tour a given resort. OPCs offer a cost-effective way to reach prospects interested enough in the destination to have traveled there. On the negative side, OPCs can be expensive in competitive areas where locations command high rental fees. In addition, OPCs require intensive management, and their obtrusive nature creates image problems that have prompted many jurisdictions to restrict such activities.

The shortcomings of the traditional techniques became evident as the timeshare industry expanded and consumers grew increasingly knowledgeable of the product; nonetheless, the techniques continue to find use today where state and local laws permit. They can be both acceptable and successful if they are well managed and properly focused in support of a desirable timeshare product.

As noted in chapter 2, the most frequent means by which current timeshare owners

The sales center at Villa del Palmar Cabo San Lucas, with a view of the arch in the rocky headland at the southern tip of Mexico's Baja California peninsula and a U.S. Navy ship visiting Cabo San Lucas Bay.

Courtesy of George Leposky, Interval International

first heard of their timeshare resort was through direct mail and OPCs.

Newer Marketing Techniques

In recent years, industry marketers have begun to use a variety of innovative, non-threatening, and respectful techniques to familiarize prospects with the timeshare product.

- Operating a visitor information center. In communities with a large influx of tourists, a timeshare resort may open a visitor information center staffed by trained professionals who provide directions, offer literature, sell attraction tickets, make hotel reservations—and offer tours of the sponsoring resort. A low-key version of an OPC, such a center may function solely as a community service project sponsored by the resort or as a joint effort of the resort and the local chamber of commerce or convention and visitors' bureau.

- Leveraging a brand name. As will be discussed in chapter 6, the 1984 entry of Marriott Corporation into the timeshare industry signaled the official debut of the hospitality-brand timeshare. Today, most of the major brand-name hospitality companies in the United States have embraced the timesharing concept. From the consumer's standpoint, a brand name makes the timeshare product recognizable and familiar in form, feel, and personality. As Robert A. Miller, Marriott's top vacation-ownership executive from 1984 to 1997, told *Vacation Industry Review* in 1992, brands also have a marketing cost advantage. "... [T]he Marriott brand ... overcomes the suspicion that people generally associate with this product, and it allows us to sell the product at a lower marketing cost. I don't think our competitors can deliver the quality level we build at a price comparable to ours. They have to put more money into marketing and selling, leaving less for the product."

- Cross-marketing of brand products. A hospitality brand usually considers its hotel customers prime prospects for its vacation-ownership products. A company may market its vacation-ownership resorts through tent cards in hotel rooms, information desks in hotel lobbies, and videos on an in-house television channel. When a hospitality company builds a timeshare resort near one of its hotels, as in the case of Marriott, Hyatt, and Four Seasons, the proximate location facilitates marketing as well as shared use of recreational amenities. Enabling timeshare buyers to participate in frequent user "awards" programs further strengthens the tie to the hospitality brand.

- Market segmentation. One sign that timeshare marketing has grown more sophisticated is the increasing tendency to target specific market segments. In the hospitality industry, market segmentation is largely a function of price. It occurs when a branded company markets to its existing customers, as discussed above. But targeting a particular market segment also occurs in the vacation-ownership industry through a focused pricing and marketing strategy. For example, Bluegreen Corporation, Peppertree Resorts, Ltd., and Shell Vacations, LLC, are among the firms that have carved out a strong price-to-value niche by targeting middle-income customers for the sale of vacation-ownership products.

- Affinity marketing. An example of affinity marketing is a Hertz rental car with a hang-tag on its mirror promoting Marriott Vacation Club International's resorts. The vacation-ownership divisions of hospitality companies take advantage of their corporate parent's strategic alliances both to create cross-promotions and to send direct mail targeted to strategic partners' customer lists. However, a hospitality brand is not a prerequisite for participation in affinity marketing. Westgate Resorts in Florida is involved

Marriott Vacation Club International has built sophisticated, high-tech features into its new timeshare sales facility in Orlando, such as wall-sized maps that illuminate specific information about the company and its system of timeshare resorts and other facilities and services.

Diane R. Suchman

Diane R. Suchman

in affinity marketing relationships with the Florida Marlins baseball team and the Mall of America in Bloomington, Minnesota. Vistana has targeted the golfer niche by establishing a liaison with the Professional Golfers' Association and is building resorts adjacent to golf courses. The Kosmas Group, a Florida-based resort development firm, operates a cruise ship from Port Canaveral to generate prospects for its timeshare sales operation. Intrawest Corporation, one of North America's largest operators of ski resorts, launched its Club Intrawest vacation-ownership product at ski centers in Tremblant, Quebec, and Whistler, British Columbia; and Marriott has agreed to develop luxury vacation-ownership properties at five alpine resorts owned by the American Skiing Company.

♦ Calling the product by another name. Although the term timeshare remains in widespread use, many industry executives—particularly at the upscale end of the pricing spectrum—now prefer to call their product vacation ownership or vacation-club membership, depending on the nature of the offering in a given instance. In part, changing the name is a way of disassociating the product from the tainted image of timesharing, but the name change also reflects the fact that vacation clubs are a different product than the traditional timeshare interval. As discussed in chap-

♦ Marketing with Mixed Media

Electronic media can play an important role in marketing timeshare projects. The old timeshare industry saying "High tech equals no check" might have been true a couple of years ago; today, however, developers need to start paying attention to inexpensive marketing opportunities provided by new technologies such as targeted Internet e-mail, CD-ROM direct-mail marketing, and interactive kiosks. After all, timeshare is not currently a sought-out product. It must be aggressively marketed and sold—and this is where electronic media come into play.

Targeted Internet E-Mail

With over 100 million Internet users worldwide, marketers everywhere are trying to figure out how to make money from the Internet's new captive audience. Unfortunately, many marketers understand neither their audiences nor their audiences' reasons for using the Internet. To begin, Internet users do not view themselves as captives of the medium in the way that television watchers are captives of television. Instead, Internet users revel in the control they exercise over what they see at any given moment. For marketers, reaching such an audience means going beyond the passive nature of television advertisements. The most appeal-ing feature of the Internet is that users do not have to see any advertisements at all.

So what are Internet users looking for? They want a sense of community interwoven with commerce. In other words, they desire access to products and services, but they would like that access to come through someone they know and trust. And that is why home pages on the Internet are so ineffective unless they offer a wanted product (such as music CDs or books) that can be easily purchased over the World Wide Web. Massive, unsolicited e-mail mailings (spam mail) also are ineffective due to their impersonal approach. If marketers want to generate leads on the Internet, they need to pay attention to the unlimited possibilities of developing one-on-one relationships with consumers via solicited Internet e-mail.

To develop these relationships, marketers and salespersons must use exactly the same techniques they have used for years: find out what they have in common with the people they want to reach, create sizzle and buying urgency, and overcome any objections to the product. Technology will never replace the relationship-building skills of the salesperson, but it can be effective in creating sizzle and overcoming objections if only because of its built-in credibility in the eyes of the prospect.

Just as salespersons now use their local churches and sports clubs to meet potential customers and forge a sense of community with those prospects, the Internet offers cross-marketing and selling channels to every interest group on the planet. Promotion is accepted on the Internet as long as it is personalized and addresses the specific wants and needs of the people receiving the e-mail messages. Never before have we had the ability to tailor every communication to the exact tastes of potential consumers. Since it costs essentially the same to send 1 million e-mails as one e-mail, marketers can customize sales promotions to the demographic profile of each prospect in the pipeline and come up with presentations that meet the personalized expectations of each profiled demographic group or online community.

Direct-Mail CD-ROM

Another example of customized electronic marketing is the much-unused CD-ROM direct-mail piece. At a per unit cost comparable to many printed direct-mail pieces, the CD-ROM offers the possibility of targeting specific groups of consumers based on their demographics and interests. By using elementary software, savvy marketers can create visually stunning, up-to-date electronic communications that employ all the best features

ter 3, the standard timeshare product is ownership of a fixed week at a specific resort, with exchanges possible through affiliation with one of the industry's exchange companies. A vacation club, on the other hand, typically involves multiple resort locations accessible through internal exchange, along with other value-added benefits, including discounts on various club products and programs as an enhancement to the club's own exchange capability. Many vacation clubs are point-based. External trades are handled through an outside exchange company that provides a full array of destinations and experiences. Today, most brand-name hospitality firms and many independent develop-

of the Internet—namely, interactive navigational tools that engage viewers and allow them to participate in their own decision-making process.

The direct-mail CD-ROM periodically sent by AOL to potential Internet users is an excellent example. This interactive CD-ROM allows the user to purchase the product immediately. Timeshare marketers can achieve similar results by linking a CD-ROM to their home page on the web, which can then be set up with e-commerce to permit transactions. E-commerce, of course, is the last piece of any successful digital strategy; it directly relates to a company's revenue stream.

For all its unrealized promise, the CD-ROM mailer, as with any other technological solution, has a couple of serious drawbacks that need to be factored into all financial projections. The first is penetration. How many people who receive a CD-ROM have a computer that is capable of running the disk at optimum speed? If half of recipients do not own a computer, then the cost of the project essentially doubles. The best solution is to undertake in-depth database profiling to ensure that the CD-ROM is compatible with all platforms and with several generations of computer hardware.

The second potential difficulty is technical support. Unlike printed pieces, which require no assistance, effective CD-ROM mailers need the support of some type of help desk that can assist prospects in overcoming any technical or educational issues. While a help desk can be expensive to maintain, the answer lies in cross-training help desk personnel to become both salespersons and technical support people, thus countering extra costs with extra income.

Interactive Kiosks

For marketers interested in off-site sales, interactive kiosks offer a tremendous opportunity to attract prospective customers without the high cost of setting up off-site sales centers. By focusing on high-traffic venues such as shopping malls, marketers can easily program stand-alone electronic kiosks to provide arresting graphics, text, video, and voiceovers that appeal to people already disposed to buy something. Once again, the primary attraction is the consumer's ability to control the content and flow of the presentation, thereby creating a personalized, no-pressure tour of the product or service.

All that is required for a standalone kiosk is a preprogrammed computer, an attractive and sturdy case that can withstand the rigors of hundreds of users each day, a full-sized touchscreen computer monitor, and a printer. The obvious advantage of a printer is that coupons, brochures, or tickets can be issued on the spot, giving customers immediate access to premiums, prizes, or special offers. Another handy kiosk add-on is a telephone that connects to a representative who can book resort tours, rentals, or attractions.

In addition to videos and photographs, a kiosk can even accommodate virtual reality walk-throughs of a resort and its units and amenities. Prospects can tour a property by simply moving their finger across the touchscreen monitor. And a sales kiosk that does not require wages, coffee breaks, or vacations is a powerful marketing tool.

Because of the untested capabilities of the new interactive technologies, it is easy to understand why developers might hesitate before investing thousands of dollars in high-tech marketing presentations. After all, will any of the new technologies ever close a single sale? Probably not. But it is not hard to see the role of interactive technologies as sales tools that can dispose a potential client to buy a product or service—and that is the most that we can ever hope to ask of technology.

Source: James Dunn, Interval International, *Urban Land* Timeshare Supplement, August 1998, p. 13.

Bluegreen Corporation maintains information kiosks in shopping malls in Myrtle Beach, South Carolina, to direct visitors to area attractions, including its timeshare resorts.

ers offer vacation clubs, with the brands tapping into the benefits of their existing loyalty programs.

◆ Database marketing. The evolution of market research in recent years has made possible the refinement of databases that permit prospective customers to be targeted with pinpoint accuracy. The process requires state-of-the-art computer technology for storing and processing large amounts of data and the use of that technology to segment large populations into recognizable groups based on demographic, cultural, lifestyle, and socioeconomic variables that reflect a propensity to purchase. Today's technological resources enable vacation-ownership marketers to analyze their buyer profile and create a model to concentrate on their best prospects, thus decreasing marketing costs while achieving higher closing rates.

◆ Reloads and upgrades. Reloading is selling more of a product to people who already own it; upgrading enables owners to turn in their existing product for a larger and/or newer product with features not available at the time of the initial purchase. Reload and upgrade programs can be extremely profitable because they involve a universe of informed and prequalified buyers and require little or no expenditures for lead generation. From a broader perspective, everything a resort does over time to keep its owners satisfied with the vacation-ownership product enhances owner receptivity to a reload or upgrade program. Some multisite developers rely heavily on reloads and upgrades to sell their newest inventory.

◆ Referrals. Most vacation-ownership marketers embrace the time-honored practice of generating prospects by asking satisfied customers to refer their friends. The customer making the referral typically receives some type of consideration or gift after the referred person becomes an owner. Large developers with extensive owner bases commonly use referral programs. For them, the referral process can be inexpensive; most cost is incurred after the sale, and referrals can yield a high closing rate.

◆ High-tech marketing to individuals. With 50 percent of American households now owning personal computers and the number of users projected to grow by 8 million each year for the next three years,[1] astute vacation-ownership marketers are beginning to employ the Internet, CD-ROM disks, cable television, and interactive kiosks in public places to achieve real-time, online communication with individual customers. By using database marketing to tailor their message and information technology to deliver it, marketers have the capability to design products for an individual market segment and then customize intensely motivating messages targeted to specific members of that segment. Web-based bookings and sales tour appointments are particularly inexpensive, and their reduced marketing costs help make product prices more competitive, although these activities raise legal issues with respect to registration requirements. Furthermore, Web-based marketing requires a commitment of resources to manage the website properly and update it periodically so that its content remains current.

Marketing Volume Requirements

In creating a lead-generation program that involves a mix of techniques, a marketer relies on market research, past experience, and industry rules of thumb to estimate both the number of contacts needed to attract one responsive prospect and the number of prospects who must be toured through the property to obtain a sale.

Figure 5-1 contains pro forma calculations for a generic timeshare marketing effort. If the marketer employs 20 salespersons and wants each to tour two prospects a day, he or she will presumably need to generate 40 prospects a day. Assuming a 1 percent response rate among contacts, 4,000 contacts are necessary to generate 40 prospects a day. To keep the sales staff busy in a year with 360 selling days, the marketer must generate 1.44 million contacts annually.

Of those 40 prospects a day, perhaps four will buy. A 10 percent closing rate is considered average for the timeshare industry, although many marketers claim more—and few will admit to less. The methods used to calculate closing rates vary widely from one operation to another, with some marketers counting and others excluding from their computations any walk-in visitors and identified prospects who do not meet specific marketing criteria.

At the rate of four sales a day, the marketing operation generates 1,440 sales during a 360-day selling year, but some buyers have second thoughts and rescind (cancel) the contract before their sale becomes final. As will be noted in chapter 6, recent in-

Figure 5-1 **Lead Generation (Hypothetical Example)**

- 100 contacts (mailings, calls, and so forth) = 1 response (prospect)
- 40 prospects per day required or 100 x 40 = 4,000
- 40 prospects per day x 10% closing rate = 4 sales per day
- Mailings per year = 4,000 x 360 = 1,440,000
- 4 sales per day x 360 selling days per year = 1,440 sales per year
- 1,440 sales per year less 20% rescission rate = 1,152 net sales per year
- 1,152 sales x $10,000 per sale = $11,520,000 total sales

dustry surveys indicate that developers average reported rescission rates of 14 to 15 percent. However, some industry observers believe that a rescission rate of about 20 percent is in fact more typical, although some of the better marketers have brought their rescissions down into the mid- to low teens.

After eliminating rescissions, the generic marketing operation concludes the year with 1,152 net sales. At an average sale price of $10,000, sales for the year total $11.52 million.

Sales

With the requisite number of leads generated and the arrival of a prospect at an on- or off-site sales center, the sales process begins. As described in chapter 4, the sales process involves welcoming the prospect, a period of relationship building, the presentation of the timeshare concept and product offering, a tour of the resort, and the close or formal presentation of the offering. The sales approach varies among developers and among individual resorts but nonetheless embodies several common considerations and techniques.

Off-Site versus On-Site Location

For years, the popular view in timesharing held that the product had to be seen to be sold. Today, however, increasing numbers of marketers are selling vacation-ownership products from off-site sales centers. At this writing, EPIC Resorts, LLC, operates a successful off-site sales center in the Franklin Mills Mall in northeast Philadelphia; EPIC sells inventory at its Daytona Beach (Florida) Regency resort. Surrey Vacation Resorts in Branson, Missouri, operates off-site sales centers in St. Louis and Kansas City, Missouri, and Tulsa, Oklahoma. Marriott pioneered off-site sales at a large sales center in New Jersey, from which it sold inventory in new resorts as far away as California and Colorado. Resorts in the Colorado Rockies have used off-site sales centers in Dallas and Denver to sell inventory while marketers with products in the Great Smokies and along the Carolina coast have opened off-site centers convenient to residents of Atlanta and other southeastern cities.

Off-site selling is inherently different from on-site selling. With an off-site setting, the consumer obviously cannot feel, see, or touch the product. Even though some off-site sales centers include a model unit, the challenge lies in conveying the experiential value and appeal of a swimming pool or beach, golf course, ski slope, and other on-site amenities. Thus, in an off-site setting, the use of video and multimedia technology is extremely important to push prospects' emotional "hot buttons."

It is equally important to employ salespersons who hail from the immediate vicinity of the sales center. The fact that salespersons live in the same community as prospective customers and thus presumably share the same geocultural values introduces a trust factor that can be highly beneficial. After the sale is completed, local salespersons are likely to maintain a relationship with their customers.

Especially for resorts in locations that are remote from the point of sale, the prospect of exchange may play an important role in the off-site sale. Prospective owners in New Jersey or Minnesota may not plan to travel to a home resort in the Caribbean or Hawaii every year, but the knowledge that desirable, alternative destinations are available for exchange can make the product far more attractive to customers who have never seen the home resort but are considering a purchase sight unseen.

The dynamics of off-site sales also differs from that of on-site sales. An off-site center is part of the community in which it is located, and its prospects are residents who live and work nearby. People generally visit the center on weeknights after work. With off-site sales, the pressure for a first-day close is not as intense, the sales staff engages in more follow-up, and a greater number of prospects come back another day for another look. Over time, the off-site sales center also may become a service center where owners make reservations, pay maintenance fees, and request assistance with exchanges.

Effective Sales Techniques

The sales techniques of the past have largely given way to a needs-focused approach in which the salesperson functions as a counselor, helping prospects optimize price and maximize the value of their vacation arrangements. Moreover, on the assumption that high-pressure selling arises in part from commission-based sales, some organizations have moved away from straight commissions to a salary-plus-commission or straight-salary arrangement.

Sales executives have increasingly come to realize that opportunities exist beyond the realm of first-day-incentive sales. The old adage that "there's no such thing as a be-back"[2] has yielded to sales practices that treat the customer with respect, encourage return visits, and offer alternative programs for prospects who choose not to purchase the primary vacation-ownership product at the conclusion of the initial tour.

At some resorts, relationship-based selling extends beyond the sales center.

The salesperson may spend an entire day with new buyers, take them to dinner, call them at home, and send thank-you cards to maintain contact beyond the time of the sale. Even where postsale relationship practices have not been integrated into the standard sales process, most resorts employ a "button-up" or "verification officer" to review with buyers in a systematic and informative way the details of what they have bought. This review ensures that

buyers understand the nature of the product and the transaction. It also helps short circuit buyer's remorse and reduce rescissions in the hours and days immediately following the sale.

Biennials, Exit Programs, and Trial Memberships

Three main categories of programs may be offered to prospects who do not choose to

Westgate Resorts's Westgate Lakes, a converted whole-ownership resort in Orlando, Florida, includes a three-story, 40,000-square-foot sales/reception/office center. At buildout, the complex will contain approximately 1,300 units.

82

Fairfield Communities's Royal Vista Resort in Ft. Lauderdale, Florida, is situated on more than three acres of beautiful beachfront property.

Courtesy of Fairfield Communities, Inc.

purchase the primary vacation-ownership product: biennials, exit programs, and trial memberships.

As described in chapter 3, a biennial provides every-other-year use of the primary vacation-ownership product. It is ideal for prospects who either want to buy a timeshare interval but cannot afford the cost of the annual-use product or prefer not to commit to an annual timeshare vacation. Where a lockoff option exists, purchasers of a biennial can, if permitted, vacation every year by occupying half the unit at the home resort one year and, during the next year, exchanging the use of the other half of the unit for a vacation in a different timeshare resort.

An exit program offers to sell something other than the primary timeshare resort product when a sale is obviously not forthcoming at the conclusion of a sales presentation. The alternative product might, for example, consist of an added-value package of savings on various travel products and services. Developed in the late 1980s, exit programs provide a way to off-

set a portion of the marketing costs associated with an unconsummated sale.

Trial membership—the current trend—is an altogether different product designed to maintain a relationship with someone not currently interested in the product but perhaps potentially interested at a future date. Some developers also use trial membership to recapture a percentage of sales from prospects who agreed to buy the primary product and then canceled during the rescission period. According to one developer, perhaps one in five cancellations —20 percent—can be recaptured through a trial membership. Trial memberships provide low-cost, time-limited travel and leisure benefits that typically include an opportunity to sample the developer's primary product line of vacation-ownership accommodations.

Exchange Programs

From a marketing and sales standpoint, the opportunity for exchange enhances the value of the resort product. Other than the resort itself, consumers cite exchange as the major reason for their purchase of a vacation-ownership product. Exchange adds value by making the product flexible and providing vacation alternatives. In recent years, exchange programs have come to include additional leisure-lifestyle benefits and services beyond vacation time at participating resorts. For instance, Fairfield Communities, Inc., has arranged with Carnival Cruise Lines for owners in Fairfield's point-based FairShare Plus program to use their points for cruises of three to 14 days' duration.

The two major exchange companies, Interval International and Resort Condominiums International, support participating resorts' marketing and sales efforts by providing a wide variety of collateral materials, including brochures, directories, kiosks, videos, wall tours, and other sales aids that help motivate prospects to buy.

Recognizing that the average vacation-owner owns 1.8 weeks and that many owners have bought additional weeks at resorts into which they have exchanged, resort operators welcome exchange guests as prospective purchasers. The cost of lead generation is practically nil, and owners already understand and have "test driven" the product at no cost to the host resort. Resorts with large amounts of unsold developer inventory may even arrange with their exchange company to fill their properties with exchange guests. Guests then receive an invitation to take a sales tour.

Resale Programs

Resales have long been the Achilles heel of the timeshare industry. Unlike a car or a house, for which a ready resale market exists, the resale market for vacation-ownership property has been uneven and fraught with ethical pitfalls. The resale issue has important implications for the willingness of prospective purchasers to buy the product. In the past, many sales-persons improperly alleged that a timeshare was a good investment that could be resold easily at a profit. Today, the onus is on all sales personnel to emphasize that vacation-ownership products are *not* an investment at all but rather leisure products to be purchased for the owner's use and enjoyment.

Four types of resale resources are available to individual owners who wish to sell their vacation-ownership product:

- In-house resale programs conducted by developers, management companies, and property owners' associations. Most such programs primarily target other owners at the resort or within the multi-site vacation club in which the resale property is available. When such a program exists, sales personnel use it as an important and reassuring selling point for new inventory.
- Independent resale companies. Resales may also be managed by an independent resale company. Independent resellers frequently charge upfront advertising or listing fees and require (and charge for) an appraisal as a condition of listing. After collecting the fees, many resale companies may do little or nothing to sell the listed property. Such inaction has prompted complaints from timeshare owners.
- Independent licensed resale brokers who charge no upfront fees and receive compensation as a commission only when a property is sold.
- Classified advertising in newspapers, in consumer-oriented special-interest publications, and on various websites.

Many individuals who try to resell a vacation-ownership product are disappointed at the low price the product fetches on the resale market and the high commission charged by the facilitator of the transaction. These factors reflect the nature of the resale marketplace, which discounts the portion of the initial price attributable to marketing expenses and the costs of sale as opposed to the product's inherent value. Furthermore, most buyers of vacation-ownership resales are consumers who already own a week and are searching for a bargain. Because these consumers know what they want and what it should cost, pricing is the biggest single factor in the entire resale marketplace. The lower the price, the faster the sale. Such price sensitivity leaves no funds available for traditional marketing and sales efforts that might attract a customer base that goes beyond current owners.

In an effort to bring order to the resale market, ARDA's Resale Task Force drafted a set of guidelines for ARDA members. The board of directors adopted the guidelines as standards of practice in October 1998. The standards prohibit an appraisal as a required condition of listing and call for extensive disclosures and explanations, including the purpose of any upfront fees that may be charged, the circumstances under which upfront fees will be refunded upon consummation of a sale, information about the resort that may affect a purchaser's buying decision, and when the purchaser will receive actual use rights and occupancy of the unit. The guidelines also prohibit the development of misleading marketing materials and require resale firms to maintain a commercial business location with a physical address.

Rental Programs

Resorts with vacant accommodations may rent units to the general public, thereby creating an opportunity to market and sell vacation-ownership interests to renters. Space available to renters may be unsold inventory from which the developer is seeking an alternative source of income or already owned units that owners wish to rent rather than exchange or occupy themselves.

Any resort operating a rental program must proceed judiciously to avoid competing with its owners. One solution is a rental pool, into which flow all rental revenues from both developer inventory and for-rent owners' units. After deducting expenses, the pool divides the net proceeds among participants on a pro rata basis.

Owing to accounting and legal considerations, including complex provisions of securities law that may be triggered by a rental pool, some developers prefer not to establish a rental pool, although such developers may still accept owners' units for rentals on an individual basis. In these instances, the developer typically avoids complaints of unfair competition by filling all the space that owners have made available for rent before placing renters in any of his or her own unsold inventory.

New Orleans developer Tom Bowes has made marketing to renters the keystone of his strategy at Hotel de L'Eau Vive, a small urban resort in the heart of downtown New Orleans. He operates the resort as a boutique hotel for transient-stay guests, renting units made available by owners but not his unsold inventory (except when special events ensure a full house). A concierge discreetly informs guests of the available vacation-ownership opportunities and is paid on commission for any sales closed. This passive selling strategy allows Bowes to price his inventory at more than 50 percent below competing products.

Ethical Standards

For more than a decade, ARDA has enforced a code of standards and ethics that contains numerous provisions dealing with the marketing and sale of vacation-ownership products. It defines marketing and sales as part of the development activity covered by the code and applies the code to all types of development activity.

With respect to marketing, the code calls for "accurate and clear" information, descriptions, and disclosures as well as "avoidance of false and deceptive statements." It prohibits fictitious contests and provides guidelines with respect to

♦ premiums, gifts, and other items that may be offered to consumers;

Cancun's Royal Resorts sponsors Mayan Biosphere stores that sell natural products and locally produced handcrafts to support nearby nature preserves such as the Sian Kaan Biosphere and Isla Contoy reef. The stores, in turn, provide visitors with information about Royal Resorts and opportunities to visit the company's projects.

Diane R. Suchman

+ programs involving chance, gaming, or sweepstakes;
+ programs involving certificates, coupons, and other documents representing something of value; and
+ electronic media advertisements.

With respect to sales, the code requires accurate descriptions and disclosures of the physical development and the nature of the interest offered for sale in that development. It provides guidelines for

+ contract documents;
+ disclosure—before closing a sale—of the provisions in place for postsale administration, management, governance, and collection of fees;
+ disclosures related to the closing and payment process; and
+ disclosure of consumers' rescission rights.

ARDA's seven-member Standards and Ethics Committee is charged with administering and enforcing the code. Allegations of code violations may be raised by members of the committee, the ARDA Board of Directors, or any firm subject to the code. The alleged violator may either acknowledge the unacceptable activity and agree to halt it or challenge the allegations. In the latter instance, the code provides for a hearing. If the committee determines that the alleged violator has failed to comply with the code, it can impose sanctions that may involve suspension or termination of ARDA membership.

Notes

1. Source: estats (http://www/ emarketer.com/estats/welcome.html).

2. A "be-back" is a customer who returns to make a purchase after leaving at the conclusion of a sales presentation without having purchased the product.

Chapter 6

The Timeshare
Development
Business

Diane R. Suchman

Though the timeshare development business is relatively new, it is now the fastest-growing segment of the travel and tourism industry. With growth has come innovation, new opportunities, more challenges and complexity, and increasing competition.

While related to both the residential and hospitality (hotel and resort) development business, the timeshare business is characterized by its own unique requirements and rewards. As described in chapter 3, timeshare and vacation ownership can take many forms —from freestanding projects to mixed-use developments to systems of resorts. Timeshare properties can be located in cities, in national or international tourist destinations, or in areas of regional interest. They may be targeted to moderate- or high-income purchasers or luxury-level buyers. And they may involve any of a variety of purchase and exchange arrangements.

Developers of timeshare and vacation-ownership properties plan and build the product and associated amenities (or convert an existing hotel, apartment building, or resort to a timeshare property), determine and structure purchase arrangements, market and sell intervals (or contract with a marketing firm to do so), and, in many cases, manage the completed development—which, upon sellout, is typically transferred to and governed by a homeowners' association. As a rule, the developer also establishes a reservation/internal exchange system and an affiliation with an exchange company for owners interested in expanding their range of vacation opportunities.

Figure 6-1 Advantages and Disadvantages of Initial Public Offerings (IPOs)

Advantages of IPOs

- Financial flexibility; public companies can sell low-cost equity and gain access to improved bank financing.
- The use of stock as currency for acquisitions.
- The opportunity to streamline a firm's corporate structure and focus its strategic direction.
- The ability to use stock options as a management incentive.
- The potential for improved liquidity and tax benefits for insiders.

Disadvantages of IPOs

- The considerable cost of an IPO, from $700,000 to $2.5 million or more.
- The executive time required to undertake an IPO, which can divert attention from a company's business, with potentially adverse effects on operations and the bottom line.
- The public scrutiny to which all aspects of a public company's activities are subjected.
- The increased rigor and diligence with which corporate formalities must be observed.
- Opportunity costs, especially the forfeiture of opportunities for certain types of development arrangements.
- Valuation of the company's stock; initially and on an ongoing basis, stock prices are subject to market volatility and other factors beyond an individual company's control.
- A short-term focus, challenging company executives to consider the long-term implications of their actions.

Alternatives to IPOs

A company seeking growth and capital enhancement can consider several alternatives to the IPO approach such as:

- Internal growth and the development of new products.
- Merger with an existing public company.
- Private placement of equity or debt with an institutional or strategic partner.
- Acquisition of or acquisition by a lodging company.

Source: Excerpted from George Leposky, "Experts Say Going Public Changes the Way a Company Does Business," *Vacation Industry Review*, Interval International, Miami, Florida, July/August, 1997, p. 22. This article was based on comments from a panel of experts who spoke at the 1997 ARDA convention.

Despite the widespread belief that timeshare development is exceptionally profitable, it is a complicated, high-risk business that requires a good deal of startup money. Both the business itself and individual projects are capital-intensive. Long-term profits can be impressive, but realization of those profits requires patient money and accurate budget and sales projections.

Without question, the market for timeshare development can be assessed in the aggregate. Nonetheless, even more than in the case of most real estate developments, the nature of the timeshare product makes it difficult to determine with precision the level and nature of demand for a specific project or even a series of resorts. As a rule, timeshare developments are developed and sold in phases, thus enabling the developer to test the market while limiting financial exposure. (The ex-

ceptions are cases involving a hotel conversion or where vacant land is scarce and a high-rise building is the only feasible option.)

Timeshare ownership is a discretionary, unsought good. Many potential consumers may be unfamiliar with the product or even have negative preconceptions that must be overcome during the marketing and sales process.

Timeshare Developers

Various types of companies develop timeshare and vacation-ownership products. They may be public or private, joint venture alliances, or small independent firms; brands or franchises of brands (see Figure 6-1: Advantages and Disadvantages of Initial Public Offerings). Firms enter the timeshare business from various directions and for different reasons. Some may be

Photo on page 86:
With 12,000 acres on the scenic Cumberland Plateau, 81 acres of golf, plus many other recreational amenities, Fairfield Glade Resort in Tennessee is an exciting recreational and residential community.

Photo courtesy of Fairfield Communities, Inc.

solely timeshare developers. Others, such as Marriott and Hilton, are building on their expertise in the hospitality business. Still others, such as Bluegreen Corporation, began (and remain) in the land development business; others were originally condominium developers or gained their initial experience in the financial aspects of real estate development. All share a common belief that timesharing is a growing real estate segment that responds to the needs of today's vacation consumer. They also recognize that timeshare developments can be built, sold, and managed profitably.

Today, the business is in a state of transition. According to a 1997 ARDA survey of U.S. timeshare developers, one-quarter had considered a merger with another regional timeshare developer, 22 percent looked at the prospect of going public, 19 percent explored some form of securitization, and 17 percent thought about selling either the company or its inventory. The fragmented nature of the industry is evident in current statistics. As of 1995, brands accounted for less than 7 percent of total industry annual sales; as of 1998, brands claimed an estimated 15 to 20 percent of total industry sales and were gaining prominence.

Despite much discussion about the entry of large, well-known hospitality brands and the associated changes in the business, most timeshare developers have been and continue to be independent entities that developed and then manage individual properties or a small number of properties. Over time, they affiliated with exchange companies to provide buyers with more flexibility in their vacation choices.

The entry of national-brand hospitality companies, such as Marriott, Hyatt, Hilton, Disney, and, more recently, Four Seasons, has stimulated a surge of interest in the timeshare development business. Marriott was the first brand to enter the business when it acquired American Resorts in 1984. In 1997, the hotel giant posted $380 million in timeshare revenue, making it the nation's largest timeshare development company. Other hotel brands have followed by creating a division or subsidiary of the parent company; by entering into license or franchise arrangements (for example, the Carlson Companies have licensed the Radisson name and Preferred Equities Corporation uses the Ramada brand); or by creating partnerships with a timeshare developer (for example, Westin, Hyatt, and Four Seasons hotels).

Courtesy of George Leposky, Interval International

Swimming pool and pool bar at Bali Clarion Suites on the island of Bali, Indonesia. A mixed-use resort with hotel and timeshare components, the 353-suite property is managed by Choice Hotels Indonesia.

It is generally believed that brand entry has enhanced the industry's credibility and engendered greater consumer awareness of and confidence in timeshare products. From the brand's perspective, developing timeshare properties is a natural extension of the hospitality industry, especially the resort hospitality industry. As with a hotel, timeshare properties offer short-term lodging, require reservations and telephone systems as well as check-in and check-out systems, operate a variety

◆ Increased Consolidation through Horizontal and Vertical Integration

The vacation-ownership industry is about to enter a period of rapid consolidation brought about by an intense and merciless competitive shakeout. That shakeout will occur as a result of both horizontal and vertical integration.

With horizontal integration, large "corporate" entities will acquire regional independent operators. By definition, the larger players will absorb the most "healthy" independent companies, leaving the remaining independents to fend for themselves in a marketplace dominated by the larger players.

Their inability to compete against the economies of scale available to the brands in the areas of marketing costs, technology, and cost of capital means that the independents will find it difficult to maintain a sustainable competitive advantage. Certainly the niche markets will remain and offer opportunity for the small independent operator, but they will be small in comparison to those available to the consolidators.

Vertical integration will occur on two fronts. First, companies already in the vacation-ownership industry will realize the benefits of control through either direct ownership or, more likely, an affiliation or alliance arrangement over multiple aspects of the vacation experience, including accommodation, air and car travel, insurance, medical benefits, and so forth.

Second, companies not currently in the vacation-ownership industry, but in other sectors such as lodging, entertainment, airlines, and cruises, will undoubtedly make significant entries into the industry. It is these companies that, through a process of vertical integration, will integrate, market, and distribute the traditional accommodation-only vacation-ownership product with a variety of other related products and services. They will offer the consumer the convenience of true one-stop shopping networks and opportunities. The days of marketing and selling an accommodation-based-only element of vacation ownership are numbered. Resort systems that provide consumers with a wide variety of use options, facilities, amenities, and geographic diversity will be the key to the future. The fully integrated resort system not only favors the consumer but also the developer. It means a faster sellout, lower marketing costs, and higher profits.

Four underlying reasons explain the trend in industry consolidation. First, to take advantage of the popularity of the points-based product, a company must be able to offer a number of resorts in a variety of locations. Second, larger companies have a higher top line of growth than smaller operators. They are able to offer more attractive product offerings, better marketing techniques, commissions up to 17 percent, and superior sales site locations. Clear evidence in the vacation-ownership industry suggests that bigger is better. Larger vacation-ownership companies have experienced higher growth rates and higher margins and are generally able to offer more than their smaller, undercapitalized counterparts. For companies with annual sales in excess of $20 million, revenues grew by 29 percent in 1995 to $1.33 billion, whereas the entire industry grew by only 16 percent in 1995.

Third, larger operators benefit from the lower costs and higher margins associated with buying power, lower marketing expenses, and the more efficient use of large owner bases. Fourth, the cost of funds for larger operators is lower than for smaller operators. Larger operators have an average spread income of roughly between 400 and 600 basis points versus 100 to 250 points for smaller operators. Obviously, consolidation cannot be avoided.

The independent operator has two options for survival: affiliate with a brand or other independent operator to form a "system" of resorts or target a narrow but lucrative niche market. The days of single sites trying to be all things to all people will soon pass. The economics simply do not make sense.

Source: Excerpted from Edwin H. McMullen, Sr., and Simon Crawford-Welch, "Looking into the Crystal Ball: Vacation Ownership 2000," *Developments*, Vol. 19, No. 9, pp. 76–78.

of guest facilities and amenities, and manage the maintenance and operations functions that characterize the hospitality industry. Brand companies can leverage their already established networks of suppliers, take advantage of economies of scale, and tap their significant financial and human resources. Because they already are well known, operate numerous properties, and have evolved into an established presence in key locations, the brands benefit from significant marketing advantages. Moreover, they are familiar with long-term management issues. And brand companies enjoy alliances with other national and international travel service providers, such as airlines, car rental agencies, travel agencies, insurance companies, cruise lines, and so forth, as part of awards or honors programs for their frequent hotel guests. They can capitalize on these alliances—and their own unused hotel rooms—to offer timeshare buyers a broad range of vacation options.

Despite these advantages, brand-name companies entering the timeshare business also expose themselves to considerable risks. Even more than other timeshare development companies, brand-name companies must be careful, ethical, and customer-driven, and they must succeed. The brand's overall reputation is at stake. If a brand stumbles, consumer perceptions of the brand's quality, reliability, and value are at risk.

With increasing competition from brands, which can offer a wide range of vacation locations and services, more and more timeshare development companies are creating networks of resorts and resort-related products and services that enable them to offer a vast menu of vacation experiences—much as the hotel brands do. Depending on the size and success of the systems of resorts, some companies have in effect created a timeshare brand. As a result, small, independent timeshare operators are finding it increasingly difficult to compete. Many observers see an

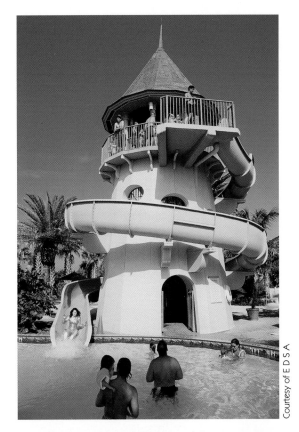

Courtesy of E D S A

Courtesy of E D S A

Disney's Vero Beach Resort's imaginative amenities provide activities and help give the resort its distinguishing character.

industry trend toward consolidation both horizontally (linking developers) and vertically (linking timeshare developers with other related service providers).

Not all timeshare developers view themselves as competing directly with hospitality brands. Some have found and pursue a specific niche; others seek prominence

Westgate Resorts's first timeshare resort outside Orlando is located in Miami, where it has attracted an international market, particularly from Latin America.

in a particular geographic area or create a network of resorts in regional destinations that are not the types of locations typically sought by the large hotel brands. Figure 6-2 lists the vacation-ownership resorts that lead the industry in sales.

How Timeshare Differs from Related Real Estate Products

Timeshare developments are similar in many respects to other types of real estate, especially hospitality products (hotels and resorts) and condominiums. As described below, however, they also evidence many significant differences.

Hotels

While both timeshare resorts and hotels may be considered part of the hospitality industry, important differences affect development and management considerations. Like hotels, timeshare developments operate a reception desk, a reservations system, recreational facilities and amenities, and housekeeping services. Though they require less public space (meeting rooms, back of the house, and so forth) than a hotel, individual guest or owner units are much larger—more on the order of a 1,200-square-foot condominium than a 300-square-foot hotel room. Timeshare

units are fitted and furnished to be as comfortable as the guest's or owner's home and feature fully equipped kitchens and amenities such as second televisions, VCRs, and whirlpool tubs.

Unlike hotels, the timeshare developer's relationship with the timeshare customer is ongoing. The hotel business rents rooms; the timeshare business sells real estate. Thus, owners are repeat customers who have purchased a lifetime of vacation experiences. As a result, their behavior and expectations differ as do their interest and involvement in the product and related services. Timeshare owners stay longer and, as a rule, take better care of their accommodations than do hotel guests. Unlike the typically solitary business traveler, timeshare owners tend to travel in family groups; as a result, occupants spend more time in the unit and use it more intensely.

Check-in times at timeshare resorts versus hotels tend to be more concentrated and more complicated. Hotels typically offer more extensive food service and a greater number of personal services such as room service, daily housekeeping, dry cleaning, business services, a beauty shop, newsstand, and the like, whereas a timeshare resort is more likely to provide an extensive array of recreational facilities and programs, travel services, and a minimarket. And hotels are expected to make a profit from the rental of rooms and sale of related services. In contrast, a timeshare development's management and operations are owner-controlled and budget-driven. The management company is expected to keep management fees in check while exceeding expectations for maintenance and service. And, finally, though their goals are related, the hotel manager's primary aim is to maximize occupancy income, whereas the timeshare project manager's primary aim is to ensure customer satisfaction.

As noted in chapter 3, hospitality brands tend to view timeshare resorts and hotels as complementary rather than competitive types of development. In many cases, they have found that there are physical, functional, and economic advantages to locating the two property types together or nearby.

Condominiums

Timeshare developments are more complicated and more expensive to develop, market, and sell than whole-owned condominiums. Construction costs are typically higher because, as with a hotel, units and facilities must be built to withstand commercial use—continuous occupancy and changing users. Moreover, additional buffering between units is required to maintain privacy and quiet. Further, the building materials selected for timeshare units —paints, wall coverings, floor treatments, and so forth—are generally more expensive than the materials specified for condominiums. With the Americans with Disabilities Act requirements more stringent for timeshares than for apartments, developers incur still additional construction costs. Jeff Jackard, vice president for development of Bluegreen Corporation, estimates that the total cost to build a timeshare unit is about 10 to 25 percent higher than for a similar condominium or apartment unit.

Given that vacation-ownership properties are typically resorts that sell vacation experiences, they are obliged to offer first-rate design features and amenities. And at least some of the planned facilities and amenities (and much of the land and infrastructure development) must be completed and ready for operation before the first sale, all of which requires a huge upfront investment. In addition, to *begin* the marketing process, the developer must typically have in place a sales office and sales force, a cadre of contract professionals, exchange capability, and administrative, maintenance, and hospitality systems. In large national (and especially international) resort systems, upfront requirements multiply with the sophisticated technological and customer support requirements associated with the properties.

Development Economics

At first glance, the development and sale of timeshare units seems to offer an easy route to financial success. A unit that could be sold as a whole-owned condominium for perhaps $250,000 can instead be sold 51 times (assuming one week for maintenance) at $10,000 per sale for a total of $510,000 per unit. Though profits can be made in timesharing, the business is not as simple—or as easily lucrative—as it might initially seem.

While ARDA has developed a uniform chart of accounts for the industry and is encouraging its adoption, it is not yet an accepted industry standard. As a result, it is difficult to obtain consistent and accurate comparative financial data. Different companies maintain their records differently, include different line items within categories of revenue or expense, and may or may not respond accurately to surveys. If accounting practices become more standardized over time, more reliable industry financial information should emerge. With these limitations in mind, some of the reported average costs and income components of a timeshare development are discussed below.

Sources of Income

Timeshare developers generally make money in three ways: development profit, financing profit, and income from operations and management. Depending on the property and the developer's philosophy, capabilities, and preferences, timeshare properties may also generate other sources of income. For example, the rental of unsold or unused units is a source of income in some timeshare developments; in others, rentals do not make money and instead are viewed as a source of new business.

Development profit is the primary source of income for a timeshare. It consists of income generated upon the sale of intervals. According to one observer, "Selling a condominium unit in one-week intervals can more than double the sales proceeds to the developer compared with sale of whole ownership, even after marketing costs."[1] George Donovan, president and CEO of Bluegreen Corporation, states that a reasonable goal for development profit before adjusting for taxes and corporate administrative costs is 15 to 20 percent.

Most buyers finance their purchases, and most developers provide financing that not only enables purchasers to buy the timeshare product but also permits developers to make a profit. To finance consumer purchases, the hospitality brands tend to rely on in-house financing, but many timeshare developers borrow money from a lender and use the buyers' mortgages as collateral. Financing profit results from the spread between the developer's cost of money and the interest rate paid by buyers to finance the purchase. For example, the developer may borrow money at 8 to 10 percent and lend it at 14 percent,

making a profit on the difference (after administrative costs). In some cases, interest rates on mortgage loans may be much higher (as, for example, loans to foreign purchasers) to reflect the developer's higher level of risk. According to ARDA, most consumer financing for vacation ownership runs for a six- to seven-year term at a fixed rate of interest (averaging 14.2 percent) with a 10 percent minimum-downpayment requirement. Industry surveys show that most developers consider their portfolios current.

One developer reported that, in his experience, the profits from financing are almost comparable to the profits from development. According to Christel DeHaan, president and founder of Christel House Inc. in Indianapolis, the ideal case is to achieve a greater profit margin on development than on financing, thus indicating that a resort is keeping marketing, sales, product, and administrative costs in line. Robert A. Miller, president and general manager of Marriott Leisure in Orlando, Florida, suggests that a good rule of thumb is that about 60 percent of profits should typically derive from development, 30 per-

Figure 6-2 **1997 Vacation-Ownership Sales Leaders**
(Annual vacation-ownership sales of $20 million or more)

Listed Alphabetically

Company	Headquarters City	Vacation-Ownership Sales (Million US $)		Number of Projects (Year-End)		Number of Units (Year-End)		Number of Owners (Year-End)	
		1996	1997	1996	1997	1996	1997	1996	1997
Anfi del Mar	Arguineguin, Spain	76	63	2	3	459	475	16,146	19,407
The Bay Club	Waikoloa, Hawaii	23	25	1	1	153	163	1,904	3,800
Bluegreen Resorts[1]	Boca Raton, Florida	27	60	3	25	280	800	5,000	32,000
CFI Resorts	Orlando, Florida	211	280	5	5	2,500	3,200	90,000	105,000
Grupo Costamex	Mexico City, Mexico	86	92	60	60	815	950	39,000	47,000
Club La Costa	Malaga, Spain	39	42	26	29	600	680	29,250	34,000
Disney Vacation Club[2]	Orlando, Florida	90	115	4	4	1,209	1,339	21,000	27,000
Fairfield Communities, Inc.[3]	Little Rock, Arkansas	195	270	20	20	3,359	3,680	161,500	182,000
Hapimag[4]	Baar, Switzerland	96	93	44	45	4,000	4,000	114,344	118,000
Hilton Grand Vacations Club	Orlando, Florida	78	85	3	5	398	566	18,000	26,000
Hyatt Vacation Ownership Inc.[5]	Chicago, Illinois	12	30	1	5	40	205	1,000	2,000
ILX Resorts	Phoenix, Arizona	20	23	8	9	378	452	11,000	14,000
Island One Inc.	Orlando, Florida	30	32	4	4	562	612	26,000	28,000
The Kosmas Group	New Smyrna Beach, Florida	45	40	13	15	600	954	21,200	29,000
Marriott Vacation Club Intl.[6]	Lakeland, Florida	290	380	30	35	2,400	3,000	80,000	100,000
Orange Lake Country Club	Kissimmee, Florida	45	55	1	1	1,052	1,212	52,000	56,000
Pacific Monarch Resorts	Laguna Hills, California	70	65	5	6	500	500	30,000	35,000
Peppertree Resorts Ltd	Asheville, North Carolina	23	31	15	16	998	1,073	42,000	46,000
Polo Resorts Inc.[7]	Las Vegas, Nevada	39	39	2	2	562	574	24,394	28,500
Grupo Pestana	Madeira, Portugal	20	20	4	4	363	363	10,500	12,000
Ramada Vacation Suites[8]		37	44	13	15	804	868	32,623	34,493
Resort Properties Group	Las Vegas, Nevada	29	32	4	4	1,020	1,020	40,000	42,000
The Ridge Tahoe	Tenerife, Canary Islands	31	28	5	5	302	378	16,595	22,000
Royal Mayan Resort Group	Cancun, Mexico	40	44	4	4	780	780	36,000	40,000
Shell Vacations, LLC[9]	Northbrook, Illinois	80	85	9	10	860	1,154	42,000	51,000
Signature Resorts (now Sunterra)	Los Angeles, California	182	281	33	70	2,905	5,038	85,000	175,000
Silverleaf Resorts[11]	Dallas, Texas	48	65	7	9	755	855	28,700	33,500
Trendwest Resorts	Bellevue, Washington	100	126	19	22	780	1,003	39,000	52,496
The Villa Group	Puerto Vallarta, Mexico	32	30	3	3	676	868	21,000	24,000
Vistana Development Ltd[12]	Lake Buena Vista, Florida	60	110	3	10	1,438	1,725	51,510	66,050
Winners Circle Resorts Intl.	Del Mar, California	11	21	7	8	428	564	28,000	30,000
Totals		2,155	2,711	358	454	31,976	39,051	1,214,666	1,515,246
Numeric increase			556		96		7,075		300,580
Percent increase			26%		27%		22%		25%

1. Bluegreen Resorts data for the fiscal year ending March 31. Fiscal 1998 data estimated by VO WORLD and include consolidation with RDI as of October 1997, when this acquisition closed. In addition to the timeshare owner base shown, Bluegreen's RDI property management division manages resorts with about 72,000 timeshare owners.
2. Disney Vacation Club. Sales volumes estimate by VO WORLD.
3. Fairfield Communities data include that of Vacation Break USA, the acquisition of which Fairfield completed in December 1997. The acquisition was on a pooling-of-interests basis. Consolidated 1997 data are estimated by VO WORLD based on a projection of nine-month results for both companies.
4. Hapimag. Chart shows sales measured in U.S. dollars and indicates a loss in 1997 versus 1996. The dollar appreciated against the Swiss franc in 1997, and measured in Swiss francs—Hapimag's home currency —there was a gain last year.
5. Hyatt Vacation Club. Sales estimated by VO WORLD.
6. Marriott Vacation Club International. Sales data are VO WORLD estimates and are believed to be conservative (1996 estimate revised upward by $25 million).
7. Polo Resorts Inc. is the developments entity of Polo Towers. Previously, VO WORLD reported on this firm under the name of the marketing entity, International Resort Group. 1997 sales and owner data estimated by VO WORLD.
8. Ramada Vacation Suites—Preferred Equities Corp., a subsidiary of Mego Financial. Data are for fiscal years ending August 31.
9. Shell Vacations, LLC, previously known as the Shell Group.
10. Signature Resorts. Data represent a consolidation of all acquisitions completed in 1997, with 1996 data restated to include that of acquired properties and timeshare firms. 1997 timeshare sales estimated by VO WORLD.
11. Silverleaf Resorts. 1997 data estimated by VO WORLD.
12. Vistana. 1997 data reflect acquisition of Success Companies and Point of Colorado.

Source: *Vacation Ownership WORLD,* January 1998.

cent from financing, and 10 percent from management fees.

Initially, most developers manage their properties either in-house or through an outsourcing arrangement. They subsequently encourage the homeowners' associations to contract with them to manage the properties on an ongoing basis. Some also manage properties developed by others. The typical fee for management services is equivalent to a fixed percentage —typically 10 to 12 percent—of the total operating budget of the homeowners' association. The management side of the business is extremely competitive; to maintain the contractual relationship with the homeowners' association over time, the developer/manager must ensure customer satisfaction.

Many developers make some money from the rental of units during the sellout period. If the project is developed as a conversion from a hotel, the developer may also receive income from hotel operations during the transition. In addition, the developer has the opportunity to offer other products and services that can earn a profit.

For example, depending on the specific market and project, an on-site restaurant, minigrocery store, travel agency, business services center, or other retail or service outlet might operate as a profit center, particularly if it is open to the public as well as to resort owners. Other resort profit centers can include video rentals, pay-per-view television channels, and charges for room safes and long-distance telephone service.

Costs[2]

The primary cost components for a time-share developer are capital construction, marketing, and sales costs along with general and administrative costs. Estimates of the proportions of unit sales price attributable to each cost factor vary by source, but most observers agree that product cost accounts for about 25 to 30 percent of unit sales price, sales and marketing about 50 to 55 percent; administrative costs about 10 percent; and gross profits about 15 to 20 percent. In addition, during the sellout period, the developer is obligated to pay annual maintenance fees for the project's

According to its architect, Fugleberg Koch, Hilton Grand Vacations Club Sea World in Orlando, Florida, has been so successful that the construction schedule was moved forward to accommodate demand.

©Michael Lowry Photography, courtesy of Fugleberg Koch

unsold, developer-owned inventory and to cover annual shortfalls in the operating budget (a cost known as the developer subsidy).

It is important to note that large, branded operators such as Marriott may realize significantly different revenue, cost, and profit results than small, independent players. Further, newer properties with less-established marketing programs and owner bases typically realize lower profit margins.

Figure 6-2 illustrates ARDA's most recently published cost estimates.

Jeffrey A. Owings, senior vice president of FINOVA Capital Corporation, reports that for successful developers, product costs have historically represented approximately 20 to 25 percent of sales proceeds, although some developers have recently brought product costs up to 30 to 35 percent of sales. Brand-name hotel companies such as Marriott, Hilton, and Four Seasons often realize product costs of 40 percent and more. Owings says that the increasing proportion of sales proceeds attributable to product cost is achieved by reducing other operating costs, primarily marketing. In addition, competition for properties from other timeshare developers and other hospitality uses (primarily resort hotels) has been a major factor in the rise in product cost.

Owings also notes that the relative cost of marketing and sales has increased over time. "Historically, a timeshare developer would aim for marketing and sales costs of 40 percent and would settle for 45 percent. Today, many developers shoot for 45 to 50 percent and settle for 55 percent. A surprising number of operators have to battle back from 65 percent."

General and administrative costs (G&A), by Owings's calculation, have typically totaled 10 percent or less of sales. He observes that many developers have been able to hold G&A to 5 to 8 percent by enhancing the efficiency of their operation. In particular, developers operating multiple

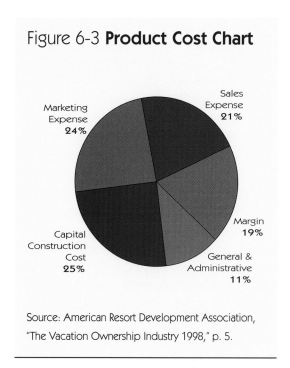

Figure 6-3 **Product Cost Chart**

Sales Expense 21%

Marketing Expense 24%

Capital Construction Cost 25%

Margin 19%

General & Administrative 11%

locations can spread administrative costs over a wider range of businesses. In any event, G&A costs tend to be more fixed in nature than marketing and sales costs; therefore, increases in annual sales (also a trend) tend to lower the percentage of G&A.

According to Owings, the developer subsidy—the developer's share of the cost to operate the resort during sellout—typically ranges from 2 to 4 percent of sales. A resort with hotel revenues or a developer who can produce hotel revenues can reduce or even eliminate the subsidy.

Risks

As with any business, certain risks are inherent in timeshare development. Obviously, timeshare developers must sell what they create. In addition, timeshare development has its own peculiar challenges. It is essentially a cash-negative business such that developers must close many more sales than a home builder or condominium developer before achieving a positive cash flow. A typical downpayment is 10 percent, but developers must pay 40 to 50 percent of the unit sales price upfront in marketing and sales costs. To close the cash-flow gap, many developers sell receivables or borrow against future sales. In addition, some developers assume more risk by borrowing at floating rates and lending at fixed rates. And, if developers hypothecate receivables (pledge receivables as collateral for debt) to obtain tax advantages, the bank's recourse is often to the developer.

Donald Harrill, senior vice president of Hilton Hotels Corporation, pointed out that although the short-term financial risk is higher for timeshare developments, the long-term risk is lower than for hotel properties. Timeshare developers incur a four- to five-year risk during the planning, development, and sales period. Once the product is sold, however, the ongoing risk associated with the payment of mortgages and management of the property is significantly reduced. With a hotel development, the initial development risk is smaller, but the long-term inventory risk is ongoing and subject to changes in the economy, the competitive environment, and other factors beyond the owner's control.

As with any real estate development venture, timeshare developers face political risks—the risks associated with obtaining permits and addressing public concerns regarding the proposed development. Such concerns are especially common in high-profile resort locations. As Art Spaulding, partner in Cox Castle & Nicholson, cautions, "Any negotiated solution to community objections will undoubtedly increase the cost of developing a timeshare product; this must be factored into the economic model used to justify the acquisition—preferably before the property is acquired and not after."[3]

As noted in chapter 7, in addition to local land use regulations and federal laws governing taxation and business practices, state law largely governs the practices specific to the timeshare industry. In general, industry leaders believe that timeshare is one of the most heavily regulated businesses. Regulations differ from state to state and continue to evolve. Indeed, wide-ranging requirements and a variety of state regulations challenge multisite developers to create an efficient system for producing and managing homogeneous products in different locations. In addition, timeshare is a young, rapidly growing business that is undergoing structural shifts, thereby creating new opportunities but also new risks—especially risks that challenge the viability of smaller development companies.

Finally, the purchaser of a timeshare assumes some measure of risk. The consumer's primary concern is that the developer will neither complete nor sell out the development (or will not complete it as promised). Purchasers are also concerned that, at some point, they will be unable to make mortgage or assessment payments on time; that other buyers will default on mortgage or fee payments, thus requiring the homeowners' association to meet the project's financial obligations; and that, for whatever reason, management, maintenance, and improvements will not be properly carried out to ensure owners' long-term satisfaction. Regulatory requirements may nullify some of these issues; nonetheless, the developer needs to understand and address all perceived risks.

Industry Issues

In addition to coping with the complexity and evolving nature of the business, timeshare developers must grapple with several key issues. Among them, perhaps the most challenging relate to image and ethics, marketing costs, resales (and the question of the investment value of timeshare purchases), and human resources. In many ways, these issues are linked to one another and are mutually reinforcing.

Image and Ethics
Image and ethics are closely connected. The image of the timeshare sector that

Courtesy of Vistana, Inc.

Market segmentation of the timeshare industry is expected to occur much as it has in the hotel industry. Vistana, Inc., an Orlando-based timeshare company, operates a multitiered system of resorts, including its Hampton Vacation Resorts line. Shown here is Oak Plantation in Kissimmee, Florida.

today's more professional industry is striving to overcome has its roots in the sometimes low-quality products and unethical sales practices that tainted timesharing's early years. With, however, the entry and apparent success of the hospitality brands and the growing number and quality of timeshare resorts throughout the world, public awareness of the product and its benefits has increased. As described briefly in chapter 5, ARDA has adopted a code of standards and ethics to promote honesty, fairness, and integrity in timeshare contracts, sales, and solicitations. Yet, even amid self-policing efforts and increasing regulation, the industry remains highly sensitive to a public image that was etched by earlier (and, unfortunately, sometimes more recent) scandals.

State regulations that govern operation of the timeshare business may affect ethi-cal practices in a variety of ways. Regulations may, for example, require developer registration and the licensure of salespersons. Bonding may be required for key personnel or to ensure the completion of developments. States may institute a mandatory rescission period as well as various disclosure requirements.

Though many in the industry feel overregulated, the industry itself must work to create a more positive image for timeshare and vacation-ownership resorts. Individual entities acting in concert through ARDA must continue to take the lead in identifying and correcting the industry's own weaknesses.

Marketing and Sales

Closely related to the image issue is one of the most frustrating aspects of the business for many developers—the high cost

Diane R. Suchman

Landscaping is essential to a timeshare resort's appeal, and ongoing maintenance of the grounds and plant life requires time, budget, and forethought. In the photograph at top, gardeners manicure designs in the lawn of the Royal Islander resort in Cancun, Mexico. Shown below is the resort's greenhouse, where several varieties of plants are cultivated continuously to maintain a ready supply of replacements so that the resort's landscaping always looks lush.

its more flexible (and presumably more desirable) forms—is complicated, and many potential customers are unfamiliar with (or may even have a negative preconception of) the product. Therefore, to sell their products, developers turn to a number of high-cost strategies, including print advertising, direct mail, telemarketing, OPCs, and subsidized minivacations (described in chapter 5).

In addition, as a cash-negative business, timeshare development is, in the words of Harrill, "a sales-driven industry, but the average salesperson in the industry knows nothing about financial performance. As a result, they tend to oversell, which leads to rescissions, and they spend too much money making a sale."

To make a profit, developers must constantly monitor and control marketing costs. To that end, it is extremely important to generate leads efficiently. Developers must do their homework to ensure that marketing dollars are spent to target, attract, and make presentations to prospects who, according to selected indicators, are most likely to buy. As explained in chapter 3, probable buyers fit definable demographic and economic profiles and exhibit certain leisure spending and travel patterns.

But the core frustration is that even though interval ownership is a feasible economic concept, it is not marketed that way. Instead, prospective clients are often sold interval weeks in a hard-sell environment characterized by the offer of premiums, price drops, and sometimes difficult-to-honor promises. Most developers interviewed for this book deplored the practice of tempting prospects with traditional rewards for visiting and/or making a purchase even when that practice is part of a gentler approach. Nonetheless, many still find it necessary to do so.

In some of the more popular resort destinations, such as Orlando, Las Vegas, and Hawaii, the proliferation of timeshare resorts has created a competitive sales en-

of marketing and sales. As noted, these activities typically represent about 40 to 50 percent or even more of the purchase price of a unit/week. At the core of the marketing cost issue is the necessity— and expense—of generating demand by bringing buyers to the product. Vacation ownership is not an essential good, and it is fairly expensive for most households; on average, it costs $10,000 for a two-bedroom unit/week. The concept—especially in

vironment where savvy consumers expect substantial gifts in exchange for touring a property—thus raising marketing costs. For this and other reasons, according to Owings, the past few years have seen a 5 to 10 percent increase in marketing and selling expenses, "which comes right off the bottom line."

Despite the problems facing timeshare developers, it is clear that the timeshare concept delivers on its promises. According to a recent ARDA survey, 85 percent of timeshare owners are satisfied or very satisfied with their purchases.[4] Seventy-two percent of surveyed timeshare owners ultimately bought another timeshare week. Furthermore, referrals from existing owners often prove to be the most productive source of new business.

Richard Sutton, general director of Royal Resorts, whose developments are featured in chapter 9, believes that the solution lies in consumer education. Educated consumers will seek out reputable and properly operated interval properties and not be tempted by gifts. Informed prospects will understand the criteria for determining a sound resort operation and make the purchase decision objectively rather than under duress. The responsibility for educating the public, Sutton believes, rests with developers, their professional associations, and the media.

The last component of the sales and marketing issue concerns the industry's high level of rescissions. Rescissions not only require developers to remarket affected units, but they also impose legal and administrative burdens. Industry studies indicate that rescission rates now hover at about 14 percent of sales. However, few in the industry believe the percentage is actually that low. Many suspect that average rescission rates are in the 22 to 28 percent range, with few developers experiencing rates below 20 percent.

To minimize rescissions industrywide, many developers now train their sales teams to think in terms of providing customers with information, counseling, and encouragement rather than pushing and promising. Often, resorts employ a quality assurance manager (sometimes called a verification loan officer) who meets with purchasers after the sale to make sure that the product and terms were properly explained and that buyers understand the purchase and its associated paperwork. In addition, at many resorts, the salesperson calls buyers during the rescission period and asks for referrals. The telephone call serves three purposes: it helps strengthen the relationship with buyers, it reinforces buyers' confidence in the purchase, and it generates valuable sales leads. To minimize the number of rescissions—and their associated administrative costs—Royal Resorts does not accept contracts at the conclusion of sales presentations. Instead, prospective buyers sign an application to purchase. Two weeks later, Royal Resorts mails a contract to the prospect's home for signature; most prospects sign and return the contracts. The result is few rescissions.

The overall goal of these strategies is to ensure that the customer makes an informed decision and leaves feeling comfortable with the timeshare concept, the company, and the value of the purchase. Sensitivity to the matter of customer comfort is so great that some of the timeshare executives interviewed for this book reported firing salespersons who continued to use hard-sell tactics, even though they were high-volume producers.

Resales

In view of the difficulties in producing sales prospects, explaining the timeshare product, and absorbing the high costs associated with closing a sale, individual owners who wish to sell their unit/weeks are ill-equipped to do so. As a result, resale prices have historically been noticeably low. Moreover, for developers, resales compete with initial sales during project sellout. After sellout, resales are expensive to consummate and yield little profit, if any, to the developer. Yet, as discussed in chapter 5, the resales issue needs to be resolved. Some owners must sell their units because of changed circumstances. If they cannot sell their units, they may simply default on payments, creating financial problems for both the developer/lender and the homeowners' association. In addition, the issue of long-term investment value remains a problem for the industry as well as a barrier to initial sales.

Some developers who plan to remain in the industry for the long term have created sales organizations that remarket resale units at sold-out resorts. Though today's prices for resales tend to be much lower than for new sales, Harrill believes that the numbers reflect prices paid for resale unit/weeks in older properties. As resort systems mature and proliferate, Harrill expects that resale prices in those systems will rise, more accurately reflecting the purchase of the various experiences offered by the properties.

Richard Ragatz, executive vice president of RCI Consulting, believes that the resales issue appears to be resolving itself as the industry matures. He notes that during the past two years, resales totaled 12 percent of all timeshare sales, up from 2 to 3 percent a few years ago.

Human Resources

According to Ed McMullen, managing director for Shell Vacations, LLC, the biggest single challenge in the current market is human resources. Timeshare is an extremely complicated business requiring highly intelligent, dedicated, and multidisciplined professionals who understand both the dynamics of the business and the market. In an era of overall economic growth and rapid industry expansion, the number of experienced people in all the major disciplines required of the vacation-ownership industry—development, marketing, sales, law, management and operations, and finance—is limited. As a result, demand for talented and knowledge-able staff—particularly in the key area of marketing—outstrips supply. And with the industry still in its infancy, there is no real locus of training to prepare professionals for the current market. McMullen observes, "Everyone steals people from everyone else."

In many markets, human resources issues extend to service staff as well. In tight labor markets such as Orlando, competition can be stiff (and thus wages high) for housekeepers and hourly workers. With timeshare development and management so strongly oriented toward customer satisfaction, careful selection, training, and retraining of employees is extremely important even where the labor pool is adequate.

Keys to Success

Several elements are generally viewed as essential to success in the timeshare development business.

- An understanding of the complexity, nuances, and economics of the business. In particular, developers need to understand the implications of the industry's cash-flow requirements and how economic cycles affect those requirements.
- Access to capital. As discussed earlier, the economics of timeshare development are such that significant upfront capital is required.
- Predictability. Adequate preparation—planning the entire project, committing to a design, locking in permits and pricing, ensuring utility capacity over time, and so forth—helps avoid expensive surprises as the project develops in phases over time.
- Design for long-term maintenance. The requirements for long-term maintenance point to the importance of providing adequate storage space or other operational areas, ensuring the easy maintainability of buildings, understanding the quality needs of and replacement cycle for interior furnishings, and mak-

Marriott Vacation Club International's Custom House Tower is an 80-unit adaptive use of a landmark historic customs building; elegant interior designs reflect the building's downtown Boston location.

ing certain that maintenance fees include adequate reserves.

◆ Human resources. Developers need to hire multidisciplinary professionals with appropriate skills and experience. Staff must demonstrate financial savvy, marketing expertise, and an understanding of the complexity of the business.

◆ Choice locations. Timeshare resorts tend to sell more easily in locations that are accessible and located in year-round markets in regional, national, or international destinations that attract considerable tourist traffic.

◆ Exchange companies. Given that the choice of exchange company strongly affects consumer satisfaction, new developers should inform themselves thoroughly about various exchange companies' offerings and requirements.

◆ Business management systems. Management systems help ensure predictability in producing high-quality sales prospects, providing adequate maintenance, and attending to all other aspects of the business.

◆ Rules. Rules should require sales and management professionals to treat all

Amenities at the Moon Palace Resort in Cancun, Mexico, include both indoor and outdoor swimming pools.

Courtesy of RCI

Courtesy of RCI

owners and sales prospects in the same respectful manner and to help control marketing operations by ensuring that no special benefits are promised.

◆ User-friendly computer systems. Appropriately designed computer systems support good customer service.

◆ Continuing assessment of the competition and an understanding of industry trends. A savvy developer can anticipate and capitalize on the evolving changes in the industry by keeping abreast of the competition and industry trends.

But the single most important and all-encompassing key to success in the vacation-ownership industry is *customer satisfaction*. Customers are the source of the developer's reputation and are the least expensive and most promising source of future sales. Timeshare developers need to understand what the customer needs and wants and then design the development plan, marketing strategy, and resort operations and management systems accordingly. Robert A. Miller stresses that the developer's goal should be to exceed customer expectations in terms of the product, the level of follow-up service, and the long-term vacation-ownership experience, or, in short, to "delight them with their purchases."

Notes

1. David M. Disick and George W. van der Ploeg, "Vacation Ownership Clubs: Planning, Financing, and Development," *The Real Estate Finance Journal*, Spring 1994, p. 44.

2. For aggregate information on current industry activities and economic impacts, readers are referred to ARDA's "The Timeshare Development Industry: Overview and Economic Analysis." ARDA also publishes information on the financial aspects of the timeshare development industry, including "Financial Performance: A Survey of Timeshare and Vacation Ownership Resort Developers."

3. Art Spaulding, "Structuring for Ownership," *Urban Land* Timeshare Supplement, August 1998, p. 21.

4. ARDA, "The Vacation Ownership Industry 1998," p. 9. Note that ARDA's figure of 85 percent satisfied consumers is somewhat higher than RCI Consulting's figure of 81.1 percent in chapter 2. The difference is attributable to differences in survey instruments, dates, and respondents; however, both surveys indicate particularly high rates of satisfaction.

Chapter 7
Legal Issues

Kurt P. Gruber and Andrew T. Marcus,
Baker & Hostetler, LLP

everal legal and regulatory implications are associated with developing and selling timeshare projects. In addition to traditional real estate development considerations such as land use, permitting, title, construction, environmental requirements, and other issues, timeshare development brings its own unique complexities to the real estate development process. By understanding and addressing the legal and regulatory intricacies at a project's outset, the developer will be better positioned to develop and sell a profitable timeshare product.

This chapter provides an overview of the legal and regulatory complexities typically encountered by a timeshare developer, including determination of the legal interest in the property, the subdivision vehicle, and the use plan; special considerations attendant to vacation clubs; registration and other timeshare-specific regulatory requirements; broker issues; and securities, tax, and finance matters.

The local laws that govern any real estate development also regulate timeshare developments. In addition, a number of federal laws enacted with broader intent affect timeshare development, sales, and operations. Nonetheless, most of the laws that specifically regulate the timeshare industry are state laws. Developers and their legal counsel need to understand the nature, extent, and likely effects of the timeshare laws in their state before proceeding with a timeshare project.

The Underlying Interest in The Property

The first task in structuring a timeshare project calls for determining the developer's legal interest in the property underlying the timeshare plan. In some instances, the nature of the developer's legal interest in the property dictates the structure of the project. In other cases, the type of timeshare plan the developer intends to develop influences the choice. For example, the developer who wants to sell a fee-based timeshare product should probably already have a fee-simple interest in the underlying property.

Almost any legal ownership structure will enable the developer to develop property as a timeshare resort. Assuming that the developer is free to choose from any of the available structures, the choice will depend on the developer's ultimate purpose and regulatory and tax consequences. The most common approach is to submit all of the developer's fee-simple right, title, and interest in the property to the timeshare plan, usually in phases to match sales. On recording the timeshare instrument encumbering the property, the developer's interest is converted to timeshare interests (e.g., timeshare weeks). Subsequently, the developer's interest in the nature of unsold timeshare inventory is phased out as that inventory sells.

An owner who wants to retain ownership of the property may create an affiliated but legally separate development entity, lease the property to the development entity, and require that entity to submit the leasehold interest in the property to the timeshare plan. This scenario often plays out in response to local laws or customs and frequently finds application in jurisdictions outside the United States where foreign ownership of property is problematic. The affiliated development entity is also favored in Hawaii; in that case, long-term leases permit the developer to retain ownership of valuable real property.

A leasehold interest is generally treated as a personal property interest. Consequently, the developer is not able to sell a fee-based timeshare interest to the timeshare purchaser. In some jurisdictions, however, a fee-based timeshare can still be created if the leasehold interest is subjected to the condominium form of ownership and the laws of the jurisdiction deem condominium ownership a real property interest notwithstanding the underlying lease. In addition, some jurisdictions require the owner of the underlying interest to place significant restrictions on its rights in favor of the timeshare plan in order to protect the rights of timeshare purchasers.

In some situations, the developer may convert existing improvements (physical structures built on the property) to the timeshare plan. While few jurisdictions have enacted timeshare regulations that specifically govern the conversion of such improvements, other applicable laws, such as condominium laws, may require the developer to meet prescribed requirements as a condition of converting the property. The timeshare law also may contain other provisions that apply to conversion projects. For example, a law mandating full funding of reserves may require the developer to spend a large sum to renovate the project, adopt a timeshare budget with a high maintenance fee that effectively impedes sales, or grant an expensive developer subsidy.

Notwithstanding the nature of the underlying interest submitted to the timeshare plan, the developer needs to consider the overall project, including the timeshare parcel. If the project is to incorporate uses other than a timeshare resort—for example, commercial development or single-family housing—a master declaration of covenants and restrictions should be recorded against the entire property. The declaration contains a general discussion of the different uses of the property and provides for critical matters such as uniform devel-

Photo on page 106:
By converting to a club system, Sunterra Corporation intends to provide buyers with greater flexibility and to establish a long-lasting relationship with them. Shown here is the company's Savoy at South Beach Resort in Miami, Florida.

Courtesy of Sunterra Corporation

opment and the sharing of common infrastructure and common-area expenses. It is essential that the developer carefully consider how a timeshare project, with its unique characteristics, is to be integrated into an overall development.

With timeshare development, as with any for-sale real estate-based product, the developer must have a clear understanding of all relevant local laws and underlying title matters. As already noted, it is unusual for local laws to address timeshare specifically. However, except in jurisdictions where timeshare development is common, laws and zoning regulations that limit the type, density, or configuration of development or that restrict the transient use of accommodations (which may include timeshares) are not out of the ordinary. A title report should uncover any recorded prohibitions or limitations on timeshare development. Some state timeshare laws require the timeshare interest conveyed to the buyer to be free and clear of liens or encumbrances. The laws also require interest holders in the underlying property to execute and record subordination or nondisturbance agreements to protect the use rights of timeshare purchasers.

Subdivision Vehicle

Once the developer has determined the underlying interest to be subjected to the timeshare plan, prepared a master plan for the property, and verified that no local laws or title documents prohibit or restrict timeshare, selection of the appropriate subdivision vehicle is the next step in the development of a timeshare project. While the timeshare plan provides for the subdivision of time, it still is important to consider the method by which the property will be physically divided. The developer typically has four options as follows:

- undivided-interest ownership;
- the condominium form of ownership;

The Vidafel Mayan Palace Hotel in Acapulco, Guerrero, Mexico.

A pond on the Riverside Golf Course mirrors both the Fairmont Vacation Villas at Riverside and the Rocky Mountains in the background. The resort is located in Fairmont Hot Springs, British Columbia, Canada, near the headwaters of the Columbia River.

◆ the cooperative form of ownership; or
◆ use of a trust vehicle.

In an undivided-interest structure, which is created by recording a declaration of covenants and restrictions, the purchaser receives an undivided interest in the entire parcel as a tenant-in-common with all other purchasers. The declaration of covenants and restrictions then restricts use of the property and the vacation accommodations located on the property.

A condominium is created by recording a declaration of condominium, which divides the property into units and common elements. The purchaser of a unit in the condominium receives exclusive ownership of that unit and a percentage share in the common elements. In a timeshare project, however, the purchaser does not buy the whole unit. Instead, he or she purchases either an individual interest in a particular unit or (in a jurisdiction that recognizes time intervals as a distinguishable interest in real property) exclusive ownership of a specific time interval.

In a cooperative, a corporation (usually a nonprofit owners' association) owns the accommodations and common areas while purchasers receive shares in the corporation. The cooperative documents govern the use and occupancy of the property. A trust vehicle operates much like a cooperative. The trust owns the property, and the purchasers are the beneficiaries of the trust. The trust documents govern the use and occupancy of the property.

Their lack of experience with the sale of shares in a timeshare cooperative and the possible treatment of such sales as securities—coupled with the fact that trusts face various regulatory and adverse tax consequences—motivate most developers to choose undivided-interest or condominium vehicles for subdividing timeshare property. The benefits to the developer of an undivided-interest structure include less regulation, reduced purchaser control and owner democracy, and fewer regulatory requirements regarding financial accountability and reserves. The benefits of a condominium structure are greater legal certainty in phasing development and avoiding developer maintenance fees; greater regulatory acceptance and certainty;

greater lender acceptance; and, depending on the jurisdiction, greater flexibility in legally separating commercial areas and developer profit centers from the project's residential element.

The Timeshare Plan

The next step in the process of structuring the timeshare project is the development of the timeshare plan, which is the legal structure through which vacation accommodations are subdivided into periods of time. The timeshare plan also delineates the purchaser's other benefits (such as access to a reservations system) that make use of the purchase possible. The plan takes the form of a separately recorded restrictive instrument or is specified in the provisions of the underlying declaration of covenants and restrictions, declaration of condominium, cooperative document, or trust instrument.

Most jurisdictions define a timeshare plan by statute as any arrangement in which a purchaser receives ownership rights in or a right to use vacation accommodations and facilities, if any, for a period of time less than a full year during any given year and which right to use occurs for more than a stated number of years. The two general categories of timeshare plans are timeshare estates and timeshare licenses, both of which include a right-to-use component. As a right to use vacation accommodations and facilities, the timeshare estate incorporates an underlying real estate interest in the accommodations and facilities. A timeshare license is similar but does not incorporate any underlying real property interest.

The laws of most jurisdictions treat timeshare estates as real property interests and timeshare licenses as personal property interests. The purchaser of a timeshare estate receives a deed and all the rights and liabilities associated with ownership of real property, such as the obligation to pay real estate taxes and bear the burden of an uninsured casualty. The purchaser of a timeshare license acquires use rights with the general legal status of a license.

Open-air lobby at Bali Desa in Bali, Indonesia.

Courtesy of George Leposky, Interval International

The timeshare license purchaser has few, if any, of the rights and liabilities associated with real property. Instead, the timeshare developer, as the owner or lessee of the fee-simple title to the real estate underlying the timeshare plan, controls the operation, management, improvement, and repair of the timeshare property; recovers the cost of the operation, management, improvement, and repair of the property from the timeshare purchasers through annual contractual assessments; and receives any condemnation awards or insurance proceeds regarding the property. The developer may freely transfer its interest in the underlying real property.[1] The terms of the purchase agreement determine whether the purchaser can transfer the timeshare license contractual interest to a third party.

As a purely practical matter, most timeshare developers would choose to sell timeshare licenses instead of timeshare estates. A timeshare license plan allows the developer to retain ownership of the underlying property; avoid owner democracy and control; maintain maximum flexibility over the use, operation, and development of the property; develop and sell a less complicated product; avoid certain real estate finance laws; and recover the timeshare license through nonjudicial means if the purchaser defaults on the purchase-money loan. Consequently, timeshare license plans were the favored structure in the early years of timesharing in the United States.

For several legal, tax, and regulatory reasons, however, most developers in the United States now develop timeshare estate plans instead of timeshare license plans. The Internal Revenue Service considers the purchase of a timeshare license a lease rather than a sale, meaning that the developer of the timeshare plan must recognize in the year of sale all the income from the sale of the timeshare license[2] and cannot deduct the costs of construction or other costs of sale (including commissions) in that year. Instead, the costs of acquisition, construction, and other deductible costs of sales must be amortized over the term of the timeshare plan.

Similarly, generally accepted accounting principles may require sales of timeshare licenses to be booked as leases. Consequently, public companies concerned about posting earnings may not be able to recognize fully the earnings from timeshare license transfers in the year of sale. In addition, given that a timeshare license is generally treated as a personal property interest, the sale of timeshare licenses may be subject to sales and use tax, with the sales tax due on the entire amount of the purchase at time of sale—even if the consumer is paying the purchase price with a note payable over time.

Regulators also prefer the more familiar deeded products. For example, some states require purchasers of timeshare licenses to be accorded open-ended rescission rights. In addition, many state timeshare laws protect the rights of purchasers of timeshare licenses by requiring the execution and recordation of some type of subordination or nondisturbance instrument. Such an instrument requires the timeshare developer (or any holder of an interest in or lien or encumbrance against the underlying property that is the subject of the timeshare license plan) to subordinate its property rights to those of the timeshare license owners for the term of the timeshare license plan.

For all of the foregoing reasons, timeshare lenders generally dislike timeshare license plans. In particular, strict laws that require open-ended rescission rights, limit installment sales interest rates, and lack holder-in-due-course protections (making it difficult to finance the paper) present problems for the financial markets. Indeed, most timeshare sales experts agree that it is difficult to sell a timeshare license. In their view, consumers prefer the perceived benefits of deeded ownership, including the right to purchase title insurance, the pride of ownership of property, and the ability to pass timeshare interests on to heirs.

Use Plan and Rules

Regardless of the underlying legal structure and type of timeshare plan, every timeshare project must have a detailed use plan. The use plan consists of the rules or covenants that govern and describe how and when purchasers may use the timeshare resort's accommodations and facilities.

Use plans vary from the relatively simple to the extraordinarily complex. As a general rule, the simplicity of a timeshare use plan is inversely proportional to its flexibility and the costs of creating and administering it. For example, a use plan that grants a purchaser the right to occupy the same unit during the same week each year is relatively simple and inexpensive to create and administer. However, it does not provide the purchaser with any flexibility in using the resort during other times of the year or for intervals other than the specified seven consecutive days. Use plans that provide more flexibility are necessarily more complex and require sophisticated reservation system rules and software. Because of their greater legal and regulatory challenges, they also cost more to create and maintain.

Most of the early timeshare resorts offered simple fixed-week/fixed-unit use plans. To give the managing entity more flexibility to perform its maintenance obligations, some developers began offering fixed-week/floating-unit plans, which granted purchasers the right to occupy a particular type of unit (i.e., one-bedroom, two-bedroom, and so forth) during the same week each year, with the specific unit to be assigned at the time of check-in. To provide purchasers with greater options for using the timeshare product, many developers also began offering use plans with an array of flexible use features. As

Many timeshare resorts incorporate retail opportunities that can benefit both the developer and owners and guests. Access to Disney's Old Key West Resort's retail and sandwich shop area is outdoors, whereas Royal Resorts Royal Islander's retail area is located within the central facilities building.

described in chapter 3, some plans offer floating-week and split-week options and, more recently, point systems and vacation clubs.

Most states, either through timeshare-specific or more general consumer protection laws, require flexible use plans to be created and maintained with at least a minimum level of integrity. In particular, the laws specify that a use plan should not allow a developer to sell more timeshare interests than there are weeks available for occupancy, even though not every purchaser will reserve accommodations at the resort every year. In the point system context, this "one-to-one purchaser-to-accommodation ratio" means that the total amount of points allocated to purchasers in a given year cannot exceed the total number of points required to reserve use of all timeshare accommodations in the system during that year.

The variations and nuances regarding implementation of the different types of use plans are limitless. In designing the use plan for a particular project, the developer must consider how much flexibility is commercially necessary and weigh it against the prospective costs and complexities associated with creating and administering the reservation system. For example, there may be relatively little benefit to a use plan that allows daily reservations in a seven-day resort destination such as Hawaii. However, for a project in an urban center such as New York City, where, in addition to seven-day vacationers, potential purchasers may include businesses and people who live in the suburbs, a use plan that allows daily reservations may be essential.

The developer must also consider how the complexity of the product may affect the sales process. If the product is too complicated, sales staff face an unhappy choice: either expand an already lengthy sales pitch and risk potential consumer backlash or omit discussion of critical aspects of the use plan, which may create problems later when the consumer encounters unexpected rules or procedures.

Vacation Clubs

In recent years, developers of timeshare projects have looked beyond the development of a single timeshare project to a long-term strategy that involves the development of more than one project. Today's most common long-term timeshare development strategy is the multisite timeshare plan known as the vacation club. With vacation clubs, developers can bring consistency and quality to their customers' exchange experiences at other timeshare resorts, capture the opportunity to sell their consumers more than one timeshare interest, and develop a distribution mechanism for marketing projects at off-site locations.

Legally, a multisite timeshare plan or vacation club is a timeshare plan in which several timeshare projects are linked together through a mandatory reservation system that operates in one of two ways. One system type pools accommodations and makes them available on a first-come, first-served basis (purchasers do not have priority rights to reserve accommodations at any particular resort). The second system type requires consumers to reserve accommodations at their home resort by a prescribed period of time, after which unreserved accommodation rights are deposited into a pool and then made available on a first-come, first-served basis to owners from all of the club's resorts.

A developer should not decide to develop a vacation club without fully understanding the associated costs and intricacies. As a general rule, a vacation club cannot *begin* to support the expense of establishing or operating a reservation network and providing purchasers with desirable reservation options until it reaches 10,000 to 12,000 owners or represents approximately 195 to 235 units in varied projects. Given the complexity involved in managing and coordinating the reservation requests of even a modestly sized system, the developer must either expend significant funds upfront to purchase the hardware and software necessary to operate the system or engage one of the few available service providers to run the club's reservation system. In addition, the developer must link the various club resorts in a way that meets both legal and practical requirements and establish rules and procedures that govern owner use of the club itself

Courtesy of Club Intrawest

Club Intrawest's Kauai resort in Hawaii capitalizes on the popularity of the state as a vacation destination.

and individual club resorts. The level of complexity involved in establishing the club affects the developer's costs as well as the sales process.

Another important consideration for the developer of the multisite timeshare product is how to balance demand. In particular, the developer needs to devote attention to the comparability of the resorts to be included in the plan. While the developer wants to provide consumers with a variety of vacation opportunities, wide disparities in the level of demand among the resorts will lead to consumer dissatisfaction. For example, too little inventory available at a resort in a high-demand destination such as Orlando, Florida, and too much inventory available at a resort in a lower-demand destination or an area with significant seasonal shifts, such as

Hilton Head Island, South Carolina, will generate owner frustration and fallout.

In addition, as resorts are added to the vacation club, the multisite timeshare plan should enable the vacation club manager to make periodic adjustments to the valuation of the various accommodations within the plan to reflect shifts in owner demands. Use of a point system that offers maximum flexibility in reserving both time and unit type helps a vacation club balance demand and manage consumers' reservation expectations, activities, and habits.

Timeshare Registration Requirements

Most states require a timeshare project's public offering documents or registration statement to be filed and approved by a

Palm trees and flowers announce the entry to Vistana Resort.

Courtesy of Vistana, Inc.

designated regulatory authority before interests in the project may be offered to residents of the state. Specific registration requirements vary from state to state but usually apply regardless of whether the project to be offered within a given state is physically located in that state. The term "offer" tends to be defined broadly. Most states require the developer to register before publishing any advertisements in the state or engaging in any in-state direct-mail or telemarketing activities. Depending on the state, registration approval can take as few as 30 days or as long as a year or more.

The documentation required by most states to complete a registration generally consists of title documents, disclosure documents, and consumer documents. Title documents are those documents that are (or will be) recorded in the public records to establish the timeshare plan and/or encumber the timeshare property. Examples of title documents include declarations of covenants, conditions, and restrictions; declarations of condominium; plats; easements; mortgages; and leases. Title documents required for various state

registrations may also include a copy of the form deed that the developer intends to use to convey timeshare interests to purchasers as well as a recent title report or attorney's title opinion with respect to the overall timeshare property.

Disclosure documents are those documents that describe fully and fairly to the purchaser the material and other aspects of the timeshare plan. Documents may include public offering statements; registration applications; reservation system rules; resort regulations; homeowners' association budgets and financial statements; and local government permits and approvals. Where applicable, state law dictates the specific information that must be contained in a public offering statement or registration application. Such information usually includes, among other items, details about the use plan; the underlying legal structure of the project; the number, size, and type of units to be constructed; the proposed date of completion of construction; the planned recreational facilities; the developer's financial strength and experience; the status of title to the timeshare property; descriptions of the general area surrounding the timeshare property; any agreements for the provision of management, utilities, or other services to the timeshare property; exchange programs that may be available for use by purchasers; and any material or other special-risk factors that might reasonably affect a prospective purchaser's decision to buy.

Consumer documents are the other documents that timeshare purchasers are asked to sign in connection with the purchase of a timeshare interest. Consumer documents may include the purchase agreement and any addenda; purchase-money financing documents such as the promissory note and mortgage and truth-in-lending disclosures; and the receipt for timeshare documents to indicate that the purchaser has received all of the disclosure documents and other materials as required by law.

In addition to the registration requirements discussed above, several states require all proposed timeshare advertising materials to contain certain disclosures and to be filed with the state regulatory authority before they are disseminated within the state. Because registration requirements differ from jurisdiction to jurisdiction and the penalties for failure to comply can be severe (e.g., the Division of Florida Land Sales, Condominiums and Mobile Homes has the authority to impose a $10,000 fine for each piece of unregistered advertising used in the state), timeshare developers should fully investigate the applicable laws in each state before engaging in any potentially regulated promotional activity.

Additional Regulatory Considerations

Once a timeshare project is registered in a particular state, the developer may still have to overcome other regulatory hurdles before proceeding with marketing and sales. Many states have enacted general consumer protection laws that are not specific to timeshare but nevertheless govern the developer's proposed promotional activities. The most common of these laws apply to telemarketing, home solicitations, promotional offers, and gambling.

Most states have enacted telemarketing laws that require any person or company that intends to telemarket in the state to register with a designated state regulatory agency. In addition, as part of the registration process, many states require the telemarketer to post a substantial bond. Various state telemarketing laws also set forth behavioral and disclosure guidelines that complement those established by federal law, to which all telemarketers must likewise adhere.

Home solicitation laws are special laws that apply to the sale of goods and services when purchasers are solicited in their home. Several states have expanded the coverage of home solicitation laws—initially enacted to apply to door-to-door salespersons—to include sales made over the telephone to purchasers in their home. Most home solicitation laws require a

The view from a balcony of one of the Royal Islander's beachfront villas in Cancun, where buyers purchase a fixed-unit/fixed-week time interval through a deed of trust.

Diane R. Suchman

Courtesy of E D S A

The blending of natural and manmade landscaping enhances the tropical environment featured at the Hyatt Regency Cerromar in Dorado, Puerto Rico.

identity of the promoter and the purpose of the promotion. Some promotional offer laws also require registration with the state attorney general's office or some other designated regulatory authority.

Gambling laws are laws that regulate or prohibit gambling, lotteries, drawings, and the like. Many promotional offers involve a giveaway, which, under some state laws, could be deemed an illegal lottery. While exemptions apply in many cases to retail-related giveaways, these exemptions often contain specific requirements regarding conduct of the drawing and disclosure requirements regarding the purpose of the drawing and the value of the prizes. In some instances, states may require a permitted promotional giveaway to be registered with a regulatory authority.

Several laws, not all of which are specifically related to timeshare, can affect a timeshare developer's activities in a given jurisdiction. To ensure that regulatory requirements are not inadvertently overlooked, timeshare developers and marketers may want to review with legal counsel, in advance, the laws that apply to promotional activities in each state where they intend to conduct business.

Broker Licensing Issues

Many real estate broker licensing issues affect the marketing and sale of timeshare interests. Some states require timeshares to be sold only by licensed real estate brokers and salespersons, even when developers offer timeshare licenses rather than timeshare estates. Further, as part of their marketing strategy, many developers compensate off-site agents and existing purchasers for referring prospective purchasers to sales presentations at the resort. Under some state laws, this compensation arrangement may fall under the real estate broker licensing law, even if developers pay compensation only for prospects referred and not for prospects' purchases. With respect to the marketing and sale of

written purchase contract and a specific cancellation period, during which the purchaser has the right to cancel the transaction for any reason. Home solicitation laws also apply to the sale of discounted minivacation packages designed to induce a prospective timeshare purchaser to visit a resort.

Promotional offer laws are generally disclosure-oriented laws designed to ensure that consumers are provided with all relevant details regarding offers that appear "too good to be true." Examples of promotional offer laws include statutory limits on the use of words such as "free" and requirements that promotional offers disclose the

out-of-state projects, several states require an in-state broker to be employed by the developer and to be designated in the various registration materials as the project's broker. As is the case with the timeshare registration and consumer protection laws discussed above, timeshare developers should familiarize themselves in advance with how real estate broker laws are likely to affect their proposed marketing and sales activities.

Securities, Tax, and Finance Laws

A number of other state and federal laws enacted for broader purposes also affect the development and sale of timeshare. Among these, securities, tax, and finance laws are especially important. The discussion below highlights major issues addressed by some of these laws.

Federal Securities Laws

Generally speaking, a security under federal law is an investment opportunity from which a purchaser expects to receive profits through the efforts of others. The more a product is pitched and designed for personal use and consumption, the less likely it will be deemed a security. Regulations tend to focus on registration requirements, approval of the securities offering circular, marketing restrictions, and disclosure requirements.

State "Blue Sky" Laws

The type and scope of state regulation of securities offerings varies across the country, but "blue sky" securities analyses generally tend to focus on marketing techniques and product.

Federal Tax Issues

As previously noted, the major federal tax issue pertaining to timeshare products involves the determination of whether the Internal Revenue Service will, for tax purposes, recognize the sale of timeshare interests to purchasers as a sale or a lease. In particular, the IRS looks to factors such as who owns and manages the property. Other tax issues include the implications of reporting timeshare sales income to the IRS on an installment basis, special rules affecting foreign corporations, and whether buyers can take a second-home mortgage interest deduction on a timeshare purchase.

State Tax Issues

The major state tax issue is whether sales taxes apply to the sale or use of timeshare products. Generally, the structure of the timeshare product determines the applicability of sales tax. In addition, some jurisdictions impose sales tax on services provided to the timeshare owners' association. Timeshare owners pay the tax as part of their maintenance fees.

Federal Financing Issues

A number of other federal laws related to financing may also apply to the timeshare developer's sales and marketing effort, including

- the Real Estate Settlement Procedures Act;
- the Truth-in-Lending Act;
- the Federal Trade Commission Trade Practice Rules and holder-in-due-course limitations;
- the Equal Credit Opportunity Act;
- the Fair Credit Reporting Act; and
- the Electronic Funds Transfer Act.

Again, the impact of these laws on the development, sale, and marketing of the timeshare project varies according to the type and structure of the timeshare plan selected by the developer.

Notes

1. Subject to the use rights of the timeshare purchasers depending on applicable state law.

2. Subject to limited installment sales reporting.

Chapter 8
Financing

Jeffrey A. Owings,
FINOVA Capital Corporation

The discussion on financing timeshare developments begins with a description of the traditional structure of transactions for financing timeshare developments and its evolution into today's financial structures. It then explains acquisition loans, construction loans, renovation loans, and receivable loans, with particular emphasis on securitization of timeshare receivables as an alternative to commercial loans secured by receivables. Finally, the chapter analyzes the economic feasibility of a new timeshare resort, evaluates a new resort's cash-flow potential, and summarizes today's opportunities and trends.

Given the significant financing needs of timeshare development, it is essential that lender and borrower establish a particularly close working relationship. The lender must structure loans to the developer in a manner that will enable the operation to succeed. At the same time, the loan structure must protect the lender in the event that problems arise.

Business Capital

Recent History

In contrast to the early days of the timeshare industry, timeshare developers looking for funds to capitalize their businesses in 1999 will find a widely available and comparatively inexpensive supply of dollars. Just five years ago, however, the pursuit of capital for timeshare development was a common topic at industry conferences.

Today, finding money is no longer an issue. The buzz words are LIBOR (London Inter-Bank Offered Rate), no recourse, securitization, warehouse line, and so forth. Particularly during the last two years, the timeshare business has undergone dramatic changes and has finally been discovered by Wall Street and major banks. The result is a dramatic expansion in the pricing and structure of financial products available to the industry's top developers.

Today, commercial finance companies, commercial banks, and Wall Street firms all compete for market share. To appreciate the shift in circumstances, it is instructive to study the roots of timeshare finance and the subsequent evolution in financing. As recently as five years ago, its poor public image and a set of perceived risks that went well beyond the comfort level of lenders made the timeshare business a pariah in the eyes of most institutional capital providers. Accordingly, commercial finance companies such as FINOVA, Heller, and Textron stepped in to fill the timeshare industry's capital void. These lenders looked beyond timeshare's poor image and recognized that the perceived risks were manageable through sound loan structures.

The industry's poor image resulted from the actions of a few disreputable timeshare developers during the 1980s. These developers were interested only in a fast buck and were willing to misrepresent the product. Clearly, the actions of a few caused a backlash of consumer protection regulations that now govern developers' business practices, particularly in Florida and California. With tightened regulations and ARDA's strong leadership, the industry's performance—and image—began to change in the early 1990s.

Despite progress within the industry, the early 1990s were nonetheless a difficult time for raising capital. As a result of the demise of the savings and loan business and the concomitant real estate recession (termed a depression by some),

capital providers avoided all real estate transactions. Timeshare developers therefore had to contend not only with a poor image but also their undeniable link to a real estate product. Yet, even in the midst of the early 1990s credit crunch that affected the real estate and hospitality industries, a few savvy commercial finance companies took advantage of their unregulated status and made well-secured loans to timeshare developers. These loans typically included a premium return to the lender. To the timeshare industry's credit, the sector performed well during the recession. While cost of capital was relatively expensive, cost of product was low and the potential for high returns was great. Many developers acquired hospitality properties from the Resolution Trust Corporation (RTC) or obtained other distressed properties from owners at deep discounts and converted them to timeshare. The success of timeshare developers in the early 1990s laid the foundation for rapid expansion of the business once the economy rebounded.

Financing Example, 1992: Orange Tree Golf & Conference Resort

A close look at a transaction booked in 1992 illustrates some of the dynamics that were in play at that time. Shell Vacations, LLC, is a premier timeshare developer in North America. In 1992, it uncovered an opportunity to acquire an existing 162-unit hotel and golf course in Scottsdale, Arizona. The hotel component of the Orange Tree Golf & Conference Resort (featured as a case study in chapter 9) was not performing, and the lender, Security Pacific National Bank (since acquired by Bank of America), was in the process of foreclosing on both the hotel and golf course. The bank was under pressure to sell the asset to reduce its real estate exposure. Shell Vacations astutely analyzed the situation and offered to buy the property for $15 million (a $10 million discount from the

Photo on page 120: **Missiones del Cabo, a mixed-use condominium hotel and timeshare resort, commands the sea from a rocky promontory at the north end of Cabo San Lucas Bay in Mexico.**

Courtesy of George Leposky, Interval International

Spanish Mission architecture characterizes the Marina El Cid Hotel & Yacht Club, part of the El Cid Mega Resort Complex in Mazatlan, Mexico.

bank's $25 million carrying amount). Shell arranged financing with its lender, FINOVA; the bank accepted the purchase offer.

Given that the golf course was making money and could support a $6 million loan, the effective cost of the timeshare portion of the property was $9 million plus approximately $2 million in improvements; the resultant per unit product cost totaled only $68,000. At an average timeshare interval sales price of $7,500, the timeshare product cost was a mere 18 percent ($7,500 x

A wise acquisition and a mutually beneficial relationship between lender and developer were key ingredients in the success of the Orange Tree Golf & Conference Resort in Scottsdale, Arizona. The resort includes an 18-hole golf course designed by Johnny Bulla.

51 weeks/$68,000). With the typical product cost for a timeshare resort running at a minimum 25 percent, Shell made an extremely opportunistic acquisition.

A review of the loan terms for the Orange Tree transaction offers a clear picture of the lending environment at the time the deal came together. Of the $15 million purchase price, FINOVA agreed to finance $14 million and to provide an additional $2 million for improvements and startup operations costs. Shell Vacations's out-of-pocket costs totaled $1 million or 6 percent of the cost to acquire the property and prepare it for operation as a timeshare resort. With respect to pricing for the deal, the interest rate for the golf course and timeshare loans was 2 percent above the published prime rate, in addition to which the lender received a 50 percent participation in the project's profits from all sources, including the sale of timeshares, golf course income, hotel income, and the financing spread. FINOVA also required that it be allowed to finance and service all receivables from the sale of timeshare interests in the resort. The pricing for the receivable loan was similarly prime plus 2 percent. The same transaction in early 1999 would probably be priced 100 basis points lower for the acquisition loan and 150 basis points better for the receivable loan, with limited (if any) profit participation.

Shell sold over 8,000 timeshare intervals in less than four years and retired all project debt (except a small mortgage remaining on the golf course). Both the developer and the lender realized a tremendous return on their investment.

Financing Example, 1998: Vistana

The following example demonstrates the types of changes that occurred in timeshare financing transactions between 1992 and 1998. Vistana, a development company based in Orlando, went public in early 1997. Since that time, it reduced its typical financing package (for all types of financing) from prime plus 2 percent to LIBOR-based financing that is well below the prime rate. Vistana has a $70 million receivable-secured transaction (secured by notes generated from sales in any of its properties) priced at LIBOR plus 100 basis points (effectively 6.5 percent) and a $20 million *unsecured* transaction with Dresdner Bank priced at LIBOR plus 225 basis points. Vistana is still the exception rather than the rule, although most public timeshare companies (Fairfield, Sunterra, Silverleaf, and Bluegreen) have also been able to command premium pricing.

Trends by Development Entity

With their acquisition of regional operators, publicly held timeshare companies have become industry consolidators. The most aggressive consolidator is Sunterra, which acquired All Seasons in Arizona, Powhatan/Green Springs in Virginia, Vacation Internationale in Washington, and LSI in Europe. Vistana expanded westward by acquiring the Success Group based in Arizona and Colorado; Fairfield absorbed Vacation Break in Florida. The public companies used their common stock as the currency to acquire the various independent developers. This type of consolidation has resulted in a timeshare industry that now consists of fewer but relatively larger and better-capitalized companies.

Too many dollars chasing too few timeshare developers has benefited strong independent operators. Developers such as Shell Vacations, Consolidated Resorts, EPIC Resorts, and the Kosmas Group are a few of the many independent developers that in 1998 negotiated capital structures previously unavailable to timeshare developers.

Hotel companies have also made a large financial commitment to the timeshare business. Marriott, the pioneer among hotel companies expanding into the timeshare business, entered the business cautiously in 1984 and, by 1998, had expanded its operations to annual sales of over $400 million. Hilton, Disney, Hyatt, and Four Seasons have followed Marriott into the timeshare business. Other hotel companies have entered the business through strategic alliances. Large real estate investment trusts (REITs) also plan to move into the timeshare business. Both hotel companies and REITs bring their existing capital sources to the timeshare business.

Clearly, the timeshare business now includes highly credible players with access to both public and private capital at attractive terms. The following discussion reviews the structure of the various types of loans available to timeshare developers by focusing on the two most prevalent loan types: acquisition and development loans and receivable loans.

Acquisition and Development Loans

While the Orange Tree transaction involved acquisition financing for an existing property along with relatively minor expenditures to convert the property to a timeshare, timeshare lenders can finance more complex acquisition and development loans. In particular, construction loans for purpose-built timeshare resorts (including land acquisition) are available. The past few years in fact have seen the development of many new timeshare resorts in major timeshare markets such as Orlando, Las Vegas, Hawaii, southern California, and Virginia. At the same time, lenders have financed the acquisition and renovation of existing properties in markets where prime land is scarce, such as New Orleans, San Francisco, and New York.

Whether a developer requests financing for startup construction, acquisition with major renovation, or acquisition with minor renovation, the lender brings the same underwriting concerns to the evaluation of the loan application. Is the project feasible? Are the costs realistic? Does the developer have experience with the product? Does the developer have experience in the market? How much cash equity is to be invested? What is the all-in product cost? What is the projected sales pace? Is it realistic? What is the projected sales price? Does it compare favorably with the market? What expenses are projected for marketing, sales, and administration? Are the developer's historical operating expenses comparable to the projections? Do projections show positive net cash flow? Is the developer making unrealistic assumptions? These and other questions are intended to help the lender evaluate the proposed resort development's likelihood of success. If a resort fails, a lender forced to foreclose is in the unenviable position of trying to sell the remaining inventory to timeshare purchasers or the entire inventory to another developer. Either way, the losses can be staggering.

Though primarily concerned with the market risk of an acquisition and development loan, a lender also needs to evaluate the likelihood that construction of the proposed new development will be completed. All construction deals carry the risk of cost overruns, work stoppages, weather delays, poor workmanship, and other issues. Construction delays or cost increases that exceed original projections can lead to budget overruns that potentially threaten the project's chances for success. Therefore, the developer and lender must agree on the final construction budget and ensure that the construction job is entrusted to highly professional contractors.

For most timeshare projects, the developer hires an experienced general contractor to budget and manage the construction job. The general contractor then manages the work of the subcontractors. Most construction projects are structured with a guaranteed price contract from the general contractor. The contract protects the developer from cost changes as the project is built. The developer, however, must protect the lender and thus obtains payment and performance bonds or otherwise provides some type of completion guarantee. The lender requires a substantial portion of the budget to be dedicated to a contingency reserve, which can cover cost overruns and significant change orders.

The lender also needs to ensure that an interest reserve is in place to cover interest payments on the construction loan during both the construction period and the first year or so of sales. With a lengthy construction period (18 months), a large project in particular will require substantial interest reserves and a large debt carry upon completion. For example, a $24 million construction loan at a 10 percent interest rate has a $200,000 *monthly* interest payment. Therefore, the construction budget may well require a $4 million interest reserve to support the project until sales reduce the mortgage to a manageable level.

When evaluating acquisition and development loans, the lender must consider the amount of cash equity the developer plans to contribute to the overall cost of acquiring and/or building the property as well as the amount of the personal guarantee the developer proposes to provide. Guarantees are particularly important when a project faces substantial risk that it will not be completed. Guarantee requirements generally become less prevalent (depending on market conditions) once a resort is completed and the sales process begins.

Equity is a give-and-take negotiation between lender and developer. At minimum, the lender likes the hard equity in a timeshare acquisition and development transaction to equate to 20 percent of cost.

The developer often tries to reduce the amount of required equity by citing previous development successes, issuing corporate or personal guarantees, securing letters of credit, leveraging the appraised value of the property as compared to cost, and providing other assurances of risk minimization. Some lenders are amenable to trading lower developer equity requirements for profit participation in the deal.

Only when a lender is comfortable with the construction budget, the contractor,

Courtesy of Vistana, Inc.

Since becoming a public company, Vistana, Inc., has been able to negotiate lower financing rates for its developments. Shown here are exterior and interior photographs of its flagship property, Vistana Resort in Orlando, Florida, which has been developed in phases since 1980.

Courtesy of Vistana, Inc.

the completion guarantees, and the contingency and interest reserves is it time, first, to evaluate the financial feasibility of the proposed timeshare resort and, second, to consider the appropriate loan structure for the transaction. The accompanying feature box provides a simplified hypothetical example of a lender's evaluation of an acquisition and development loan.

Receivable Loans

While it is essential to structure the acquisition loan to suit the economics of a particular resort, a developer must also be concerned with the amount of capital required to finance sales. Given that most sales in the timeshare business are developer-financed, a developer must maintain a positive cash flow to ensure a source of capital for consumer mortgages. Without appropriate end-loan structures, a successful sales operation can literally sell itself out of business. Figure 8-1 illustrates a generic consumer financing scenario.

The example shows that, at the time of the sale of a timeshare interval priced at $10,000, the consumer makes a $1,000 downpayment while the developer carries a $9,000 note for seven years at a 14 per-

---

◆ Hypothetical Lender Evaluation of a Proposed Timeshare Resort

Assume that a lender is reviewing an acquisition and development financing opportunity for any of three types of developments: a $20 million purpose-built project, a $10 million acquisition and $10 million renovation project, or an $18 million acquisition and $2 million renovation project. In all cases, the loan amount put at risk by the lender at project completion is $20 million. The risk of finishing the project on time and on budget is assumed to be equal for all three developments, even though a large renovation project carries a higher probability of cost overruns while the level of risk rises with the size of the construction loan. For this analysis, the lender is indifferent to these risks.

Of primary importance to the lender is the repayment of the loan in concert with the sale of the timeshare inventory. The information provided to the lender shows that the resort will encompass 150 timeshare units at an average sales price of $10,000. Product cost is approximately 26 percent. The lender evaluates these numbers based on comparable resorts in the market and the developer's

Hypothetical Analysis

Acquisition and development loan	$20,000,000
150 units x 150 intervals	7,650 intervals
7,650 intervals x $10,000 average price	$76,500,000
7,650 intervals x 85% (loan repayment trigger)	6,500 intervals
$20,000,000/6,500 intervals	$3,077 release payment

experience. Analysis reveals that a price of $10,000 is conservative and that the developer has proved its ability to market similar timeshare inventory in other properties.

The lender now establishes the release payment—the amount required to repay the mortgage as each timeshare interest is sold. Since the lender will place a blanket lien on the property, the release payment will allow consumers to receive clear title to their acquired timeshare interest. The lender and the developer have agreed that the loan will be repaid when 85 percent of the resort's available timeshare inventory is sold. This structure gives the lender some cushion by allowing the loan to be retired in full before the inventory is completely sold.

As the data show, the average release payment is $3,077 for each sale, approximately 30 percent of the sale price of each timeshare unit. (In a typical scenario, the timeshare inventory is a mix of different unit sizes—e.g., one- and two-bedroom units, with different prices for different seasons. In this simplified model, however, the calculations that determine the appropriate release payment are an average interval price and an average proportion of product cost.) If all goes as planned for the hypothetical development, the developer will repay the acquisition and development loan in full when the resort's 6,500th interval is sold. The developer will have generated nearly $65 million in timeshare sales in order to retire the $20 million acquisition and development loan.

Figure 8-1 **Hypothetical Consumer Financing**

Interval sales price	$10,000
Downpayment	−1,000
Note	$9,000
Advance rate	x .9
Loan advance	$8,100
Downpayment	+1,000
Cash received from sale	$9,100
Operating expenses	(6,000)
Release payment	(3,000)
Cash remaining	$100

cent interest rate. Assuming that the developer's operating costs (i.e., sales, marketing, and administration) account for 60 percent of the sales cost ($6,000) and that the mortgage release payment totals 30 percent ($3,000), the receivable loan will need a 90 percent advance rate to generate sufficient cash to permit the developer to break even.

If the advance rate were 80 rather than 90 percent, the developer would have a negative cash flow of $800 with each financed sale. Indeed, in the early years of the timeshare business, developers frequently abandoned projects when lenders failed to provide the advance rates that would permit a project to realize a positive cash flow. Even worse, some developments began construction but failed because of poor underwriting skills on the part of both lender and developer. Fortunately, those problems are history. Today, timeshare receivables from reputable developers routinely receive 90 percent advance rates from lenders. In fact, timeshare receivable collateral as a commodity has attracted attention from Wall Street and any number of investment vehicles.

Hypothecation

This section discusses the structure of a typical hypothecation loan and the various forms of securitization structures that are available to large developers who generate $50 million in timeshare receivables annually. Hypothecation refers to a loan made to a developer by a lending institution and that the developer guarantees with a portfolio of consumer loans. The cash flow generated by the consumer loans is used to repay the hypothecation loan.

With hypothecation, most developments generally require a 90 percent advance rate to cash-flow the business; that is, the lender provides 90 percent of the value of the consumer loans in advance within a loan structure that ultimately results in the satisfactory repayment of the loan. The loan structure includes, for example, a provision requiring the developer to replace delinquent notes with paying notes to maintain eligible receivable collateral at an amount that will keep the borrowing base within 90 percent. The lender also establishes in its name a separate lockbox as the depository for consumer payments. The lender collects payments on a regular basis and applies them to the interest and principal on the receivable loan.

Typically, with a receivable-secured loan, the interest rate paid by the developer—whether fixed or floating—is lower than the interest rate the consumer pays to the developer. For example, if the loan to the developer carries an interest rate of 9.5 percent and the average rate on the contracts is 13 percent, the 3.5 percent difference collected through the lockbox permits rapid amortization of the loan. In the present hypothetical structure, a receivable loan secured by contracts with an original term of seven years is repaid in fewer than five years. The developer and the lender may agree to a loan structure that allows the loan to revolve, permitting readvances to the developer if rapid payment of current receivables creates a loan advance percentage that drops below 90 percent. In that case, the developer could borrow more money against good contracts, up to 90 percent.

As noted in chapter 7, hypothecation enables developers to spread their income tax liability from the receivables over the term of the consumer contracts and deduct the interest paid on the loan.

Terms of Consumer Loans

The developer and lender must agree on the terms of the consumer notes and the level of consumer underwriting to be performed by the lender. To facilitate a rapid sales pace, the developer's sales organization often asks for terms that ensure low monthly payments to the consumer (i.e., contracts with long terms and low interest rates). Lenders, however, typically prefer shorter-term notes and higher interest rates that accelerate loan repayment. Accordingly, developers must find a balance whereby the terms of the consumer contracts neither inhibit sales nor raise lender concerns.

In most developments, consumer contracts have the following characteristics: a 10 percent downpayment, seven-year term, and an interest rate between 12 and 16 percent. Many variations are also available, such as ten-year terms, variable-rate notes, and/or low interest rates when downpayments total 50 percent or more of the selling price.

Consumer underwriting is a major issue for both developers and lenders. Lenders prefer developers who run credit reports at the point of sale and make immediate decisions regarding a prospect's probable payment performance. For their part, many developers find that point-of-sale credit reports reduce the costs associated with accepting buyers who are likely to default. Lenders often run their own credit report before accepting a contract if the developer does not rely on point-of-sale reports.

The lender's requirements for accepting contracts as collateral are of primary importance to the developer. In particular, strict underwriting of consumer loans can be just as problematic to a develop-

er's cash flow as a low advance rate. On the other hand, a delinquent portfolio of consumer notes negatively affects cash flow and can result in a problem loan. One approach that has worked well over the years for FINOVA is to encourage developers to underwrite their own contracts and to rely on the replacement requirement to maintain the borrowing base.

Other Loan Considerations

Regardless of loan type, all loans that finance timeshare properties include several specific components such as financial covenants, guarantees, environmental assurances, and insurance protection. Financial covenants typically establish the operational bounds within which the borrower may conduct business. Lenders usually want to ensure that the developer's net worth is maintained at an agreed-upon level. In fact, financial covenants often specify maximum expense ratios to ensure the developer's operating efficiency. For example, marketing, sales, and administration costs are the primary operating expenses in a timeshare business. A developer who cannot stay within a certain agreed-upon limit (e.g., 65 percent of net sales) will likely experience cash-flow problems and ultimately ask the lender for concessions or waivers under the loan documents. A quarterly (or even monthly) review of operating performance allows the lender to monitor the developer's performance trends.

In the early years of timeshare lending, personal guarantees were almost always required. Today, however, they are less frequently requested as additional security for receivable loans.

When making loans secured by real property, lenders are concerned about inheriting environmental mitigation and remediation responsibilities and therefore routinely require Phase I environmental reports that detail the environmental risks

Club Intrawest, a large Canadian public timeshare company, is renowned for its ski resorts. Shown here is its Blackcomb ski resort dressed in its summer finery.

associated with a given property. If the risks are great or potential cleanup is unduly expensive, the developer and/or lender may choose not to proceed with the timeshare development. In addition, hazard insurance and business interruption insurance can be expensive or difficult to obtain in coastal or earthquake-prone areas or other environmentally sensitive locations.

A favorite topic of negotiation between developers and lenders is pricing. A developer typically pays points to the lender upfront at the time of loan commitment —generally 1 percent of the committed amount of a receivable line of credit. In the past, the best rate a proven timeshare developer could expect to obtain was prime plus 2 percent. As more developers went public and Wall Street analysts and money center banks began tracking the timeshare business, new sources of capital entered the industry; as a result, the spreads paid to lenders have shrunk.

Many lenders do not hold assets for their own books but rather originate loans for the sole purpose of selling them in a securitization to generate a gain. These lenders typically are less concerned about the yield on the loan because a loan with a thin spread does not remain on their books long enough to create earnings problems. Balance sheet lenders (i.e., lenders who intend to hold an asset through the life of the loan), however, have had to adjust pricing to remain competitive. In early 1999, it is not unusual to see pricing to the public companies at LIBOR plus 100 to 200 basis points (approximately 6.5 to 7.5 percent) and to well-capitalized, private companies at LIBOR plus 250 to 350 basis points (roughly equivalent to prime plus 0.5 percent).

In early 1999, the pricing cycle favors developers, just as the previous cycle favored lenders. Many developers feel that today's pricing is long overdue and that, in the past, lenders received an unfair share of timeshare profits from fat pricing structures. A traditional lender's viewpoint is that pricing reflects risk and that the high prices of the past resulted from either working out problem timeshare loans or accepting loan losses when performance did not match expectations. In the future, pricing will likely cycle back

◆ Development and Consumer Financing Trends

According to a recent ARDA survey of timeshare developers' financial performance, financing has become increasingly easier to obtain in recent years. In 1996, nearly 90 percent of timeshare developers obtained construction loans compared with just over 70 percent in 1994. Among developers surveyed, just 32 percent worked with lenders that required more than 20 percent of equity in the projects they financed. The percentage of developers obtaining acquisition loans decreased from 68 percent in 1994 to 47 percent in 1995.

Almost 80 percent of timeshare developers report a minimum downpayment requirement of 10 percent for financed sales, exclusive of special financing packages. In fact, over 75 percent of developers have required the 10 percent minimum during the past five years. Nonetheless, 92 percent of consumers now make downpayments that exceed 10 percent. In 1995, by contrast, approximately 75 percent of surveyed consumers made downpayments of 10 percent or less.

Approximately three-quarters (77.3 percent) of developers—compared with 96 percent in 1995—disclose that their consumer receivables portfolio is extended on a fixed rather than variable basis. Slightly more than half of surveyed developers (53 percent) charge an interest rate between 13.1 percent and 15 percent. In 1995, only 37 percent charged interest in this range. The industry is witnessing a substantial increase in longer financing terms: 63.6 percent of developers report that the average terms of their receivables exceed six years as compared with only 40 percent in 1995.

Only 36 percent of developers report selling any portion of their 1996 contracts to a lender. The industry has witnessed a dramatic increase in the proportion of developers who have not hypothecated any of their contracts, from none in 1995 to 28.9 percent in 1996. This trend sharply underscores developers' focus on portfolio profitability and points to liquidity in developers' operations. Almost half (45.2 percent) of developers report a weighted average floating interest rate of 200 to 250 basis points above the prime rate. Developers note that they consider more than 85 percent of their receivables to be current. A little more than half (51.3 percent) of respondents claim an average actual bad-debt expense of 3.1 to 6 percent of 1996 net sales.

Source: American Resort Development Association, "Backgrounder," *Vacation Ownership: Financial Performance of the Industry,* n.d.

to a level that is more balanced between developers and lenders.

Securitization

The above discussion focused on converting timeshare receivable collateral to cash in the form of a secured loan from a commercial lender. Alternatively, large pools of receivables can be securitized (sold to investors) through Wall Street outlets. However, the securitization of receivables is typically available only to note holders with a minimum aggregate principal balance of $50 million or greater. This size requirement eliminates virtually all developers except those who produce annual sales of $30 million or more. The transaction costs associated with originating a securitization make smaller transactions uneconomical.

Nevertheless, for developers with significant receivables portfolios, securitization can be an attractive source of capital. Securitization enables developers to lock in a relatively low cost of capital (depending on market conditions, low cost means three- to five-year Treasuries plus 90 to 250 basis points), to eliminate any requirement for personal recourse, and to circumvent the obligation to replace delinquent notes. On the other hand, securitization transactions involve terms that, once in place, cannot be modified later. In addition, the transactions carry high upfront expenses and involve significant legal, tax, and rating agency due diligence.

The period from 1992 to mid-1998 saw the completion of approximately 16 transactions for the securitization of timeshare receivables. The amount of the placements totaled approximately $1.3 billion. The typical deal structure is a Duff & Phelps—rated private placement, with a senior securities piece at Treasuries plus 90 to 150 basis points and a subordinated piece held by the developer. The subordinated piece absorbs losses before the senior piece is affected.

Credit enhancement for a securitization requires overcollateralization (i.e., ensuring that the receivable balance is higher than the amount advanced), an excess spread account (i.e., capturing the interest-rate differential between consumer notes and the rate of the transaction), a cash reserve, and the aforementioned developer subordinate piece. The amount of required credit enhancement depends on the payment history of the collateral pool as well as on the quality of the developer, the resort or resorts, and the servicing agent and other judgments.

A transaction that is fairly typical of recent timeshare securitization is the Vistana deal closed in September 1998. In that deal, Vistana raised $66 million by pledging $71 million of notes into the trust owned by investors (a 93 percent advance rate). Specifically, the transaction involved the issuance of two senior securities: a Class A AAA-rated tranche of $32 million and a Class B A-rated tranche of $34 million. Vistana effectively held a junior subordinated security of $5 million. The transaction was further enhanced by a 5 percent excess spread account while the underwriter and placement agent (Dresdner Kleinwort Benson) provided a letter of credit supporting 12 percent ($8.5 million) of the deal. The all-in cost of the financing (excluding fees and costs), including the letter of credit, totaled approximately 6.3 percent, or 190 basis points over the three-year Treasury note.

Economic Feasibility of a New Timeshare Resort

Developers and lenders in the timeshare industry need to work cooperatively to assess new development opportunities. Evaluating the feasibility of a timeshare developer's business plan requires an

Fairfield Communities's most recent oceanfront resort is SeaWatch Plantation in Myrtle Beach, South Carolina, a destination resort.

Courtesy of Fairfield Communities, Inc.

understanding of the economics of time-share development and, in particular, how developers earn a profit. While it is relatively simple, the sources of profit are fundamental to judging whether a new project will generate sufficient cash flow to ensure success and whether the likely returns make the venture worth pursuing.

As discussed in chapter 6, timeshare developers rely on three sources of profit: profit from development and sales, profit from financial arbitrage, and profit from resort management income. Of the three, it is most important to generate profit from development and sales. In cases where development and sales generate little or no profit, the lender will probably come out fine in the deal, but the developer's return will be low relative to the risks assumed and the time spent developing and selling the resort. As noted elsewhere, the major cost component of a timeshare resort is marketing and sales (40 to 65 percent of gross sales), followed by product cost (20 to 35 percent), general and administrative (G&A) costs (8 to 10 percent), and resort subsidy[1] (2 to 4 percent). Development profit generally falls in the range of 12 to 20 percent.

Cash-Flow Analysis

An important consideration is whether a resort that generates a 12 percent profit margin will produce sufficient cash flow to operate successfully. The cash flow for a timeshare resort tends to break even in the first year or two and then turn positive in the later years, thus placing pressure on the early years of operations.

A comprehensive cash-flow model is an excellent tool for evaluating the likely success or failure of a particular timeshare resort. Figure 8-2 provides a sample cash-flow model that includes the first-year analysis performed on a monthly basis plus a complete sellout and debt repayment analysis performed on an annual basis. When dollars are at risk, both developer and lender turn to a cash-flow model to analyze project performance on a per month basis from the resort's inception through sellout. For purposes of this chapter, the analysis covers only the first year on a per month basis and then evaluates the full impact of the cash flow on an annual basis. The sample analysis is based on a hypothetical 100-unit timeshare resort with an average sales price of $10,000 per

Royal Resorts finances its resorts through Mexican banks, with assistance from Fonatur, an agency of the Mexican government that assembled and sold prepared land in Cancun's "hotel zone." The interior of a villa at the company's Royal Islander resort is furnished with marble floors and rattan in a cool, sand-colored monochrome.

Diane R. Suchman

Figure 8-2 **Cash-Flow Model**

	Assumptions	Total Year 1	Total Year 2	Total Year 3	Total Year 4	Total Year 5	Totals
Assumptions							
Number of intervals sold per month	100	1,120	1,120	1,060	1,100	700	5,100
Cumulative intervals sold	5,100	1,120	2,240	3,300	4,400	5,100	5,100
Percent of intervals sold		22%	44%	65%	86%	100%	100%
Average interval sales price	$10,000	$10,000	$10,000	$10,000	$10,000	$10,000	$10,000
Timeshare sales revenue		$11,200,000	$11,200,000	$10,600,000	$11,000,000	$7,000,000	$51,000,000
Cash Sources							
Borrower equity		$2,000,000	$0	$0	$0	$0	$2,000,000
Acquisition debt		$8,000,000	$0	$0	$0	$0	$8,000,000
Receivable loan advances	90%	$8,064,000	$8,064,000	$7,632,000	$7,920,000	$5,040,000	$36,720,000
Cash sales and downpayments	20%	$2,240,000	$2,240,000	$2,120,000	$2,200,000	$1,400,000	$10,200,000
Total cash sources		$20,304,000	$10,304,000	$9,752,000	$10,120,000	$6,440,000	$56,920,000
Cash Uses							
Project acquisition		$10,000,000	$0	$0	$0	$0	$10,000,000
Marketing and sales	50%	$5,600,000	$5,600,000	$5,300,000	$5,500,000	$3,500,000	$25,500,000
G&A	10%	$1,120,000	$1,120,000	$1,060,000	$1,100,000	$700,000	$5,100,000
Resort operating shortfall		$600,000	$450,000	$300,000	$150,000	$0	$1,500,000
Release payment	30%	$2,419,200	$2,419,200	$2,289,600	$2,376,000	$1,008,931	$10,512,931
Total cash uses		$19,739,200	$9,589,200	$8,949,600	$9,126,000	$5,208,931	$52,612,931
Net Cash Flow		$564,800	$1,164,800	$1,102,400	$1,144,000	$1,231,069	$5,207,069
Acquisition Loan							
Beginning balance		$8,000,000	$6,888,205	$5,044,417	$3,152,586	$983,744	$8,000,000
Interest @ 9.5%		$1,307,405	$575,412	$397,769	$207,158	$25,187	$2,512,931
Subtotal		$9,307,405	$7,463,617	$5,442,186	$3,359,744	$1,008,931	$10,512,931
Payments		$2,419,200	$2,419,200	$2,289,600	$2,376,000	$1,008,931	$10,512,931
Ending balance		$6,888,205	$5,044,417	$3,152,586	$983,744	$0	$0

unit/week and 50 weekly intervals sold for each unit—thus, the total sellout value is $50 million.

The key to successful evaluation of pro forma cash flows is accurate assumptions. The first section of the cash-flow model shows assumptions for the number of intervals sold, their average price, and cumulative sales revenue. All sales are net of cancellations. The sales assumptions are based on the developer's previous performance in the market in which the proposed timeshare resort is located. If the developer has no previous timeshare experience or no experience in the particular market, the lender will find it difficult to judge the reasonableness of the assumptions. For this reason, developers without timeshare experience present lenders with a major finance challenge. However, developers with timeshare experience in other markets are usually able to rely on their track record to establish their credibility. In such cases, lenders evaluate comparable resorts in the market where the resort is to be developed and thus determine the

Sunterra Corporation's Sedona Springs Resort in Sedona, Arizona. Since going public in 1996, the company has expanded rapidly through a combination of development and acquisition.

Courtesy of Sunterra Corporation

proposed facility's likely sales and operating performance. With the sales revenue assumptions established, lenders can determine the cash sources for the proposed resort.

Cash sources in this example include borrower equity, an acquisition loan, receivable loan advances, and cash sales and downpayments. The first two involve the capital required to purchase an existing property. For simplicity, the sample analysis assumes a straight acquisition with only modest improvements, although the model can be easily adapted to include a construction loan or any other type of product acquisition and renovation. The purchase price of the property is assumed to be $10 million. The property is acquired with $2 million in equity from the developer and $8 million in debt from the lender. The receivable loan will provide a 90 percent advance rate. Based on the developer's previous experience, it is assumed that 20 percent of the transactions will be cash sales and that downpayments for the remaining purchases will total 10 percent of the sales price.

In the example, cash is used for resort acquisition, marketing and sales expenses,

G&A expenses, the resort operations shortfall, and release payments. The resort acquisition cost is assumed to be $10 million while marketing and sales expenses account for 50 percent of total sales and G&A for 10 percent.

As with the probability of sales success, the assumed operating expenses are evaluated in terms of the developer's previous performance and the similarity of the proposed resort's operations to those of the developer's other resorts. Resort operations shortfall is the net cost (expenses minus revenues) the developer incurs while selling the resort inventory. In this example, which involves an existing 100-unit resort, the operations shortfall would be much greater than for a development built and sold in smaller phases.

To offset operations costs, the developer must rent unsold inventory. In rare cases, an existing facility will generate sufficient rental income to offset all resort operations expenses. In the example, the resort operations shortfall is assumed to be $600,000 in year one, $450,000 in year two, $300,000 in year three, and $150,000 in year four. The release payment (calculated as described earlier) is assumed to be 30 percent.

For a real-world timeshare resort, the cash-flow model would include additional line items that represent the totality of resort activity. For example, delinquent timeshare intervals would need to be replaced and ultimately resold. The example omits such considerations in favor of focusing on the primary components of a cash-flow analysis.

An additional component of the analysis is the status of the acquisition loan shown at the bottom of the model. By including this information in the pro forma, the developer can demonstrate to the lender the status of the loan throughout the sellout period. For example, the loan has a beginning balance of $8 million in year one and is reduced to $6.88 million at the end of that year. The developer repays the loan in full in year five.

Once the cash sources and uses are established, sellout of the resort produces the net cash flow and cumulative cash flow. In the example, the resort enjoys positive cash flow from the first year through sellout in the fifth year. Year-one cash flow is $564,800 but improves to over $1 million in each of the next four years. Cumulative cash flow for the resort's five-year sellout is $5.2 million.

Through modern computing capabilities, a cash-flow model lends itself to repeated testing to evaluate the resort's cash flow if certain assumptions are modified. For example, what if sales were 25 percent per month slower than projected? What if the average price per unit/week were $8,000 instead of $10,000? What if marketing costs were 55 percent, 60 percent, or more?

The final component of the cash-flow analysis is the repayment of the acquisition loan. This component shows the original balance, interest accrued, release payments, and ending balance on a monthly basis.

Used properly, the cash-flow model allows lenders to analyze the likelihood of a timeshare resort's success and the probability that the associated loans will be repaid in full. It permits the developer to evaluate what acquisition price is financially feasible, what operating ratios must be achieved to guarantee the desired profits and cash flows, and whether the deal is even worth pursuing.

Looking Ahead

Between 1996 and 1998, the timeshare business experienced dramatic changes. In particular, in 1997 and 1998, Wall Street and major banks finally discovered the industry and triggered a major evolution in the pricing and structure of financial products available to the top developers. More recently, however, foreign currency collapses, liquidity shortages in the commercial mortgage-backed securities (CMBS) markets, and significant volatility in stock prices in the equity markets have rocked the capital markets. Public timeshare companies have seen their valuations cut in half or more, limiting their ability to use stock as currency for further consolidation within the timeshare industry. CS First Boston, a relatively large industry player, has become less active in timeshare finance because of problems with international currencies and CMBS spreads.

A look to the industry's future raises several questions. Will other "new money" sources remain interested in the timeshare business if current market conditions prevail? What opportunities exist for traditional lenders who tend to have higher pricing but are more likely to provide the flexibility needed by borrowers? Will market conditions reverse course and return to the fever pitch that characterized 1997 and the first half of 1998?

Note

1. The developer's cost to operate the resort during sellout.

Chapter 9

Timeshare and Vacation-Ownership Case Studies

Timeshare and vacation ownership properties encompass a wide variety of product types, locations, structures, and project developers. This chapter features ten developments that were selected to illustrate different project or company approaches or features in geographically diverse locations. Three are international examples. The projects include

- Deer Valley Club, Park City, Utah, developed by Silverlake Corporation;
- Cypress Harbour Resort, Orlando, Florida, developed by Marriott Vacation Club International;
- Royal Resorts, Cancun, Mexico (multiple projects);
- Club Asia International, Malaysia, developed by Sarawak Economic Development Corporation International;
- Hotel de l'Eau Vive, New Orleans, developed by Benjamin Harrison Interests;
- Orange Tree Golf & Conference Resort, Scottsdale, Arizona, developed by Shell Vacations, LLC;
- Hilton Grand Vacations Club Flamingo Hilton, Las Vegas, developed by Hilton Grand Vacations Club;
- The Bay Club at Waikaloa, Hawaii, developed by the Nikken Corporation;
- Shore Crest Vacation Villas, Myrtle Beach, South Carolina, developed by Bluegreen Corporation; and
- Pacific Shores Nature Club, Vancouver Island, British Columbia, Canada, developed by Andrew and Susan Pearson.

Each case study provides a description of the project, its location and developer, the project planning process, important design features, purchase arrangements and pricing, the sales and marketing effort, management and operations, and lessons learned. Project data, photographs, a site plan and unit plan, and directions to the property complete each case study. All information presented was current as of fall 1998.

Deer Valley Club

Park City, Utah

Deer Valley Club, a 30-unit resort outside Park City, Utah, is a private enclave owned by its members. In contrast to the typical unit/week timeshare sale arrangement, the 195 members of Deer Valley Club own an undivided deeded interest (UDI) in the club, which includes a 1/195 interest in all the common areas, facilities, and amenities such as furnishings, fixtures, and equipment—virtually everything that exists on the property's two-thirds of an acre.

Deer Valley Club was developed by Silverlake Development Corporation, a wholly owned subsidiary of Richmond Properties, Inc., with headquarters in Tampa, Florida. Richmond Properties is a multifaceted real estate company experienced in commercial, office, multifamily, and resort development.

Location and Site

The club is located on one of the major ski runs at Deer Valley Resort, a 1,750-acre multiple-use residential and resort development that opened in 1981 in the Wasatch Mountains, 40 minutes from Salt Lake City. Averaging more than 300 inches of snow per season, Deer Valley Resort was recently rated the third-best ski resort in North America by *Mountain Sports and Living Magazine* (formerly *Snow Country*). It is said that the only time visitors find ice in the area is when they order drinks. The resort features 18 chair lifts as well as a high-speed, mile-long gondola that whisks skiers to the top of Little Baldy in less than six minutes.

Accommodations at Deer Valley Resort include one- to four-bedroom condominiums as well as hotels and private homes. With more than 84 trails, including the longest at 2.1 miles, the resort's new snow-making equipment serves 475 acres and 800 acres of graded skiing along the terrain. Deer Valley Resort will host the men's and women's slalom, combined slalom, aerials, and moguls during the 2002 Salt Lake City Winter Olympics. The resort offers eight on-mountain restaurants, including the Mariposa, McHenry's, and the Seafood Buffet. Silver Lake Restaurant, Snow Park Restaurant, and Bald Mountain Pizza serve lunch. Two ski-up, on-mountain eateries, Snowshoe Tommy's and Cushing's Cabin, offer skiers a quick snack.

Located directly on the Homestake Ski Run in Silver Lake Village, Deer Valley Club commands one of the resort's premier sites. It is surrounded by ski trails, panoramic vistas, and luxury shopping and dining. The development strategy for Deer Valley Club called for more services and amenities than other area residential developments, ample and flexible use, hassle-free vacation homeownership, and pricing correlated with actual use. Members are typically high-echelon professionals, corporate executives, and entrepreneurs who say their most precious asset is time. When they do vacation, members want a high level of services.

According to Len Scaglione, vice president of Silverlake Development Corporation, Deer Valley Club contains 14 two-bedroom townhomes, 12 three-bedroom townhomes, and four four-bedroom townhomes, all of which are fully furnished and equipped. Club facilities include a heated outdoor pool; the cozy 46-seat Sai Sommet Restaurant, whose centerpiece is a large flagstone fireplace; heated underground parking; a members-only clubroom and lounge; a health club with steam room

and sauna; a game room with a pool table, arcade, and video games; and a ski locker with direct ski-in/ski-out access. Club services include long-term ski equipment and clothing storage for members, airport and in-town shuttle service, shopping service, and full housekeeping.

Member ownership of Deer Valley Club takes the form of UDI; at sellout, the club will be entirely owned by its 195 members. Owners do not buy a specific unit or access to a specific time period. Rather, each member owns a fee-simple, debt-free, undivided deeded interest in the club. Ownership is evidenced by a fee-simple real estate deed, which is a special warranty deed recorded and insured by a title insurance policy. And, as noted, all 195 members share equal ownership of the club's common areas, including furnishings and accessories.

With a membership/units ratio of 6.5, each member is entitled to a little more than four weeks of annual use. About 30 percent of the time in a given year is allocated to additional visits as well as to two scheduled maintenance periods. Members can reserve time whenever they wish, subject to the club's reservations policies and procedures. In addition, members can generally obtain last-minute, space-available reservations for themselves and their guests.

Project Planning and Development

In 1989, Silverlake Development Corporation purchased the 0.66-acre Deer Valley Club site from Deer Valley Resort as an investment. A year later, the company formulated plans to develop the property as a condominium project to be called Silver Lake Inn. According to the initial strategy, Silverlake would erect 30 condominiums to sell to area residents and skiers.

Construction began in spring 1991 and was proceeding on schedule when the project focus abruptly shifted from whole-

Photo on page 140:
The warm lights of Deer Valley Club at night against a winter backdrop.

ownership condominiums to the UDI concept. At that time, a vacation-ownership development across the street—also named Deer Valley Club—was attempting to sell a form of timeshare to high-income households but found itself facing development and financing difficulties. Officials at Deer Valley Resort, which had sold land to both developers, and at the Highland Resort Group, which was marketing the Deer Valley Club project and was one of the creators of UDI, approached Silverlake Development about adapting its Silver Lake Inn condominium concept to the UDI approach. Believing that UDI owners would use their units more frequently than condominium owners, Highland asked Silverlake to sell the project in 195 memberships rather than as whole-ownership condominiums. In agreeing to Highland's proposal, Silverlake reasoned that the economics made sense and that the change would make the project more salable. According to the terms of a license agreement, the resort permitted Silverlake to use the Deer Valley trademark; in addition, it promised Deer Valley Resort's full support in marketing the project. Silverlake also retained the Deer Valley Club moniker. (The property across the street is currently under development as the Châteaux Lodge.)

Silverlake honored the original purchase contracts executed by individuals already under contract in the struggling condominium venture across the street. That proved to be a boon for some—presales in the troubled project were priced at $94,000 for a three-bedroom unit while Deer Valley Club's price for the same villa was $104,000.

Because the original condominium design included full kitchens, the initial plan did not call for a restaurant. Silverlake quickly revised the design to incorporate an eatery.

Work began in 1991 and was completed several years later. The first phase was a heated, 52-stall parking structure. Deer Valley Club's soft opening (before completion of all amenities and villas) occurred in February 1993, with the grand opening eight months later.

Project and Unit Design

The goal in creating Deer Valley Club was to combine the advantages of vacation homeownership with the services of a fine hotel. The 30 condominiums, built of cedar, alder, and flagstone, are clustered together in an environmentally beneficial design midway up the mountain and adjacent to one of the more popular ski runs. The location turned out to be an excellent selling point.

To provide the ski-in/ski-out feature so highly desired in ski resorts—guests walk from the club directly onto the slope—the units are designed to fit the mountain topography. Seven levels of buildings surround the clubhouse, an indoor spa, and a swimming pool. The project's nine separate buildings are connected by hallways; three elevators serve the buildings.

Each unit takes advantage of the area's spectacular mountain and valley views. Typically, five to seven large windows distinguish the living room, with two doors leading to a wraparound deck finished with magnificent large-log railings. Each unit is furnished with a leather sleeper-sofa, a large overstuffed chair with ottoman, an armoire, a wood dining table, and six log chairs in a rustic motif. Twenty-foot cathedral ceilings with a cedar ceiling fan and a brass chandelier in the dining area complement the Western-style décor, along with a fireplace and log mantel, wood-trimmed windows, and parchment lampshades. Roman shades with coordinating fabric valances round out the effect. Most living-room fireplaces are wood-burning units with gas starters. Master-bedroom fireplaces (where applicable) are gas-burning units in conformance with local building code requirements.

Each bedroom is furnished in Western-style décor and is outfitted with a four-poster bed, complete bathroom, separate

The club lounge is rustic yet elegant.

shower and bathroom, whirlpool tub, and portable humidifier. Kitchens offer an eating bar and service for 12, side-by-side refrigerator, microwave oven, food mixer, four-burner gas stove, oversized oven, and small appliances such as a blender and toaster oven.

The project totals 120,000 square feet—40,000 square feet of living area and 80,000 square feet of amenities. Silver Lake Development financed the development and received a construction loan from American Centennial Insurance Company (ACIC).

The final development costs exceeded the original budget by 50 percent. The cost overrun largely resulted from the Park City Building Department's determination that Deer Valley Club had evolved into a commercial project and thus had to comply with the more expensive requirements of the commercial rather than the residential building code. In addition, because it functions more as a hotel than a true con-

dominium project, Deer Valley Club was required to incorporate changes mandated by the Americans with Disabilities Act (ADA), such as installing bars around the bathtubs, lowering counters and light switches, and so forth. Instead of the two handicap-accessible units originally envisioned, the club includes four such units. Finally, the cost of the club's various amenities totaled more than $1 million.

More specifically, the commercial building code's stringent fire regulations necessitated additional points of access and a modification of construction standards and materials. For instance, instead of installing one layer of sheet rock, the developers were required to install two layers and to add a single layer of sheet rock to the entire external shell of the buildings before installation of the siding. The regulations also mandated a different type of fire sprinkler system and required sprinklers in the parking garage. The project's change

The club's ski-in/ski-out feature affords skiers immediate access to the slopes.

Courtesy of Deer Valley Club

in status to a club meant that a state-of-the-art restaurant kitchen was required, along with a more extensive exercise room. In addition, Silverlake had to furnish the project with a front desk, shuttle vans, guest amenities, and other conveniences.

While the developers incurred significant additional building costs, they also realized a tremendous increase in project salability. After the changes, Deer Valley Club went from a $12 million sellout value to a $20 million sellout value. Silverlake had found a new market niche, selling living space at an average price of $500 per square foot.

Purchase Arrangements And Pricing

Deer Valley Club offered 91 club (two-bedroom) memberships, 78 grand (three-bedroom) memberships, and 26 royal (four-bedroom) memberships as well as 35 associate memberships that grant use of the common areas. Associate members

pay annual dues applied to the club's general operating budget.

In addition, the developer sold corporate memberships, which provide more than one individual or family with club privileges. Corporate members can reserve 21 days of planned vacation per membership—not per person—per season. The corporate club membership enables two individuals to share a membership while the corporate grand and corporate royal memberships permit three and four persons, respectively, to share a membership. By charter, corporate memberships cannot exceed 20 percent of the total number of memberships.

One of the club's main selling points is its flexibility in accommodating a wide variety of vacation needs. By providing owners with floating time during a club year that runs from October 1 to the following September 30, the club permits each owner to reserve up to 14 days of planned winter vacations and 14 days of planned summer vacations. There is no limit to the number of days a member may use the club; the only constraint is use by other members. If some members use the club less than their allotted time, others can use it more. A computerized reservation system ensures that all members have equal access to peak-period lodging over the years.

A rotating priority system determines reservation confirmations when the number of reservation requests for a certain period exceeds the number of available townhomes. Each membership is assigned a number before confirmation of the vacation period. To allocate planned vacation periods equitably over the year, each member's reservation priority number changes annually based on the original membership number assigned at closing. The original priority number is also included on the special warranty deed.

All members pay housekeeping fees associated with their stay. For a nightly fee and with some restrictions, members can reserve townhomes other than the type they purchased, subject to availability. Members can also pay a fee (in addition to the normal housekeeping charge) and upgrade to a unit of a different size, subject to availability. In addition, members can use the club amenities and common areas when not staying overnight.

Initially, prices for a two-bedroom townhome membership were $84,000; for a three-bedroom, $94,000; and for a four-bedroom, $104,000. The three- and four-bedroom units have sold out. Because of the project's success, a two-bedroom membership is now priced at $99,900 while resales of four-bedroom memberships range from $200,000 to $220,000.

At the outset, Silverlake financed membership purchases. It recognized that financial institutions were unfamiliar with the concept of undivided deeded interest and thus hesitant to finance UDI purchases. As a practical matter, more than half (55 percent) of members have financed their membership purchases. In time, Silverlake sold its entire mortgage portfolio to First Bank and Trust of New Orleans under an agreement whereby the developer will continue to provide member financing, subject to individual loan approval.

Deer Valley Club owners can arrange to stay at two other club projects—Ships Watch in Duck, North Carolina (a UDI resort), and Intrawest Resort Club Blackcomb in Whistler, British Columbia. The manager at Deer Valley Club arranges exchanges between owners at Deer Valley and the other projects. Ships Watch is a 25-acre beachfront enclave on the Outer Banks. The 53 seaside homes range in size from 2,400 to 3,800 square feet. Amenities include an Olympic-size swimming pool with pavilion, tennis courts, reception center, and a 200-foot pier on a sound. Like Deer Valley Club, Intrawest Resort Club Blackcomb in Whistler, British Columbia, is steps from the ski lifts. Towering over the club are Blackcomb and Whistler mountains, which offer more vertical rise than any other ski mountains in North America. Intrawest Resort Club residences vary in size; many feature private balconies that afford magnificent views of the surrounding mountains and village.

Members who cannot or do not want to exchange an interval at Deer Valley Club can rent any one of their scheduled weeks except Christmas and Presidents' weeks. Unused time for those periods must be returned to Deer Valley Club management. Members with the highest priority numbers for a particular season reserve the prime weeks. Members cannot, however, rent these weeks; only they or their guests may use the interval. The weeks do not sell as fixed time periods. Rather, the rotating priority reservation system determines the allocations of the intervals.

Rentals are coordinated and managed by the club management with the assistance of a local property management company. During ski season, a two-bedroom town-

Unit interiors are rustic, with wood trim, 20-foot-high ceilings, and wood-burning fireplaces.

Courtesy of Deer Valley Club

Floor plan for the Royal Townhome. Each unit is approximately 2,000 square feet.

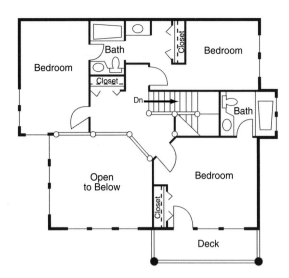

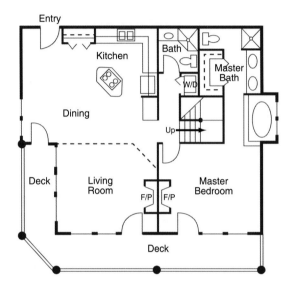

home can rent for $800 a night, or $5,600 a week. The revenue is split 70/30, with the owner taking the higher percentage. Deer Valley Club collects 20 percent and the property management company receives the remainder.

Sales and Marketing

Marketing at Deer Valley Club began in 1992 with 20 presales. The first sale closed a year later. Judy Nowlin, one of the top salespersons at Silverlake Realty, says that Deer Valley Club's sales and marketing strategy has not changed since the memberships went on sale in 1993. Given that Deer Valley Club's prices are higher, its clientele more affluent, and the project's

UDI concept difficult to comprehend, Deer Valley Club has adopted a marketing strategy that differs from that of the typical timeshare project.

Marketers decided against a national marketing promotion in favor of targeting visitors who had already decided they wanted to spend their vacations in Deer Valley and would likely return. The target audience included families who could not afford to own a typical Deer Valley condominium (priced at more than $1 million) as well as families who could but did not want to invest in a home that would see limited use. Half the current owners live on the East Coast while most others live in California. Only a few hail from the Salt Lake City area.

The process of identifying buyers took place in the resort area itself as well as in nearby luxury hotels and through drop-ins from ski traffic, information booths at ski lodges, and so forth. Local real estate brokers played a limited role in club sales. The developers determined that the learning curve for the UDI concept is high and that most brokers would make more money by selling higher-priced lots, homes, and condominiums.

Memberships at Deer Valley Club are sold as a luxury item. Deer Valley Club promotes its wide range of amenities, including free airport pickup, a health club, a heated outdoor swimming pool, heated walkways, a gourmet restaurant, prearrival grocery delivery, concierge services, and business services. In addition to price, one of the club's biggest selling points is its ski-in/ski-out location. While the complex is located directly on Deer Valley's ski trails, the surrounding greenery and landscape foster an environment conducive to rest and relaxation. Owners and guests never sense that they are vacationing in a highly traveled area.

In the beginning, Deer Valley Club scheduled local events such as A Day at the Club to attract individuals interested in learning more about the UDI concept.

Participants received a free one-day ski pass and were invited to ski in for lunch. A salesperson would then show prospects around the club. As more and more memberships sold, salespersons came to depend almost exclusively on referrals from satisfied owners.

From a sales and marketing viewpoint, the only major problem encountered at Deer Valley Club has been the lack of familiarity with the UDI form of ownership. Initially, salespersons experienced difficulty in convincing high-income individuals that UDI was a concept that would benefit them.

To date, 175 of 195 memberships have been sold. In 1997, Deer Valley Club sold about 12 memberships at an average sales price of $115,000. Over the past six years, prices have ranged from a low of $68,000 to a high of $225,000 for a four-bedroom unit; the former figure honored a contract from the failed project across the street. About 20 percent of the purchase price is earmarked for marketing and sales expenses and about 8 percent for sales commissions.

Deer Valley Club has a phenomenal closing rate of 99 percent. Clearly, one reason is the club's high sales price, but the low-key approach of the sales staff, who make certain that potential owners receive all information they desire, also contributes to Deer Valley Club's sales success.

Although Silverlake Realty stresses that it does not warrant or guarantee the appreciation in value of any membership interest in Deer Valley Club, the club's resale history has been impressive. A two-bedroom membership purchased in 1993 sold two years later for a 29 percent premium. A three-bedroom membership also purchased in 1993 sold four years later for a 65 percent premium. And a four-bedroom membership that sold in spring 1998 after being held for five years realized an 89 percent return on investment. Corporate memberships often performed even better—a two-bedroom resale yielded a 50 percent return

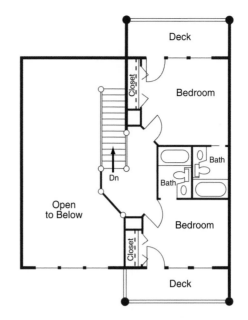

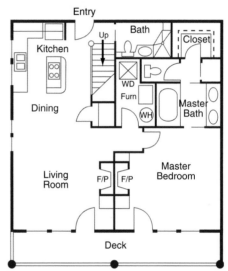

Floor plan for the Grand Townhome. Each unit is approximately 1,500 square feet.

on investment (ROI) and a three-bedroom resale a 98 percent ROI in three years.

Operations and Management

Deer Valley Lodging, a subsidiary of Premier Resorts, currently manages Deer Valley Club under the direction of a seven-member board of trustees, which also serves as the owners' association. Board members, who are elected by the owners, represent owners' home regions. The developer turned over control of the project in winter 1997 upon the sale of 75 percent of the project. The key management challenge is to keep the club's high-income,

Site plan.

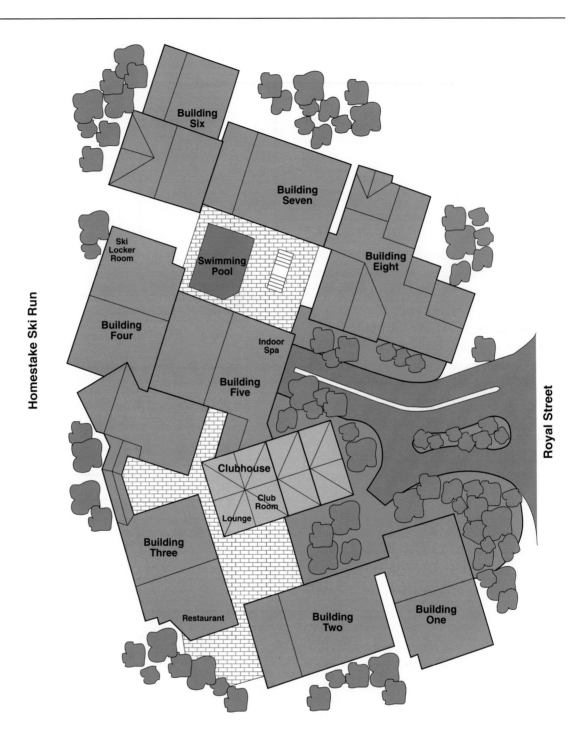

high-demand members content during their stay at the resort.

Annual income for the club during the 1997–1998 fiscal year totaled $1.4 million from assessments and $231,000 in other revenue. Major expenses included $758,000 for personnel, $156,000 for reserves, and $194,000 for utilities. Management fees totaled $86,000.

Contributions to the 1997–1998 budget included annual membership fees of $5,554 for a two-bedroom unit, $7,142 for a three-bedroom unit, and $9,254 for a four-bedroom unit. Corporate annual owners' fees ranged from $6,665 for a two-bedroom unit, to $8,572 for a three-bedroom unit, to $11,104 for a four-bedroom unit. Membership fees are assessed annually and are inclusive of property taxes, insurance, reserves, and normal operations expenses.

Daily housekeeping fees cover daily towel replenishment, bed making, and trash pickup and range from $130 for a two-bedroom unit to $175 for a three-bedroom unit and $235 for a four-bedroom unit.

Experience Gained

Silverlake Development is considering the development of additional UDI properties and has selected a site for another project. The company is extremely pleased with the financial success of Deer Valley Club.

Looking back over the past several years, the developers of Deer Valley Club say that they would have constructed few, if any, two-bedroom units. Instead, they would have concentrated on three- and four-bedroom townhomes. The reason, according to Scaglione, is that affluent individuals typically use different decision rules than less affluent buyers when purchasing vacation properties. A family with only one child—or no children—still wants the extra space afforded by a three- or four-bedroom unit so that relatives and friends can visit. In addition, if the difference between a two- and a three-bedroom unit is only $20,000 or $30,000, potential owners typically opt for the more expensive accommodation because they are accustomed to larger homes and a more gracious residential feel. Most affluent individuals seek the best in their lives, and the owners at Deer Valley Club are no exception.

◆ Project Data[1]

Development Schedule

Total number of units	30
Planning started	1989
Construction started	1991
Construction completed	1993
Sales started	1992
Sales completed	ongoing

Land Use Information

Site area	1.527 acres
Total number of timeshare units planned	30
Total number of timeshare units completed	30
Gross density	19.65 units/acre

Unit Information

Two-bedroom, two-bath

Floor area	1,000 square feet
Average price per day (1999)	$800

Three-bedroom, three-and-three-quarter-bath

Floor area	1,500 square feet
Average price per day (1999)	$915

Four-bedroom, three-and-three-quarter-bath

Floor area	2,000 square feet
Average price per day (1999)	$1,160

Administrative, Recreational, and Commercial Facilities

	Square feet
Lobby	750
Clubhouse building	3,200
Restaurant/food service	3,700

Developer

Silverlake Development Corporation
Park City, Utah

Architect

James L. Carroll & Associates, Inc.
Salt Lake City, Utah

Interior Design

Don Brady Interiors and LaVell Klobes Interiors
Park City, Utah

Note

1. Project cost information is not available.

Date of site visit: September 30, 1998
Author of case study: Mike Sheridan

Cypress Harbour Resort

Orlando, Florida

Cypress Harbour Resort is a 510-unit vacation-ownership resort in Orlando, Florida, developed and managed by Marriott Vacation Club International (MVCI). The residential-style development, which opened in 1991, is situated on 67 acres and includes 22 four-story buildings arranged around a 15-acre lake. The project, which also features a clubhouse complex, three swimming pools, an activities center, and a variety of other recreational amenities and services, has earned Interval International's five-star rating.

MVCI is a wholly owned division of Marriott International, Inc., a hospitality company founded in 1927 that today has more than 1,600 operating units worldwide. Since its inception in 1984, MCVI has become one of the world's largest vacation-ownership companies. It operates 38 resorts in 18 destinations around the world, which together represent more than 3,100 villas and over 120,000 owners; and more resorts are planned.

Cypress Harbour was Marriott's fourth vacation-ownership development in Orlando and its first freestanding vacation-ownership resort in the area. The first three developments, Sabal Palms, Royal Palms, and Imperial Palm Villas, are all located on the site of the Marriott Orlando World Center and share amenities with the Marriott Hotel at that location. A fifth project, the Grande Vista Resort, is under construction and features the Faldo Golf Institute, a golf learning center.

Location and Site

According to Alan Bernstein, senior project manager, in timeshare as in other forms of real estate, "Location is everything." As a year-round resort with several vacation attractions, Orlando is a popular location for timeshare resorts. In addition to the area's continually expanding entertainment and theme park offerings, Orlando offers easy access to beaches and has become a world-renown golfing center.

The Cypress Harbour site was selected for its location in the "resort corridor" near the powerful Disney theme park magnet. It is readily accessible from Interstate 4 and an easy drive to and from the airport. In addition, the site is large enough to accommodate a resort campus. Moreover, it is surrounded by the International Golf Course, which gives the property both definition and a buffer of green space.

At the center of the site is a 15-acre lake that was reconstructed as part of the area drainage system. The lake serves not only as a visual amenity but also as the project's thematic organizing element. In addition, it is the locus for a variety of recreational activities, including boating, fishing, and remote-controlled boat races.

Marriott now owns the International Golf Course. Therefore, if Marriott and the Cypress Harbour Condominium Association should ever decide to expand the resort or if Marriott should ever decide to build another resort nearby, it can reconfigure the golf course to obtain the needed land.

Project Planning and Development

Site preparation and land development were uneventful. Except for a few stands of trees by the lake, which were retained, on-site vegetation was largely scrub. Few environmental issues affected the development, though the lake was reconfigured to enhance its design value. A small beach was built, with some of its edges also reconfigured.

Cypress Harbour was built in five phases. During the second phase of development, Marriott decided to construct a serpentine bridge across the lake as part of a walkway system that would connect the development's residential and amenity areas. In the course of bridge construction, Marriott discovered that the south end of the lake was only two to three feet deep in contrast

The two primary amenity areas within Cypress Harbour are connected by a walkway bridge.

©Courtesy of Marriott Vacation Club International

to 14 to 20 feet at the north end. The shallow depth necessitated construction of a temporary dam and excavation of the south end of the lake in advance of the bridge construction.

Construction of the resort's buildings began in spring 1989, and the on-site sales office opened in December 1990. The first four buildings were occupied in March 1991, the same month that the clubhouse complex opened. The last building was completed and ready for occupancy on December 25, 1994. Development costs totaled approximately $120 million over the five-year period. Like other Marriott projects, Cypress Harbour was self-financed.

According to Bernstein, managing construction phasing was the major development challenge. With a hotel, development occurs all at once. With a timeshare development, however, the costs and risks associated with carrying large amounts of unsold inventory typically demand development in manageable phases.

At Cypress Harbour, development proceeded four buildings at a time. The first phase called for construction of four residential buildings, the central facilities building (or clubhouse, which contains the reception center), and the sales campus and the installation of the telephone system. The first-phase 88 villas represented a large initial cost commitment for a timeshare development but helped foster the desired sense of arrival.

Bernstein explained that, as far as possible, construction areas were kept physically separate from completed units so that buyers and guests would not sense that they were vacationing at a construction site. The decision to construct the first buildings close to the clubhouse complex meant that future buyers would not have to drive by a construction site to reach their units. Subsequent buildings were constructed outward from the initial cluster. The buildings' access road, along with underground utilities and curbs, was in-

Many villas feature water views.

Cypress Harbour's buildings, which reflect an "Old Florida" architectural style, are heavily landscaped and convey a residential ambience.

stalled first and topped with a one-inch asphalt pour to provide a finished appearance. As buildings were completed, the second inch of asphalt was added to complete the access road. Where possible, a temporary access road separated construction and visitor traffic.

Project and Unit Design

Cypress Harbour is designed with a "Key West" or "Old Florida" theme that is reinforced with gazebos, latticework, and lush, tropical landscaping. Once planners determined building size and density, they let the shape of the site dictate building placement. The four-story buildings are arranged around the lake; each features a Galvalume[1] roof accented with louvre effects and a gray or beige-and-white color scheme. Buildings completed in the early phases of development contain 22 villas; changes in roof articulation permitted 24 villas in later buildings. Walkways and bridges connect the various buildings and project amenities.

To complement the Orlando-area focus on theme parks, the resort's look suggests luxury and relaxation in a residential setting. The low-rise buildings are heavily landscaped and sited in a quiet environment of water, trees, and greenery well apart from the busy entry street.

In addition to the stocked lake, project amenities include a central facilities complex with a clubhouse that features a lobby, lounge area with large-screen television, offices, and indoor/outdoor bar. A Pizza Hut and a TCBY franchise offer quick, limited service and delivery menus. The central facilities complex also houses the Marketplace, a small store that offers fresh produce, packaged foods, incidentals, movie rentals, toys, souvenirs, and clothing with the resort logo; the Marketplace deli counter prepares fresh salads and sandwiches.

The pool area includes a large, heated freeform pool with a bubbling shallow end, a separate children's pool, small spa pools separated from the children's activity area, and large, lakeside sun decks. Across the lake via the bridge, an "island pool" features a waterfall tower that encloses a sauna, a heated pool with lap lanes, and a children's

Unit interiors are cheerful and homelike yet luxurious.

sports equipment and various types of boats and bicycles for rent. Volleyball and tennis facilities, playgrounds, and barbecue grills and picnic areas complete the recreational facilities. In addition to a wide variety of planned activities for children and adults, the resort offers concierge services, same-day valet service, and discounts for use of nearby golf courses. A nominal fee for some of the activities covers operations expenses.

Units, which are called "villas," total approximately 1,240 indoor square feet. All have two bedrooms, two bathrooms, and two sleeper-sofas and can sleep eight. None includes a lockoff. Each villa has a utility room with washer and dryer; a fully equipped kitchen with a breakfast bar, microwave oven, and dishwasher; a private, screened-in porch; and three televisions and a videocassette recorder. The master suites contain a king-size bed, security lockbox, circular whirlpool bath, and separate shower. Linens and towels are provided.

Some minor adjustments to the units' design during development were largely a response to changes in the Americans with Disabilities Act (ADA) guidelines.

Purchase Arrangements And Pricing

But for a few exceptions, such as Christmas week at a ski resort, which is sold as fixed time, Marriott sells "floating" time. Both time and units float. In other words, owners can vacation at no additional charge at their home resort for a week at any time during their chosen season on a first-come, first-served basis. "Floating" time accommodates people who like to vacation within a certain season but want some latitude in planning their vacation. The fact that units are not preassigned gives the resort flexibility in managing its inventory as if it were a hotel—for example, to clean units when they are vacated or to enable guests to check in upon arrival. The key to mak-

pool. A third pool caters to adults in a quiet, secluded lakeside location.

Nearby, at the water's edge, is an activities center building with rooms for children's activities, a room filled with electronic games, a pool room, an exercise room, large deck areas for outdoor activities, and an activities desk that provides

ing the floating system work is ensuring that all units are desirable—that there are no "bad" units. The actual purchase is for a deeded interest and is tied to a specific unit and a specific week, though the buyer may in fact never stay in that unit at that time.

Cypress Harbour Resort is part of the Marriott system of vacation-ownership resorts. The underlying concept is based on the recognition that most people do not care to vacation at the same place every year, especially as they move through the various stages of the life cycle. For a fee of $69, a Marriott resort owner can exchange a week of time for a week in the same season at a different Marriott resort. The Marriott system is intended to offer a variety of beach, urban, ski, and island/exotic experiences and, in addition to Orlando, includes properties in Longboat Key, Singer Island, and Ft. Lauderdale, Florida; Boston; the Newport Coast and Palm Desert, California; Aruba; Nassau, Bahamas; Williamsburg, Virginia; Breckenridge and Vail, Colorado; Hilton Head Island, South Carolina; Kauai, Hawaii; Park City, Utah; Absecon, New Jersey; and Majorca and Marbella, Spain. More resorts are planned both domestically and worldwide.

Typical pricing for Marriott's core product, a two-bedroom, two-bath unit, is around $17,000 for a week during the high season and $14,000 for a week during the medium season. (In most cases, there is no low season.) Occasionally, if price is an issue for an otherwise motivated buyer, Marriott will sell a biennial interest (a week every other year).

Sales are for cash or 10 percent down for ten years, with no prepayment penalty. Interest rates are pegged to a certain amount over the average Treasury bill. The interest rate as of October 1998 was 13.1 percent. Interest rates for international buyers are higher, reflecting a higher level of risk.

Reservations are made through Marriott's Owner Services Department at Marriott headquarters and are managed separately from resort operations. To avoid crowding, delays, and logistical logjams, check-ins take place over a five-day period, though Fridays and Saturdays are still busy times.

In addition, owners can use the Interval International exchange system, with its more than 1,600 resorts in 65 countries, to broaden their choice of vacation experiences. Or, for maximum flexibility, owners can participate in the Marriott Rewards Program (SM). Under the program, each week purchased is assigned a point value. Points can be exchanged for a menu of travel options, including more than 1,300 Marriott hotels worldwide and, through affiliated partners, air travel, cruises, car rentals, and more. The program gives buyers tremendous flexibility in designing their desired vacation while enabling Marriott to use empty hotel rooms to benefit its customers. The major challenge in operating the program has been inventory control.

Within Florida, Marriott has created the Florida Club, an arrangement whereby owners in Orlando, Ft. Lauderdale, Palm Beach, and any future Marriott vacation-ownership resort in Florida can exchange time among themselves. Time can even take the form of split weeks; such an arrangement is more complicated but fits buyers' needs. The exchange is free for individual weeks; for split weeks, a $50 charge applies.

Sales and Marketing

According to Bill Coker, director of sales for Latin America, sales for Cypress Harbour began in a showroom adjacent to the Marriott World Center. The project was also marketed to owners of Marriott's earlier Orlando vacation-ownership developments. When Cypress Harbour broke ground, it had already attracted $10 million in sales. Once it opened, a team of salespersons was hired to market to in-house guests.

Marriott's sales philosophy is to develop a good relationship with the potential buyer, listen to client needs, earn trust, offer guidance rather than pressure, and undersell the product so that the company actually delivers more than it promises, thereby producing high rates of owner satisfaction. To find and motivate people who can successfully follow the Marriott sales philosophy, the company contracted with the Gallup organization to develop a battery of interview questions that screen for the best candidates. Once identified, the candidates are hired as Marriott employees instead of contractors. Marriott recognizes and rewards employees through a structured career path that is designed to keep good salespersons in sales but also provide a sense of forward momentum. In addition to receiving excellent company employee benefits, salespersons earn a fixed commission plus bonuses, incentives, and annual rewards; and they participate in sales contests.

In positioning itself vis-à-vis the competition, Marriott recognizes that the true focus of competition within its quality tier is not quality or price but rather service. In particular, Coker says, "Owners want to pick up the phone, call the '800' number, have it answered, and get instant confirmation that they can vacation where and when they want."

Cypress Harbour is sold out. Resales, underway since March 1997, are handled by Marriott Resort Hospitality Corporation, which charges a 25 percent commission on each sale. Resale prices are not deeply discounted, averaging only about 10 to 15 percent below final developer pricing.

Villas may also be rented. Owners interested in offering their villas for rent may list them with Marriott, pay a housekeeping fee (about 20 percent of the nightly rate), and split the remaining portion of the rental payment with Marriott on a 65/35 basis. Owners may also rent their villas through an independent source.

Operations and Management

The Cypress Harbour Condominium Association, Inc., contracts with Marriott to manage the property. By maintaining a relationship with Marriott, the association helps ensure that Marriott quality will be sustained over the coming years. It also permits owners to participate in Marriott Vacation Club International's internal exchange program and the Marriott Rewards Program.

The annual operating budget for the Cypress Harbour Resort is $10 million plus $4 million in property taxes. Of this, annual maintenance accounts for $1 million. The yearly maintenance week varies from building to building and is determined in part by use patterns. Annual unit/week maintenance fees and taxes for 1998 ranged from $547 to $563 depending on the week's season.

Marriott performs most general management functions itself, although it contracts out landscaping, laundry, street and parking lot cleaning, any cleaning of high locations (such as roofs), and major construction jobs.

The property is secured by a 24-hour entry gatehouse. On-site safety, security, and first aid are handled by 20 loss prevention officers who roam the property at all times. Special sensors enable the

Among the resort's amenities is an activity center that includes this playroom for children.

officers to "mark" where they have been to ensure regular coverage of all areas of the resort.

The buildings constructed in the initial phase of development were undergoing renovation at the time this case study was written, and plans are in place to renovate buildings constructed in the subsequent phases. All units will be renovated on a rolling schedule every six years. Now that the cycle of renovations has begun, the resort's management will make adjustments to handle the challenge of running a resort while overseeing a major program of annual refurbishment.

Experience Gained

With experience, Marriott has been able to determine the proper size for the resort store as well as the appropriate level of food and beverage service for a large, free-standing resort such as Cypress Harbour. Initially, because Orlando is a mecca for every type of restaurant, Marriott planned no food service (except for a small deli counter). In response to customer feedback, however, the company expanded the deli counter into a convenience store and added a small fast-food operation to serve residents and visitors who do not want to leave the property for a quick lunch or dinner. And an indoor-outdoor bar was added to the clubhouse. The company is also considering the addition of a snack bar at the island pool complex. But, based on its extensive experience in the food service industry, Marriott does not believe a full-service, on-site restaurant is justified.

One of the most difficult management challenges facing all hotels and resorts in the Orlando area is the retention of housekeepers in a market with an unemployment rate of only 3 percent. Not surprisingly, the wage scale has continually crept up; in 1999, wages for housekeepers began at $7 per hour. Spreading out check-in times enables Marriott to offer more housekeepers full-time employment, but the

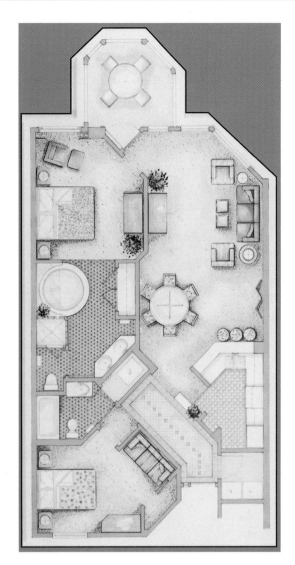

Floor plan.

company still needs to contract for additional help during busy periods. Approximately 13 percent of the housekeeping budget ($0.5 million) is contract labor.

According to Robert A. Miller, president and general manager of Marriott Leisure, Marriott's well-known and respected brand name has benefited the company's timeshare development and management efforts. It has generated interest in the product and given the company access to potential customers through its traditional marketing channels. Both brand recognition and the Marriott reputation engender buyer confidence in the company's staying power and thus its ability to fulfill its commitments. In addition, Marriott has benefited from its long experience in the hospitality business. For example, it understands the requirements for planning for long-term refurbishing and preventive maintenance. It has been able to leverage the procurement side of the business. And its corporate reputation and track record give Marriott access to capital for the fund-

ing of purchaser receivables and, in particular, better access to capital markets.

Quality is extremely important to customer satisfaction, and the company has found that owners are generally willing to pay for the maintenance services nec-

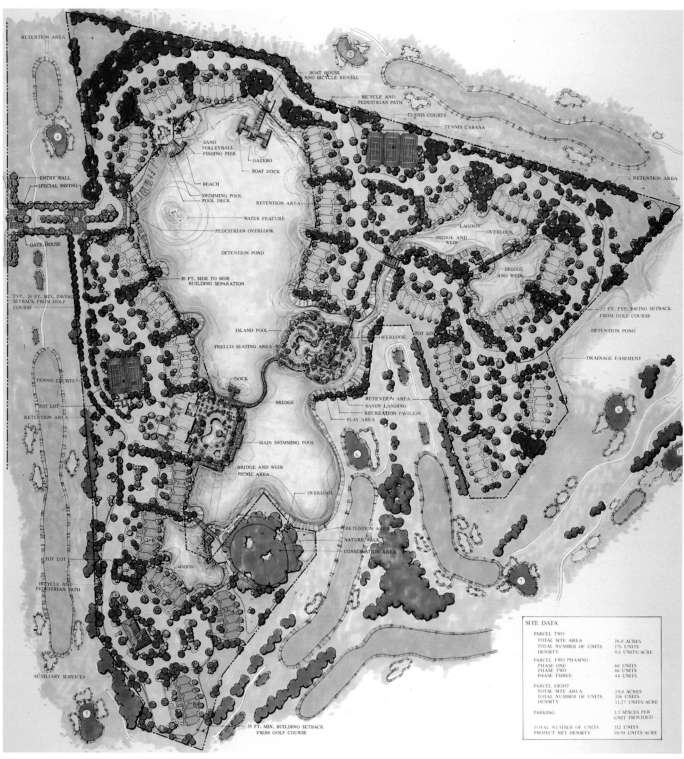

Site plan.

◆ Project Data[1]

Development Schedule

Total number of units	510
Planning started	1989
Construction started	1989
Construction completed	1995
Sales started	1990
Sales completed	1996

Land Use Information

Site area	67 acres
Total number of timeshare units planned	510
Total number of timeshare units completed	510
Gross density	7.6 units/acre

Unit Information

Unit type	two-bedroom, two-bath
Floor area	1,240 square feet
Average price per week (1997)	$13,500
Number of unit/weeks sold	26,000

Administrative, Recreational, and Commercial Facilities

	Square Feet
Reception building	8,560
Activities building	4,554, plus 3,720 of patio space
Restaurant/food service	620[2]
Marketplace store	1,447

Annual Assessments per Unit/Week (1997)

Operating costs[3]	$354.94
Reserves	$44.00
Subtotal	$398.94
Property tax	$148.30–$165.60[4]
Total—all fees	$547.24–$564.54

Developer

Marriott Vacation Club International, Inc.
Ft. Lauderdale, Florida

Architect

Helman, Hurley, Charvat & Peacock
Maitland, Florida

Interior Design

Design Continuum, Inc.
Atlanta, Georgia

Notes

1. Project cost information is not available.

2. Includes the pool bar and the Pizza Hut/TCBY outlet.

3. Includes maintenance, utilities, administrative costs, insurance, and miscellaneous fees and expenses.

4. Depending on season.

Date of site visit: October 19, 1998
Author of case study: Diane R. Suchman

---

essary to ensure that quality. Miller advises that in addition to building a high-quality project in the first place, the key to maintaining a high-quality environment in a vacation-ownership development is a professional maintenance program. Marriott's goal is to perform at a level that exceeds customer expectations. As Miller explained, "In timesharing, just as in all other businesses, customer satisfaction is the key to success."

Note

1. Galvalume is a Bethlehem Steel product.

Royal Resorts

Cancun, Mexico

The Royal Resorts Group is a Cancun, Mexico–based timeshare development, operations, and management company. It is distinguished by its customer-service orientation and an ownership arrangement that guarantees buyers return of their purchase price plus a share of any net profits when the development is sold upon maturation of the project's deed of trust. The company has developed four luxury properties in Cancun. The first, in 1977, was Club Internacional de Cancun (VCI). The next three—the Royal Mayan (1981–1987), the Royal Caribbean (1986–1991), and the Royal Islander (1991–1996)—are the primary focus of this case study. They are located adjacent to one another and share amenities and facilities. A fifth property, the Royal Sands, is under construction at a different location. Each of the four completed Royal Resorts has earned Interval International's five-star rating.

As a year-round resort with easy (and comparatively inexpensive) air access from the United States, Cancun is a prime location for a timeshare resort. The area is also a popular summer vacation destination for Mexicans and, to a lesser extent, for South Americans. It offers white sand beaches, turquoise Caribbean waters, the allure of Mexican culture, and nearby Mayan archeological sites.

Project History and Description

In the mid-1970s, Fonatur, an agency of the Mexican government, targeted Cancun, which was then little more than a barren strip of sand and swamp, as a location where it wanted to encourage tourism. Fonatur bought and subdivided land in what is now known as the hotel zone, provided the needed infrastructure, and built a golf course. The agency went on to establish development standards for the zone and, using a fund for the development of tourism, financed developers' purchase of land trusts and helped developers obtain construction and permanent loans from Mexican banks. (In Mexico, foreigners cannot purchase land within 50 kilometers of the seashore; a Mexican bank must be the trustee.)

Royal Resorts was the brainchild of four former U.S. Air Force officers and four Mexican nationals. According to Richard Sutton, Royal Resorts's general director, he and his investor-partners created a concept of timesharing based on their observations at Treetops resort in Hilton Head, South Carolina, in the early 1970s. In the absence of real estate experience, the investor-partners based the concept on their belief of what a consumer would want—an approach that continues to dominate all of the firm's activities. In 1975, the group began incremental development of VCI—seven units followed by 22 and, finally, 200 units, in five phases. Learning as they went, the investor-partners remained fixed on how to make their customers happy so that they in turn would refer their friends. VCI's purchasers were avant-garde travelers who were "discovering" Cancun—sophisticated, adventurous people who had money and were willing to take risks.

Development of the Royal Mayan, the Royal Caribbean, and the Royal Islander followed, building on VCI's success and referrals from its customer base. Each resort is designed in a "U" shape, with the open end facing the ocean, and with a restaurant and swimming pools located in the center of the "U." Lushly landscaped with tropical plants, flowers, palm trees, and cooling ponds and waterfalls, the three resorts are connected to one another with covered walkways. A free trolley shuttles members and guests among the resorts and to and from the resort-owned restaurant and water sports center across the street.

Each resort incorporates a restaurant, three tennis courts, beach frontage, swimming pools with wading areas, swim-up bars, and poolside food and beverage service. Each offers daily maid service, a gift shop, minigrocery stores, a beauty shop with massage services, and a full program of activities for children and adults. There are no extra charges for tennis courts (including racquets), snorkeling gear, pro-

grammed activities, beach towels, crafts materials, sailboats, or bicycles. The resort rents space to a doctor who maintains an on-site office. A business center provides a variety of fee-based personal services such as copying, fax services, Internet access, birthday cakes, flower delivery, stocking of kitchens before guest arrival, and even wedding arrangements. Because water and electricity are so expensive in Cancun, each resort operates a staffed, central laundry for owners' use.

Units, which are called villas, feature two bedrooms, two baths, balconies, marble floors, generous closet space, two safes, and full kitchens with dishwashers and microwave ovens. At 1,200 to 1,400 square feet, the units accommodate six people, two in each bedroom and two on a sleeper-sofa in the living area. In each villa, the second bedroom can be locked off; either the master suite or the second bedroom can be rented or exchanged as a separate unit. To accommodate the lockoff, all second bedrooms have a separate entrance, a full bath and dressing area, a small refrigerator, and a safe.

Purchase Arrangements And Pricing

Royal Resorts sells fixed-time/fixed-unit intervals—and, according to Mark Carney, marketing sales director—it is the only timeshare resort in Cancun that offers such an arrangement. Members can exchange their unit/weeks for different units or time intervals within the Royal Resorts system for a $75 fee, or they can use the services of Interval International to reserve intervals at other resorts worldwide. (Owners at VCI and the Royal Mayan can also use RCI.) Carney noted that most owners occupy their units rather than exchange them for time at other resorts.

In Sutton's opinion, point systems generally work to the disadvantage of consumers primarily because resort management cannot guarantee the use of a specific prop-

Photo on page 160:
The Royal Mayan, the Royal Caribbean, and the Royal Islander resorts sit side by side on the beach in Cancun's hotel zone, a configuration that enables owners and guests to enjoy easy access to the amenities of all three resorts.

erty at the time desired by the buyer. In addition, the complicated accounting and reservation systems required of a point system carry high costs that ultimately accrue to consumers. Sutton believes that it is hard to maintain a good balance between availability and sales and that there is a strong—and tempting—potential for developers to oversell. Other problems can arise if and when the developer wants to increase the cost or value of points. With a fixed-unit/fixed-week system, however, owners arrive at their vacation destination confident that they will occupy the desired unit for the desired interval. As noted, if owners prefer, they can exchange their unit/week for another at the same or a different resort.

Ownership arrangements at the three adjacent developments (and VCI) are based on separate 30-year deeds of trust. As each deed of trust expires, the associated property will be sold. Upon consummation of the sale and after deducting taxes, commission, and other appropriate expenses, the available funds will be distributed to members and the developer in accordance with specific priorities. For VCI, the Royal Mayan, and the Royal Caribbean, members will receive their original cash

membership investment while the developer will receive an equal amount. Any funds remaining after satisfying the initial member and developer requirements will be divided as follows: one-half to the developer and the remaining share distributed on a pro rata basis among members. Owners at the Royal Islander (and the Royal Sands, which has a 50-year deed of trust) will receive equal shares of the sales price when those properties are sold at the end of their respective trust periods, with no distribution to the developer.

Marketing and Sales

VCI, the Royal Mayan, and the Royal Caribbean have completely sold out. The Royal Islander is 96 percent sold, and preconstruction sales are underway at the Royal Sands. Internal sales account for 75 percent of all sales and include sales to renters and exchangers and the sale of additional time to existing owners.

In addition, the resort maintains three OPC locations in nearby shopping malls. The OPCs are colocated with stores that sell natural products and handicrafts through a resort-sponsored nonprofit organization dedicated to the preservation of the Mayan

Like its sister resorts, the Royal Mayan is designed with villas surrounding the resort's restaurant and swimming pool.

Biosphere. People who patronize the stores are introduced to the Royal Resorts and invited to tour the properties in exchange for a choice of gifts (such as coupons for tours of nearby archeological sites) and a $50 voucher for purchases in Royal Resorts's shops. OPCs generate 20 percent of purchasers.

The resort also places print advertisements that likewise offer premiums in exchange for tours; the advertisements account for about 5 percent of all purchases. And Royal Resorts is beginning to experiment with telemarketing to a targeted list of people referred by current owners.

From the outset, Royal Resorts has operated a resale program. The company charges a 25 percent fee for the service but realizes no profit from the transactions. The service does, however, provide a means of exit for owners who choose to separate from the resort. In any event, an owner cannot list a unit/week for resale unless his or her membership is fully paid and all obligations to the resort are current. Resales, which are generally priced at about 60 percent of the cost of a new unit/week, account for about 20 to 25 percent of all sales. According to Carney, resales do not compete with new sales because most people prefer new product. In addition, given that Royal Resorts sells from a fixed price, resales serve as a legitimate price drop. By facilitating the resale process, Royal Resorts achieves high collection rates on annual dues.

For Royal Resorts, the sale process is based on customer satisfaction and relationship-building activities that unfold over the course of a week. To begin, each owner and guest is assigned to a personal concierge, who greets the arriving party at the door at Saturday check-in, facilitates registration, and assists with a wide variety of services throughout the stay. On Sunday, each owner and guest is invited, first, to a morning orientation on what to do and not do in Cancun and, second, an after-

At the Royal Mayan, the Mayan theme is carried through with touches such as carvings on villa doors. Elsewhere, stone stellae with Mayan images adorn the resort's gardens.

Diane R. Suchman

noon party that is videotaped and replayed on in-house television throughout the week. (The video is also available for sale.) To build rapport, the personal concierge invites each owner and guest to three additional free events: breakfast or lunch, a Monday night cocktail party, and a cruise around the lagoon. The entire resort staff is responsible for seeing that the facilities are in good condition, that the resort operates flawlessly, and that each owner or guest receives first-rate service during the week. By the end of the week, customers usually ask questions about purchasing. At that time, the personal concierge introduces the customer to a sales agent. According to Carney, the sales system is designed to be free of pressure; the strongest selling point is the quality of the customer's experience at the resort.

Depending on individual experience and capability, each of the 29 personal concierges is assigned to 14 to 25 owners or guests each week and is expected to deliver 90 percent of his or her assigned parties to a salesperson for a sales presentation. The salesperson, in turn, is expected to convert 15 percent of prospects into purchasers.

Royal Resorts will not sell a timeshare interval on site. Instead, prospects inter-

Club Internacional de Cancun is Royal Resorts's first time-share resort and its only low-rise development. Built in 1977, the resort has been beautifully maintained.

Diane R. Suchman

ested in purchasing an interval complete an application and reserve a unit/week. Subsequently (within a specified time), they confirm the reservation by establishing the form of downpayment—check or credit card. In approximately two weeks, they receive a contract mailed to their home. Of those who file applications to purchase, 95 percent sign and return the contract. The two-week waiting period between signing the application to purchase and receiving the contract helps the resort build credibility with buyers and ensures that prospects feel no undue pressure to purchase. That, in turn, holds down the after-contract rescission rate to about 2 percent and minimizes the costs and administrative burdens associated with rescissions.

Slightly more than half (52 percent) of purchases are for cash; Royal Resorts self-finances the other purchases, requiring 10 percent down with terms up to ten years. Interest rates vary from 10 to 16 percent, depending on the financing arrangement. By financing the member directly, Royal Resorts has successfully assisted its members through difficult financial times. Sutton emphasizes, however, that the company is "in the resort development and hospitality business, not just the finance business."

Royal Resorts prides itself on keeping marketing and sales costs low so that it can offer buyers good value for their money.

The marketing team is encouraged to offset its costs through entrepreneurial ventures such as the sale of videos and the services of the business center. As a result, about 35 to 37 percent of the purchase price of a unit/week at Royal Resorts is attributable to product cost; the industry standard is 25 percent.

Management and Operations

The Royal Resorts Group is organized as a series of legally separate businesses that are affiliated by common or overlapping ownership. In particular, Royal Resorts operates its own construction company and provides its own in-house architecture, interior design, marketing, sales, administration, and resale services. To minimize the potential for legal liability, Royal Resorts maintains no presence in the United States. It contracts with Interval Servicing Company (ISCO) of Ft. Lauderdale, Florida, to provide a variety of member services, such as internal exchanges, changes of title, airline reservations, unit rentals, and other functions. The developers own all of the restaurants, including the three on site and Captain's Cove, a seafood restaurant open to the public and located across the street on the lagoon. Royal Resorts also operates a travel agency that books discounted tours and airline tickets for resort owners and provides ground transportation for wholesalers (tour operators).

Though each resort is a legally separate trust, management of resort operations is centrally controlled; written policies and procedures govern every aspect of resort management. To keep costs down, the company does almost everything itself rather than contract with others. In addition, it creates efficiencies wherever possible, both in management and operations. In management, for example, all four resorts share the services of key staff such as the heads of the accounting, security, maintenance, human resources, food and beverage, computer systems, internal audit, and legal services departments. Each resort obtains the services of these staff by contract. Nonetheless, each resort is a stand-alone operation in the sense that it employs its own accountant, housekeeping staff, and such. Efficiencies in operations—for example, use of the heat generated by air-conditioning units to heat water in the villas and use of recycled swimming pool backflush water to irrigate lawns and gardens—also cut costs. To cut costs and minimize loss and damage, the resorts run their own laundries. The resorts also maintain their own water purification system and impose strict standards of cleanliness to ensure safety in food service operations. In fact, Royal Resorts employs Cancun's only in-house chemist.

Maintenance and repair of physical facilities is ongoing. A storeroom of spare parts and extra equipment, furniture, and appliances makes repairs and replacements quick and easy. Certain spare parts and equipment are stocked on each floor of the villas so that management can meet the goal of responding to repair calls within 15 minutes. Each resort has its own greenhouse.

Resort members and guests receive a magnetically coded card that functions as their room key and must be presented to obtain towels, sports equipment, and ser-

vices. It is also used to pay for meals in resort restaurants and purchases at the resort-owned retail outlets. All charges are settled at checkout. The card-based system has several advantages. It is efficient, reduces opportunities for theft, ensures that people using the resort facilities are owners or guests, and is easily changed as occupancy changes. Perhaps most important, the card is simple to use, thereby encouraging people to spend more money at the resort.

The company rents unsold weeks and operates a rental service for owners who do not plan to use their villas. It rents blocks of rooms to wholesalers, but only on the company's own terms, thus ensuring that owners' needs are served first. The volume of rentals varies by season; on average, though, about 30 percent of the resorts' villas are occupied by renters.

Over time, Royal Resorts has grown from one to two parallel operating rental systems. During its first 15 years, the resort company created a rental pool run by Vacation Club Rentals (VCR) in San Antonio, Texas. Owners wishing to rent would place their units in the pool. VCR would then seek renters for the various units. For their part, owners in the pool would share the rental income with VCR after deducting 35 percent for expenses. Since 1993, ISCO has operated a first-come, first-served rental system with a fixed price for each unit depending on season and location. The system puts the owners in control. If owners change their mind about renting their unit, they call ISCO to inquire whether the unit has rented. If the unit is still available, owners can remove it from ISCO's list and use it or rent it themselves. In addition, owners continue to have the option of participating in the rental pool, which is still operated by VCR.

Though member participation in resort management has only recently become mandatory in Mexico, each Royal Resorts property has operated with a five-person membership advisory board since its in-

The Royal Islander site plan.

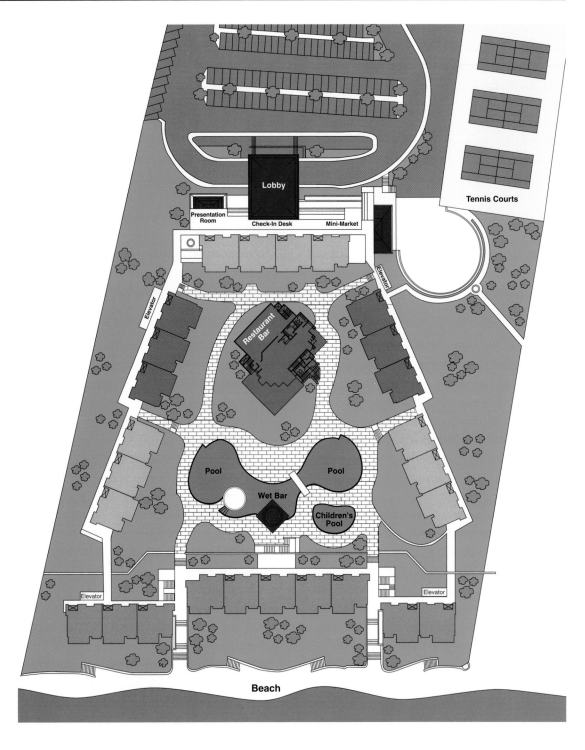

Labels in image:
Lobby
Presentation Room
Check-In Desk
Mini-Market
Tennis Courts
Elevator
Restaurant Bar
Elevator
Pool
Pool
Wet Bar
Children's Pool
Elevator
Elevator
Beach

ception. Royal Resorts operates each resort for a management fee of 10 percent (5 percent at VCI) of the annual club service fees billed to resort members. The company's philosophy is "management in the sunshine." All activities related to the properties' management and budget are open to members' inspection.

In 1998, club service fees (annual dues) totaled $465 for the Royal Mayan, $475 for the Royal Caribbean, and $468 for the Royal Islander. As noted, collection rates for annual dues remain high, and each resort has more than $1 million in its reserve account. When in the past the surplus exceeded that amount, the membership advisory boards elected to give a fixed rebate per week to owners who had paid their management fees on time. In 1997, the Royal Mayan and Royal Caribbean issued rebates of $103 and $107, respectively. (The company finds it is easier to rebate excess money rather than decrease dues; if dues are cut, it is difficult to raise them again when needed.)

Experience Gained

Working in Mexico poses special challenges. The extensive documentation required by the federal government makes for a circuitous and time-consuming development process. (It took Royal Resorts 30 months to establish the first trust and start construction.) Environmental laws have become burdensome. Most important, Mexico is beset by periodic economic crises, interest rate fluctuations, and monetary devaluations, all of which undermine local buyers' ability to pay. In such circumstances, the company works with buyers to refinance their purchase, extend their payment term, or make other arrangements to avoid default. Resort operations are also affected. On one occasion, when an economic crisis converted a resort's reserve fund from a $0.5 million surplus to a $0.5 million debt, the developers loaned the fund $0.5 million at no interest to enable it to meet its budget. Since then, all four resorts have built up a considerable surplus.

Members have also come to the aid of Royal Resorts. In 1982, as the company was completing VCI and beginning the Royal Mayan, it learned that the bank that was to finance the project had no funds for the construction loan. Royal Resorts offered VCI's 3,200 members the opportunity to invest in the Royal Mayan for a minimum of $30,000 at 25 percent interest. Alternatively, investors could choose to take the villas, which the company would then resell for a 40 percent rate of return upon completion of the resort. (Most investors chose the villas.) The company soon raised $4 million, and construction went forward.

The company has found that the best way to deal with Mexico's capricious economic environment is to anticipate changes

The Royal Islander floor plan.

and stand ready to respond rapidly. In other words, the company must be financially conservative and never overleverage itself. And, as in any foreign environment, in Mexico it is essential to work with a trustworthy, well-connected local partner who functions as the company's political presence and helps navigate a path through the bureaucracy.

Another important lesson is that homeowners' associations (HOAs) charged with maintenance responsibilities must contract with a reputable management company to ensure a resort's upkeep. According to Sutton, HOA management is a potential weakness in the timeshare industry. Understandably, homeowners want to cut costs and keep annual fees low, but a resort can deteriorate rapidly if cost-cutting goals undermine maintenance requirements.

Good management, Sutton has learned, requires fair rules and regulations that ensure equal treatment of all owners. It also demands control of the relationship between marketing and operations to make certain that the marketing team does not promise buyers special benefits. Finally,

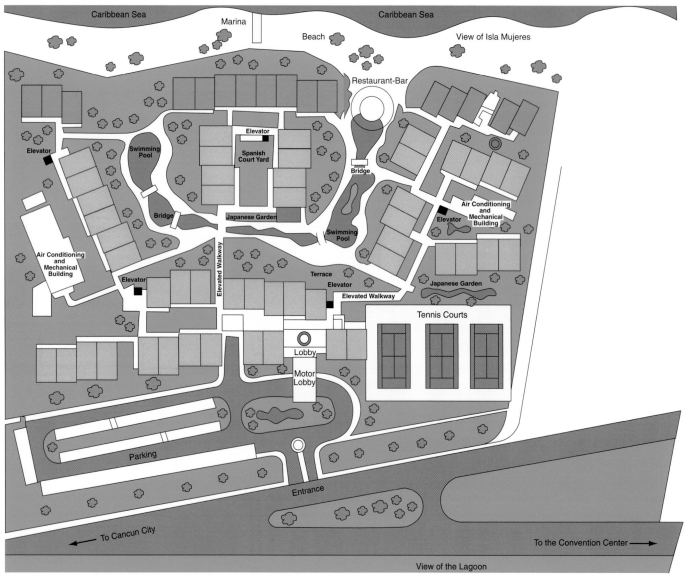

Club Internacional de Cancun site plan.

good management means remembering that "people are your biggest asset" and, most important, recognizing that a resort's primary mission is to provide owners and guests with a memorable vacation.

Sutton's main frustration after 23 years in the interval ownership business is the excessively high cost of sales and marketing and the associated overhead costs. A review of the data released by the industry's publicly held companies reveals that these expenses account for 50 percent or more of gross sales prices. In the case of Royal Resorts, however, sales and marketing expenses are much lower, thus enabling the company to invest the savings in product quality and maintain a competitive market price. As a result, Royal Resorts provides greater value while achieving an acceptable profit margin.

The Royal Resorts properties' consistently stellar ratings and the company's outstanding record of customer satisfaction are largely the product of Sutton's personal philosophy and management style. The challenge is how to ensure continuing success when Sutton retires three years hence. The current plan calls for Royal Resorts to focus on management and operations of resorts throughout the Caribbean rather than on development of new resorts, and Sutton is grooming his successors.

◆ Project Data[1]

Development Schedule

Club Internacional de Cancun

Number of units	201
Construction started	1977
Construction completed	1982
Sales started	1977
Sales completed	1986

The Royal Mayan

Number of units	200
Construction started	1983
Construction completed	1987
Sales started	1984
Sales completed	1987

The Royal Caribbean

Number of units	207
Construction started	1986
Construction completed	1990
Sales started	1986
Sales completed	1992

The Royal Islander

Number of units	179
Construction started	1990
Construction completed	1996
Sales started	1992
Sales completed	1998

Note

1. Project development costs not available.

Prices per Unit/Week (August 1998)

	Average Price per Unit/Week
The Royal Islander	
Member	$17,500–$41,000
Nonmember	$18,800–$46,000
The Royal Sands (under construction)	
Member	$17,100–$43,800
Nonmember	$19,100–$48,900

Annual Operating Expenses (1997)

The Royal Mayan	
Total	$5.2 million
Per unit/week	$510
The Royal Caribbean	
Total	$5.1 million
Per unit/week	$483
The Royal Islander	
Total	$3.7 million
Per unit/week	$405

Developer

The Royal Resorts
Cancun, Mexico

Date of site visit: October 12, 1998
Author of case study: Diane R. Suchman

Land Use Information

	Club Internacional de Cancun	The Royal Mayan	The Royal Caribbean	The Royal Islander
Site area (acres)	7.41	8.41	9.55	8.42
Timeshare buildings (square feet)	416,824	455,371	500,882	451,700
Lobby (square feet)	3,579	3,553	7,357	7,144
Restaurants (square feet)	11,582	10,441	11,453	10,904
Retail space (square feet)	1,822	1,703	7,976	3,204
Offices/sales facilities (square feet)	1,884	1,054	2,988	5,480
Open space (square feet)	117,330	103,336	139,397	139,935
Swimming pools (square feet)	9,010	11,399	22,454	10,527
Sun decks (square feet)	16,272	26,221	31,453	19,128
Tennis courts (number)	2	3	3	3
Off-street parking spaces	70	38	86	99

Club Asia International

Sarawak, Malaysia

In the western hemisphere, participation in the timeshare industry by large brand-name hospitality companies has enhanced the industry's legitimacy and spurred consumer acceptance. In Southeast Asia, where many governments play an extensive role in commercial and economic development, involvement in timesharing by a government entity sends an equally positive signal.

The state of Sarawak, Malaysia, provides a premier example of government involvement in the timeshare industry. The state-owned Sarawak Economic Development Corporation (SEDC) has launched the world's first government-owned vacation club—Club Asia International—for the express purpose of increasing occupancies

in three SEDC resorts: a Crowne Plaza Hotel in the heart of bustling downtown Kuching and two Holiday Inn resorts in the Damai Beach resort district 22 miles from Kuching. (It should be noted that Asia's economic crisis has severely restricted the amount of money the Sarawak state government is prepared to commit to marketing and selling Club Asia memberships. Thus, while the physical product and club structure are good examples of timeshare development practice, the marketing and sales results have been less than spectacular.)

Sarawak is Malaysia's largest state, encompassing 48,050 square miles of mountainous rainforest along the northwest coast of Borneo, the world's third-largest island. Close to 2 million people live in Sarawak, with about half a million in the state capital, Kuching.

SEDC was established in 1972 to promote the commercial, industrial, and socioeconomic development of Sarawak. It provides a central source of advice on business opportunities and has become involved as a joint venture partner in many sectors of the state's economy, including hospitality and tourism. Through SEDC, the government has invested over 550 million Malaysian ringgit (US$144.8 million) since the mid-1980s for the development of tourism infrastructure, including hotels and resorts, shopping complexes, a country club and championship golf course, and Sarawak Cultural Village, a tourist attraction featuring the domestic crafts and performing arts of seven indigenous ethnic groups.

In 1995, SEDC allocated a total of 222 units in the three aforementioned properties—30 percent of its hotel inventory at the time—to the vacation club concept. SEDC leases the accommodations to the operator of Club Asia International, Sara Worldwide Vacations Senderian Berhad (Sdn.Bhd.), an independent, wholly owned subsidiary of SEDC that markets and sells memberships, issues membership certificates, and maintains club records. A trustee —a subsidiary of a bank—receives purchasers' money and manages the club's funds, including trust accounts and a sinking fund (reserve account) to cover the anticipated costs of future refurbishment and repairs. The hotels and resorts are managed by H.I.-Sara Hospitality Sdn. Bhd., which is 70 percent owned by Sara Resort Sdn. Bhd. The Holiday Inn Group owns the remaining 30 percent.

In late 1998, the club counted more than 500 members. Although it lacks an owners' association of the type that would govern a deeded condominium-based project in the United States, it has a liaison committee formed by club members to serve as a channel of communication among Sara Worldwide Vacations Sdn. Bhd., club members, and the trustee.

Product Description

Club Asia International is the first point-based vacation club in Malaysia to receive approval from the Registry of Companies, the Malaysian federal government agency that regulates timeshare resorts. Purchasers of a Club Asia International membership pay RM13,800 (US$3,632) for a package of "vacation points" allocated in annual increments over a 48-year period. Buyers also pay an annual maintenance fee of RM280. "Sara Worldwide Vacations Berhad ventured into a point-based vacation program to create flexibility and maximize club members' satisfaction," explains Kevin Chong Heong Thiam, chief executive officer of Sara Worldwide Vacations Berhad and Club Asia International. Vacation points entitle club members to 48 years of guaranteed use of the three resorts' accommodations, amenities, and facilities.

Through a partnership that provides access to four additional SEDC-owned resorts—a Holiday Inn in downtown Kuching and ecotourism resorts in three separate rainforest locales—club members also may exchange their vacation points in any year for "leisure points." In addition, members may use their leisure points for

- green fees, caddy services, and golf cart rental at Damai Golf & Country Club, an 18-hole, 7,030-yard, par-72 course designed by Arnold Palmer;
- visits to Sarawak Cultural Village;
- recreational activities at or organized by participating SEDC hotels and resorts, including bird watching, camping, canoeing, cave exploration, deep-sea fishing, hiking, jet skiing, jungle-survival training, kayaking, mountain biking, motorcycling, parasailing, river cruising, rock climbing, scuba diving, snorkeling, squash, surfboarding, tennis, and water skiing; and

Photo on page 170:
Chalets surround the largest lagoon-style freeform pool at Sarawak at Damai Lagoon Resort.

- participation in home-stay programs that involve an exchange of personal residences.

Club Asia International's affiliation with Interval International makes additional worldwide exchange options available to members.

In addition to these leisure-lifestyle features, the Club Asia International vacation club product includes a payback arrangement under which club members are promised repayment of the initial amount of the membership fee plus interest—a total of RM26,000 (US$6,843)—at the end of the 48-year membership period. Thus, beyond congenial hospitality and high-quality accommodations at prices held constant as of the purchase date, the program offers members the expectation of an eventual return on their investment in the club. This arrangement is not unique. Other resorts in Malaysia and at least one resort in the Caribbean operate similar investment programs. Such a feature would not be feasible in the United States, however, because U.S. law would consider the investment a purchase of a security and thus require a filing with the U.S. Securities and Exchange Commission—a complication and expense that most U.S. timeshare developers prefer to avoid.

Yet another aspect of the Club Asia International program is a personal accident insurance policy that covers club members against accidental death or total and permanent disability caused by an accident—on or off club property—for the first five years of the 48-year term.

Other key features of the Club Asia International membership program include

- the ability to bank and/or borrow vacation points from year to year, to purchase additional points, or to amass the points needed for a particular vacation itinerary;
- transferability of vacation points or the entire membership;
- use of vacation points for guest reservations;

- flexible use, including choice of hotels or resorts, of length of stay, of weekdays and/or weekends, and of season; and
- the Club Asia International Privilege Discount Program, which provides members with discounts at participating merchants upon presentation of the membership card.

Marketing, Sales, and Financing

Sara Worldwide Vacations Berhad employs a sales staff of 15 vacation consultants who work on site at the resorts in Kuching and Damai Beach and in an off-site sales office in the Sarawak Shopping Mall in downtown Kuching. The firm plans to open another off-site sales location in Kuala Lumpur, Malaysia's federal capital. Each vacation consultant is responsible for seeing three qualified prospects a day, or 60 a month, and for closing at least four sales a month. About 30 percent of sales revenues defray marketing and sales expenses, including a sales commission of 10 percent.

Club Asia International targets Malaysians employed in a business or professional occupation. Prospects are married and have at least one child and a monthly household income of at least RM3,000 (US$790). The company relies on direct mail and telemarketing to offer a complimentary dinner for two or another incentive of similar value to prospects who agree to attend a presentation at the off-site sales center. Prospects who purchase on the day of the presentation receive a free night's stay at an SEDC property.

Another source of leads is the Club Asia International Eversharing Program, a referral program through which club members earn redeemable bonus vouchers by inviting their friends to "member-get-member functions" organized by Sara Worldwide Vacations Berhad. These promotional gatherings may take place on site at a resort or at a tea party in a member's home or a community meeting room.

Sometimes the events include a magic show for the children. "During these functions, the club's vacation consultants explain the program and seek to close sales," explains Mary Tay, Club Asia International's operations officer. The bonus vouchers may be used to pay the member's yearly club maintenance fee, reduce outstanding finance payments, purchase additional ownership, or pay for amenities and activities at participating SEDC resorts.

End-loan financing is available through financial institutions at an interest rate based on the current market rate set by Bank Negara, the Malaysian central bank. With a 10 percent downpayment, purchasers may qualify for a four-year in-house installment payment plan provided by Sara Worldwide Vacations Berhad, with a below-market interest rate (banks lend for five years at a higher rate). Because the market is primarily domestic, recent exchange rate fluctuations in Southeast Asian currencies have had practically no effect on Club Asia International's payment regime. The few non–Malaysian purchasers are responsible for exchanging their own currency into Malaysian ringgit.

Urban Hotels and Beach Resorts

As noted above, the SEDC-owned hotel and resort properties that constitute Club Asia International's inventory of accommodations fall into three general categories: urban hotels, beach resorts, and ecotourism resorts.

The urban hotels—Crowne Plaza Riverside Kuching and Holiday Inn Kuching—face each other across Jalan (Boulevard) Tunku Abdul Rahman, a main thoroughfare in the heart of Kuching that parallels the broad Sarawak River near the upstream end of the city's public waterfront promenade. SEDC spent RM89 million (US$23.4 million) to demolish dilapidated warehouses along the waterfront and create the 1.9-mile-long promenade.

The Crowne Plaza Riverside Kuching (formerly the Riverside Majestic Hotel) overlooks the Sarawak River near the upstream end of Kuching's waterfront promenade.

The Crowne Plaza Riverside Kuching is a 19-story, 250-room hotel connected to the adjacent five-story Riverside Shopping Complex, an air-conditioned mall with 182 retail shops. The 11-story Holiday Inn Kuching has 305 rooms and a secluded poolside pavilion overlooking the river. Both urban hotels offer executive floors, extensive athletic and fitness facilities, gourmet dining, conference facilities and services, and access to many of the recreational activities available through Club Asia International's leisure points.

The beach resorts—Holiday Inn Resort Damai Lagoon and Holiday Inn Resort

Royal Mulu's buildings and walkways rise on stilts more than nine meters (30 feet) above the jungle floor, well above the Melinau River's high-water mark.

Damai Beach—occupy a scenic location along the South China Sea at the foot of Gunung Santubong (Sleeping Princess Mountain). The Holiday Inn Resort Damai Lagoon consists of 226 rooms and suites and 30 chalets. The "lagoon" is the largest freeform swimming pool in Sarawak and features its own beach, waterfalls, and swim-up pool bars. The Holiday Inn Resort Damai Beach climbs the steep foothills above Teluk Bandung Beach; its 302 units include Malay-style bungalows with spectacular hilltop views and chalets and suites designed and decorated in the style of indigenous tribes, the Bidayuh, Iban, and Orang Ulu. A gift shop in the lobby sells locally made tribal craft items. Both resorts offer diverse dining facilities and extensive recreational facilities and services, and both are located within two miles of the Damai

Golf & Country Club and within walking distance of Sarawak Cultural Village.

Ecotourism Resorts

Club Asia International's three ecotourism resorts—Damai Rainforest Resort, Bukit Saban Resort, and Royal Mulu Resort—provide SEDC and the Sarawak state government with a base for attracting visitors from all over the world. Damai Rainforest Resort, in the Damai Beach resort district, offers a readily accessible ecotourism experience in a naturalistic setting close to Kuching. Bukit Saban and Royal Mulu, located deep within Borneo's interior rainforest, provide a comfortable base for more remote ecotourism adventures.

Though they are miles apart, all three resorts share a common attribute: the lush tropical rainforest that cloaks 75 percent of Borneo's landscape. Borneo's incomparably beautiful and diverse virgin forests; plunging waterfalls and surging rivers; muscular, mist-shrouded mountains; and vast, largely uncharted cave systems appeal to scientists and adventurers alike and, increasingly, to ordinary people seeking an extraordinary vacation experience.

Damai Rainforest Resort consists of 29 log-cabin chalets and ten treehouses sited on a forested hillside overlooking the South China Sea. The 44-acre resort embraces an outdoor activity center where expert instructors teach survival skills, including the use of ropes as an aid to movement and identification of edible jungle fruits and plants. Conference facilities and programs designed to build self-confidence and interpersonal skills are available to families, students, and corporate groups.

Bukit Saban is a 50-unit resort built in 1995 on a 14-acre site in the Paku district of Betong, 180 miles from Kuching. The buildings that house the accommodations resemble the apartment-style longhouses of the Iban tribe; in fact, the inhabitants of nearby Iban villages welcome visits from resort guests. Tribe members share aspects of their indigenous culture, such as cockfighting matches, traditional dances, arts and crafts, and cuisine. At the nearby Betong Handicraft Centre, young Iban women weave pua kumbu fabric and create batik designs.

Bukit Saban Resort also offers guided bicycle, boat, and foot trips in the surrounding region, including a trek through rugged terrain to a jungle waterfall. Guests can fish in the crystal-clear waters of the Paku River and observe wildlife from elevated platforms without disturbing the forest's natural systems. Nearby destinations include rice paddies and cocoa, oil palm, and pepper plantations. In addition, within 12 miles of the resort, a government-sponsored agricultural research center welcomes visitors and showcases a freshwater fish hatchery and the cultivation of wild fruits, ferns, and durian and rubber trees.

Royal Mulu Resort offers 149 units, 76 that opened in 1992 and 73 that were completed in 1996. The entire resort is built on stilts more than 30 feet above ground, well above the high-water mark of the river's annual rainy-season floods. The property occupies a 200-acre site along the Melinau River adjoining Gunung Mulu National Park, six to seven hours upriver by boat from the coast of the South China Sea. Malaysia Airlines transports most of the resort's food and visitors on 45-minute flights aboard 19-seat Twin Otter aircraft from the nearest city, Miri, to a small local airport.

Royal Mulu's visitors stay in longhouse-style structures that resemble the architecture of a nearby Penan tribal village. The structures are connected by boardwalks along which bellmen transport luggage on pedal-powered rickshaws and security staff patrol on bicycles. Guest rooms and suites, built to international standards of quality, feature air conditioning, parquet flooring, meranti wood décor, "en suite" baths and showers, refrigerated mini-bars, color television for in-house movies, and an open-air veranda facing the jungle.

The resort also includes a large, shaded open-air lobby and an air-conditioned restaurant and lounge with a separate terrace for open-air dining. Near the lobby, a sun deck surrounds an ample swimming pool with a fountain in the center, underwater lighting that changes color at night, and a built-in whirlpool spa on each side. As might be expected by virtue of its remote location, the resort generates its own power, purifies its own water, and treats its own sewage.

Without even leaving the grounds of Royal Mulu Resort, the nature-oriented visitor finds much to appreciate. Forest rangers have labeled the resort's orchids, fruit trees, and other landscape plants. A net-draped walk-through aviary is home to a representative assortment of native birds, including the state bird of Sarawak, the hornbill; huge moths and other intriguing insects flutter around the exterior light fixtures at night. Easy trail walks in the jungle meander around the resort. Visitors also may climb a local limestone outcropping that provides a view of the surrounding area.

The main attraction at Royal Mulu, however, is the vast Gunung Mulu National Park. Roughly the size of Zion National Park in Utah, Gunung Mulu National Park encompasses 210 square miles of sandstone and limestone mountains crowned with verdant rainforest and bisected by rivers and streams. The park offers visitors the opportunity to scale three major moun-

A bedroom at the Holiday Inn Resort at Damai Beach—in a chalet built in the style of an Iban tribal longhouse—is decorated with native fabrics woven by the Orang Ulu River tribe.

George Leposky, Interval International

tains—Mulu (7,796 feet), Api (5,611 feet), and Benarat (5,200 feet); climb to a rain-sculpted rock formation called the Pinnacles on Mt. Api; canoe and raft on the Melinau River; and explore the world's largest limestone cave system, in which more than 125 miles of passages have been surveyed and perhaps another 375 miles await exploration.

Park officials have established four "show caves"—Deer, Clearwater, Wind, and Lang. Guests may make arrangements at Royal Mulu Resort to tour any or all of the caves. Accompanied by guides from the nearby Orang Ulu tribe, visitors depart from the resort and travel upriver—via longboats powered by outboard motors—to Clearwater and Wind. Boardwalks lead from the park headquarters to all four caves. Besides easing the way of visitors over uneven terrain, the well-defined pathways help protect the surrounding jungle. Within the caves, well-lit concrete paths and stairways accommodate visitors while reducing the impact of tourism on the caves' rock formations and indigenous animal and plant populations.

Deer Cave is the world's largest known underground chamber, 394 feet high and 328 feet wide. Five buildings the size of St. Paul's Cathedral in London could fit inside the cavern. Among Deer Cave's notable rock formations are a profile of Abraham Lincoln, the face of a hook-nosed monkey, a life-size Buddha squatting on a ledge, and flowers of rock carved by falling water. Two million wrinkle-lip bats reside in the cave; every evening they fly out to feed, forming swirling black ribbons in the twilight sky. At the far end of Deer Cave, a valley called the Garden of Eden contains two additional caves, a forest, a stream, and several waterfalls.

Clearwater Cave is the longest cave passage in Asia and the seventh-longest known cavern in the world, extending at least 66 miles and with much more as yet uncharted. Through it flows a maze of sparkling crystal-clear rivers. At the cave's

George Leposky, Interval International

Entrance to Deer Cave in Gunung Mulu.

mouth, reached by a climb of 250 steps up the side of a cliff, grow plants of a unique species with no stem or apparent roots. A short distance within the cave, a solitary stalagmite casts a shadow known as Our Lady.

Wind and Lang caves, though smaller, are renowned for the superlative quality of their rock formations. Wind Cave takes its name from the constant cool breeze that blows through it. A narrow passage leads to the King's Chamber, which is noted for its intricately carved stalactites and stalagmites that resemble giant chessboard figures—all surrounded by wall "tapestries" washed by minerals of various hues and textures. Lang Cave, named after the guide who happened upon it in 1977, contains some of the world's most beautiful rock formations, many of which have evocative names such as Cave Curtain, Jellyfish, Rainforest, and Totem Pole. In one part of the cave, a covered passageway that protects low-hanging stalactites offers visitors a close look at these intriguing formations.

Cavers who seek to roam beyond the beaten path may apply in advance to the national park for permission to visit seven "adventure caves" wherein exploration may entail abseiling (rappelling), climbing, crawling, and/or swimming. In addition, at least 18 separate routes, ranging in length from 2,900 feet to 15.5 miles, have been mapped. Many expeditions require knowledge of technical rope work for abseiling and climbing.

Lessons Learned

Club Asia International's experience points to the value of ecotourism as a focal point for sustainable tourism development. It also demonstrates that timesharing can add value to a sustainable ecotouristic enterprise.

More generally, timesharing creates a reservoir of owner-members who, through their purchases, commit to a given resort property or a multisite vacation club. By virtue of their commitment, owners are likely to return to their home resort or to

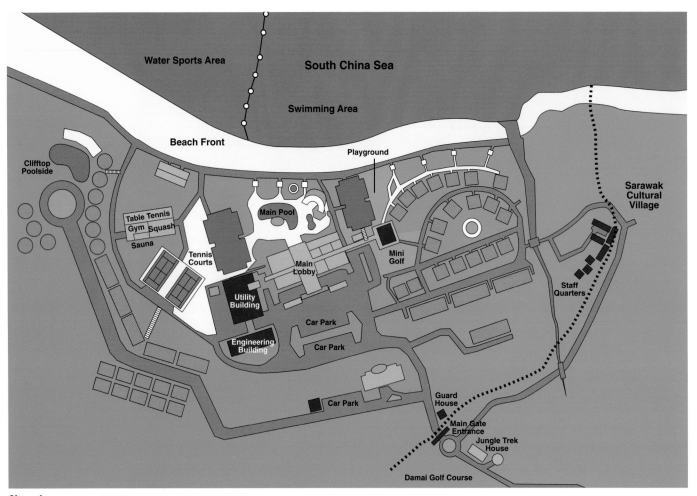

Site plan.

their club's various venues with greater frequency than the average transient guest, as shown by studies in the Canary Islands, the Caribbean, Mexico, and other destinations.

The propensity of owners to use their vacation accommodations is one reason that timeshare resorts and mixed-use (hotel and vacation-ownership) properties tend to experience higher occupancies than most hotels and resorts without a vacation-ownership component. Moreover, when owners do exchange away from their home resort, they create an exchange-network inventory that meets the needs of other owners. Exchanges help maintain occupancy rates as well as ensure the generation of revenues from food and beverage operations, guide services, boat and bicycle rentals, and other fee-based amenities

and activities. Indeed, timeshare owners and exchange guests may be expected to spend more on ancillary items because their accommodation costs, already paid for, do not figure into their current vacation budget.

Timeshare exchange also has the potential to attract to ecotourism resorts timeshare visitors from all parts of the world. The comparability aspect of the exchange process makes exchange especially attractive to timeshare travelers from distant locations. Owners are assured that, no matter how wild and remote the destination, the accommodations awaiting them will meet the same standards of comfort and overall quality that they have come to expect at their own timeshare unit or through their vacation club membership.

◆ Project Data

Development Schedule

	Construction Completed	Number of Units
Crowne Plaza Riverside Kuching	1992	228
Holiday Inn Resort Damai Lagoon	1994	253
Holiday Inn Resort Damai Beach	1986	302
Holiday Inn Kuching	—-	305
Damai Rainforest Resort	—-	45[1]
Bukit Saban Resort	1995	50
Royal Mulu Resort	1992 and 1996[2]	149

Land Use Information

Site Area	Acres
Crowne Plaza Riverside Kuching	(not available)
Holiday Inn Resort Damai Lagoon	25
Holiday Inn Resort Damai Beach	90
Holiday Inn Kuching	(not available)
Damai Rainforest Resort	44
Bukit Saban Resort	14
Royal Mulu Resort	200

Point Values and Prices[3]

Price of a Club Asia International membership	RM13,800 (US$3,632)
Number of points per membership	10,000
Total number of points in project	108,454,252
Total number of memberships	108,846
Potential project revenues	RM150 million (US$40 million)

Developer

Sara Worldwide Vacations Berhad
(a wholly owned subsidiary of Sarawak Economic Development Corporation)
Sarawak, Malaysia

Notes

1. Excluding four tents, which would have brought the total to 49.
2. Two phases.
3. December 10, 1998, exchange rates in the *Wall Street Journal:*
RM1 = US$.2632; US$1 = RM3.8.

Date of site visit: August 6–10, 1996; information updated December 1998
Author of case study: George Leposky

Hotel de L'Eau Vive

New Orleans, Louisiana

Hotel de L'Eau Vive (house of the living waters) is a small, purpose-built timeshare development in a series of restored historic buildings in the heart of downtown New Orleans. Two phases of construction have been completed, a third is underway, and a fourth phase is under consideration. In addition to 31 one-, two-, and three-bedroom time-share units that will be completed in the first three phases, the restored historic buildings include sun decks; a small, lushly landscaped interior patio with a bathing pool; and a clubroom where morning coffee and croissants are served. Developer Tom Bowes is considering the construc-

tion of an indoor swimming pool in the fourth phase. Services include 24-hour room service and concierge service and access to the New Orleans Athletic Club. Time is sold in fixed unit/weeks.

Hotel de L'Eau Vive is located in the center of the New Orleans tourist district on the Riverfront Streetcar route—two blocks from the Riverwalk, three blocks from the convention center, three blocks from the French Quarter, two blocks from the aquarium, and eight blocks from the Superdome.

Bowes has organized his vertically integrated business into a series of privately held corporations that include a construction company, a management company, and a sales company as well as a development company for each project. Hotel de L'Eau Vive is his third timeshare development.

Project Planning and Development

Bowes describes himself as "one of the last small boutique developers." Originally a stockbroker who also bought and renovated apartments in the French Quarter of New Orleans, he became a full-time developer in 1976. In 1978, amid rapidly escalating interest rates, Bowes realized that he would lose money if he continued to build condominiums. In the meantime, he had met a successful timeshare marketer in North Carolina and decided to try timeshare development in New Orleans, working in partnership with the marketing specialist. The result was Château Orleans, a 45-unit historic rehabilitation that is now sold and operating. His next project, Hotel de la Monet, located across from the mint, was a 54-unit, purpose-built development that is also sold and operating.

Hotel de L'Eau Vive was formerly a right-to-use timeshare project developed through the rehabilitation of a historic building. The original developer was in jail at the time the property attracted Bowes's interest while the project itself was in Federal Savings and Loan Insurance Corporation receivership. Three savings and loans were fighting over loan amounts and positions, and the property lacked an experienced timeshare development manager. At the time, 100 unit/weeks of time had already sold. Bowes applied to and received approval from federal court to become the keeper (operator) of the property. A few months before the 1988 Republican national convention in New Orleans, the city's entire hotel stock was booked, but Hotel de L'Eau Vive stood vacant, prompting Bowes to lease the building for the convention. Soon afterward, he negotiated the purchase of the structure.

As part of the 1988 purchase agreement, Bowes promised to honor the 100 right-to-use lessees for the term of their leases, offering them the option of converting to fee-simple deeded ownership. Today, 40 of the original lessees remain. When purchased by Bowes, the building contained 17 suites. Today, it comprises 31 suites built in two phases, with eight more under construction in Phase III.

Not surprisingly, there are about only four or five other timeshare developers in New Orleans. Expansion of an existing timeshare development in New Orleans takes six to eight months because the application to the city planning commission requires a presentation to and approval of the city council and ratification by the mayor's office. Moreover, Louisiana's complicated 1985 Timeshare Act makes it almost impossible for new timeshare developers to enter the market. The law requires developers to put $1,000 in escrow for every unit/week in a development. The state holds the money for one year following sellout of the entire project. Thus, timeshare development is limited to entrepreneurs with very deep pockets. In addition, the Timeshare Act requires a state-chartered bank to act as the escrow agent for the developer; bankers are reluctant to perform this function. Fortunately for Bowes, the law grandfathers adjacent expansions of existing projects and thus did not cover Hotel de L'Eau Vive.

The project consists of three historic buildings located on the same city block. Two are attached; the third is separated from the others by an intervening parcel. (The intervening parcel is scheduled for development by the Windsor Court Hotel, which is located across the street, and will include a walkway connecting the two parts of Hotel de L'Eau Vive.) Bowes is considering developing a fourth phase in an adjacent historic building on the same block. The first phase of the project, developed from 1988 to 1991, primarily involved interior rehabilitation and redecorating. The

Photo on page 180: **Located just steps from the river and the Vieux Carré, Hotel de L'Eau Vive draws on the amenities of the city of New Orleans to attract buyers to its door.**

Phase II building required significant exterior work, including construction of a new facade and a new foundation in the front of the building. The Phase III building requires interior work only.

Design and Financing

With successive phases, Hotel de L'Eau Vive's units have become larger and the newer units include lockoff units. Each

An interior patio and garden with a small swimming pool offer owners and guests a cool, quiet respite from city streets.

lockoff is designed to be as comparable as possible to the primary unit. The first phase consisted of three one-bedroom units. Of the units in the subsequent phases, one-third are two-bedroom, one-bath; one-third are two-bedroom, two-bath; and one-third are three-bedroom, two-bath units with a lockoff unit. In Phase III, all eight units include lockoffs, which means that each is exchangeable through Interval International as two one-bedroom suites. In fact, Interval International has bestowed five-star status on the project.

Units feature exposed-brick walls, fully equipped kitchens with wood cabinets, living and dining rooms, sleeper-sofas, color television, private telephones, and full baths with whirlpool tubs. Furnishings are simple, emphasizing natural materials such as wrought iron, glass, and pine.

At first, Bowes sought passive investors to finance his projects. Now, he acquires and develops the properties with his own money. All project financing is cash. There is no lender participation, and buyers know that the property carries no debt.

Marketing

The offering price for a unit/week is determined by Bowes's cost of doing business and producing the unit and the prices charged by the competition. Certain weeks, such as Mardi Gras, Jazz Fest, and the Sugar Bowl, sell at premium prices.

Early in the development, prices started at $11,800 for a fixed week in a two-bedroom unit. Current prices range from $7,000 to $8,000 per unit/week for a three-bedroom, two-bath suite with a lockoff unit. The competition in the timeshare industry—a comparable unit in another five-star resort—costs $14,000 to $18,000. Prices at Hotel de L'Eau Vive are low because Bowes incurs almost no marketing costs.

At one time, marketing costs accounted for 50 percent of the sales price of Bowes's units. By cutting marketing costs and

Diane R. Suchman

passing the savings on to the consumer, Bowes found that he could sell the product easily and earn the same profit.

Throughout the marketing of the first two phases and during the beginning of Phase III, Bowes employed about 50 full-time street solicitors. The solicitors offered prospective buyers incentive gifts such as telephones, tents, pots and pans, and even aerial tours of the city in exchange for listening to a sales presentation. One problem associated with urban timeshare developments in general is that city ordinances often prohibit street solicitation—the most common means of attracting prospective buyers. Of late, New Orleans has enacted such an ordinance.

Despite the ordinance, the major impetus for changing the project's sales strategy was expedience. While organizing a Grand Prix race in New Orleans in 1990–1991, Bowes was unable to devote full attention to marketing the timeshare development. To generate income during that period, he tapped into New Orleans's strong demand for hotel rooms and rented units to overnight guests. At the same time, he marketed timeshare purchases to pleased customers. The strategy proved so successful that, today, the sales process is entirely passive. The project runs as a hotel operated for the benefit of its owners. Bowes rents units for owners not using their time. (He does not rent unsold time except during major events; such rentals would undermine service to the owners.) Renting is easy because of the project's excellent location; in addition, nearby hotels refer their overflow guests. Referrals also come from former renters. The project is fully occupied every Friday. Other sales prospects are guests who exchange time through Interval International.

Bowes relies on a highly qualified concierge to use no-pressure tactics to inform overnight guests about the potential for time purchase. The concierge receives a small commission on every sale. Some walk-ins also purchase time. The goal is to

Unit interiors are simply but comfortably furnished and warmed by wood and brick walls.

sell intervals at less than half the price the competition charges for a similar product. Reservations to purchase weeks in future units are accepted for a $1,000 deposit.

In 1997, Bowes sold 150 weeks. When he used more extensive—and typical—marketing, he sold 500 weeks in a year. Though the sales volume now is lower, the marketing costs that offset the higher sales income are not there, and the bottom line is the same. In addition, the passive sales strategy requires fewer employees and less management time and attention.

First-floor unit floor plans.

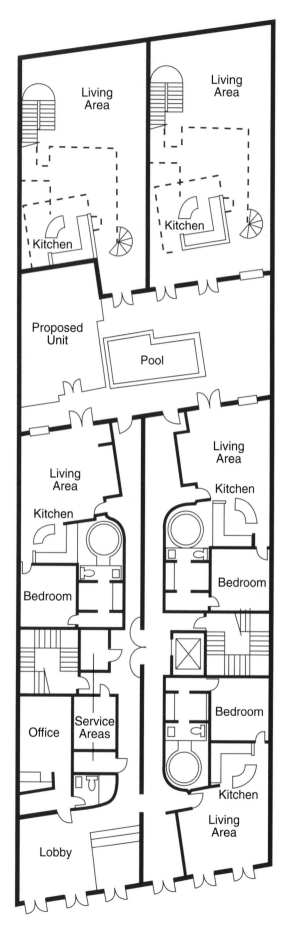

Management

Each property is ultimately owned by an owners' association. Bowes owns a management company that manages his first two projects under contract to the owners' associations. With a project that is developed in phases, each phase establishes its own owners' association. When a phase sells out and the owners of that phase assume control of their association from the developer, the owners' associations merge. A phase that is under construction operates under a "services and servitude agreement" whereby it pays a fee for use of the common amenities until the owners' associations merge. The annual assessment (including management fees and property tax) is currently $450 per unit week.

As management by the developer is handed over to an owner-controlled board, board members assume staggered terms. In this way, the association never operates with an inexperienced board, and new members have an opportunity to learn about management of a timeshare development.

Experience Gained

The most successful aspect of Hotel de L'Eau Vive is its almost nonexistent marketing costs. Bowes has learned that he can compete successfully with larger, better-known timeshare developers simply by offering a high-quality product at a much lower price.

The market for timeshare products is constantly changing and the product offered must be adjusted or upgraded to meet evolving market expectations. For example, the units in Château Orleans were small—400 square feet—and consisted of a living room, small kitchen, bedroom, and small bath. As an indication of industry changes, the units in Hotel de L'Eau Vive total 1,000 square feet or more, with two or three bedrooms, two baths, and a full kitchen—and some feature lockoff units or exchange units.

Because the market depth for timeshare development in New Orleans—indeed, in the nation—is untested, Bowes prefers to "take small bites" of eight or ten or 12 units at a time. Moreover, in urban settings, expensive land and buyer expectations dictate fewer on-site amenities and fewer services directed to children and families.

To cut costs and maintain control, Bowes provides almost all services in-house. He frames all the construction himself and personally selects interior furnishings. Because good maintenance is essential to customer satisfaction, Bowes replaces all upholstered furnishings every two years and redecorates common areas every five years.

Though resales remains a major long-term issue for the industry, resale potential has not been a problem for Hotel de L'Eau Vive. Bowes suggests that perhaps timeshare developers could offer resale services to owners in the same way that he sells units of time. He has found that timeshare development is more profitable than condominium development. (A reasonable profit would be $5,000 on each unit/week.) And, according to Bowes, "It's a lot more fun."

◆ Project Data

Development Schedule

	Phase I	Phase II	Phase III
Number of units	22	9	8
Planning started	1987	1991	1997
Construction started	1988	1992	1998
Construction completed	1989	1993	1998
Sales started	1989	1993	1998
Sales completed	1991		

Land Use Information

Site Area

Phase I	50 feet x 150 feet
Phase II	25 feet x 110 feet
Phase III	50 feet x 100 feet

Total number of timeshare units planned	60
Total number of timeshare units completed	31
Off-street parking spaces	none

Unit Information

Unit Type	Square Feet
One-bedroom	700
Two-bedroom	820
Three-bedroom	1,000

Unit Prices		Average Price per Week
Phase I	$11,800 (using former marketing program)	
Phase II		$6,000–$7,000
Phase III		$7,000–$8,000

Total Project Costs (hard and soft costs)

Phase I	$1 million
Phase II	$1 million
Phase III	$1 million

Annual operating expenses (Phases I and II, 1997)	$554,000
Annual maintenance fee (Phases I and II, 1997)	$423.85

Rental Rates (1997) per Night

One-bedroom suites	$170
Two-bedroom suites	$210
Two-bedroom, two-bath	$225
Three-bedroom, two-bath	$285
Presidential atrium suites	$285

Developer

Benjamin Harrison Interests, LLC
New Orleans, Louisiana

Date of site visit: July 8, 1998
Author of case study: Diane R. Suchman

Orange Tree Golf & Conference Resort

Scottsdale, Arizona

Orange Tree Golf & Conference Resort is a 160-unit urban regional timeshare project in Scottsdale, Arizona, one of the country's most popular resort destinations. The project is built around rather than near a golf course. Designed in 1953 by Johnny Bulla, a prominent golfer and golf course architect, the course has become one of Arizona's five most popular golf courses and is noted for its mature, tree-lined links and 108 acres of verdant beauty and strategic challenges. The 18-hole course is a par 72 with a slope rating of 120 and a course rating of 71.3 (both about average for a golf course). The resort includes a full driving range, one of the largest golf shops in the state, attended

locker rooms, two practice putting greens, and two bunkered practice chipping greens. Facilities include 7,000 square feet of lobby and restaurant space, 10,000 square feet of meeting space, and indoor and outdoor restaurants.

Orange Tree is owned by Shell Vacations, LLC, a developer of timeshare units, with corporate offices in Northbrook, Illinois, and Orlando, Florida. Founded in 1963, the company has developed more than 40 vacation-ownership projects with more than $2 billion in sales to over 150,000 families. One of the largest of the world's independent timeshare developers, Shell Vacations entered the timeshare industry by accident. It purchased a foreclosed condominium project in Orlando for little money down and converted it to a time-share development. Known as Vistana, the development became one of the largest timeshare developments in the world. Shell later sold Vistana to General Development Corporation; today, Vistana is a public company.

Officials at Shell describe their initial corporate strategy as "opportunistic development." In other words, they sought out opportunities to acquire projects that were available at favorable prices. Because few inexpensive projects are now available for purchase, Shell is shifting its emphasis from a price- to a location-driven strategy, seeking to acquire or build projects situated in areas where rapid growth is expected in the next several years.

Each Shell resort is a separate legal entity within a network of companies operated under the guidance of Shell Vacations. For instance, Shell Vacations owns Shell Orange Tree, LLC. In turn, Shell Orange Tree, LLC, owns the golf course and hotel and, at one time, owned OTIOR, LLC, a company that once held title to the Orange Tree timeshare units but continues to perform all sales and marketing functions. Shell also provides services for its own companies and others in a wide range of areas, including real estate acquisition, financing, asset management and consulting, investment, and management of commercial, hotel, resort, and vacation-ownership properties.

Orange Tree is one of the industry's stellar success stories. Shell's inventory of 8,100 interval units sold out in three and one-half years—18 months ahead of schedule—generating more than $60 million in total sales.

Location and Site

Located in Arizona's Valley of the Sun, Orange Tree is adjacent to Scottsdale's western boundary with Phoenix. A resort town with a population of 200,000, Scotts-dale lies within the Sonoran Desert at the base of the McDowell Mountains, a location influenced by the area's dynamic and diverse Southwestern culture and great natural beauty.

Boasting more than 60 hotels and resorts, the area accounts for 11,000 hotel rooms. More than 6.7 million people visited the area in 1997, attracted by Scottsdale's average median temperature of 70 degrees and an abundance of sun (the sun shines on 86 percent of the days). Accordingly, the Valley of the Sun has evolved into a world-renown mecca for golfers, with more than 100 courses. In addition, it attracts families who do not play golf but enjoy other amenities such as swimming, tennis, and hiking.

Project Planning and Development

According to Franklin Khedouri, regional vice president of Shell Vacations, LLC's western division, Orange Tree has experienced several incarnations during the past four decades. It opened as a private country club in 1955 but failed. Later, an entrepreneur purchased all the club memberships and opened Orange Tree to the public. A 14,000-square-foot conference center was added in 1986, and a 160-room luxury hotel, designed in the style of noted architect Frank Lloyd Wright, was built two years later. Because of Arizona's depressed economy and the owner's serious operating mistakes, the luxury hotel business proved unsuccessful. By 1990, Orange Tree was in default to its lenders.

About that time, representatives of Shell struck a deal with the owner to purchase the property through an arrangement that would alleviate the debt problems and provide the owner with a minority interest in Orange Tree. The owner agreed. Shell arranged for financing with FINOVA, a local lender that has since established a national presence. Days later, the proprietor had seller's remorse and backed out

Photo on page 186:
Originally built as a hotel, the property has become a time-share success story.

of the deal, forcing the property into foreclosure. Shell representatives contacted the lender, Security Pacific (later bought by Bank of America), and made an extremely low bid for the property, offering a large nonrefundable deposit and agreeing to close the deal in 90 days. Representatives of the lenders, doubting that the transaction would be closed in three months and hoping to make a quick profit, accepted Shell's offer.

Based on earlier negotiations with the owner, Shell knew that cash flow from the golf course, food and beverage service, con-

The resort's most stellar amenity is its legendary Johnny Bulla golf course.

ference center, and hotel would service the debt, allowing the company to establish an extremely favorable price structure for a timeshare venture. According to Khedouri, Shell obtained the entire property—which included 160 suites similar to an Embassy Suites product, an 18-hole golf course, and restaurants and other facilities—for a mere $15 million, a significant discount from the $25 million loan Security Pacific held on the facility. Not only was the purchase an inexpensive acquisition of hotel accommodations and facilities, but the arrangement also included a prized golf course that attracted $1.8 million a year in business. (Today, the golf course alone is probably worth $14 million.)

As already noted, FINOVA provided funding for acquisition of the Orange Tree Golf & Conference Resort; Shell contributed about $4 million in equity. The financing involved several different types of mortgages. According to Khedouri, the acquisition loan for the commercial facilities totaled $2 million while the debt for the golf course was about $6.5 million. Shell borrowed $6 million for the units themselves and sought another $1 million in working capital. Shell also arranged a hypothecation loan of about $19 million to fund sales and marketing efforts and to finance timeshare buyers' purchase of the units. Shell spent $6,000 per unit on renovating the one-bedroom suites, making the cost of the timeshare units around $68,000 per key, which is extremely low by current standards.

Khedouri notes that because sales and marketing costs can account for up to 50 percent of a unit's cost—and Orange Tree buyers put down only 10 percent—developers just starting out experience a cash shortfall of 40 percent for every unit sold. For example, for each week at Orange Tree that sold for $7,000, Shell collected a downpayment of about $700. Shell then had to pay FINOVA an agreed-upon release fee of $1,000 on the deed for each unit sold. Commissions, front-end marketing costs, administrative overhead, and other expenses added another $3,500. Thus, Shell was spending about $4,500 more than it was receiving upfront from the purchase. Obtaining the hypothecation loan enabled the company to continue operations until the project sold out.

Project and Unit Design

The 160 one-bedroom suites at Orange Tree are a 30-foot putt from one end to the other. All but one of the suites are identical, consisting of one bedroom and 780 square feet of living space. Units are clustered in a geometric architectural pattern—reminiscent of Frank Lloyd Wright's Southwestern style—in eight two-story buildings of 20 units each. (The noted American architect worked in the Phoenix area and his winter headquarters, Taliesin West, is a few miles down the road.)

The interiors are designed in a pink-and-gray color scheme, with semi–Southwestern color patterns, offsetting fabrics in vivid colors, and beige carpets. Amenities include a 25-inch television, AM/FM stereo, VCR, telephone with computer modem, refrigerated wet bar with coffee maker, six-foot shower, third telephone in the bathroom, double vanity, color television in the bathroom, and whirlpool spa. A French patio door leads to a private terrace.

Originally designed as hotel rooms, the units lacked a dividing wall between the living area and bedroom, a limitation that would normally have made them ineligible for a standard interval exchange. But the interior designer came up with the idea of a "soft separation"—a curtain effect. As a result, the exchange company accepted Orange Tree as a one-bedroom timeshare property. In addition, the units did not originally have full kitchens; microwave ovens were installed instead. If the interval exchange company had not approved either the soft separation or the microwave option, Shell would not have proceeded with the project. In addition to the micro-

Before or after a game of golf, vacationers can gather in an attractive linkside setting.

Courtesy of Shell Vacations, LLC

wave oven, the kitchen areas include a toaster and refrigerator.

Purchase Arrangements And Pricing

The first 40 units went on sale February 1, 1993. At that time, Orange Tree was the only property selling timeshare on site in Phoenix, and the only timeshare in Arizona located on a golf course. Even so, Shell officials proceeded cautiously. Rather than earmark all 160 units for timeshare, they

The resort accommodations are outfitted with comfortable furnishings in muted colors.

converted the clusters to timeshare in phases and initially offered only 20 units for timeshare purchase. By phasing sales, Shell could use the remaining units as a hotel if the timeshare concept proved unsuccessful. Thus, Orange Tree reduced its risks by adopting an exit strategy—something few other projects do. As it turned out, the project succeeded as a timeshare development.

At Orange Tree, Shell divided the year into various periods, or "seasons," each of which had a different price: $8,000 for the high season, $7,000 for the shoulder season, and $5,900 for the low season. Shell sold time in one-week intervals that floated within a season rather than in fixed weeks. Purchasers could, however, secure a fixed time period for a $1,000 premium. The legal interest purchased was a deeded interest in perpetuity, and owners received a fee-simple deed, just as if they had purchased a condominium.

Currently, the resort is affiliated with Interval International, and owners who choose to join that organization can exchange their unit/times through the system's worldwide exchange network. Although Orange Tree's timeshare plan currently involves only unit/week intervals, Shell is formulating plans to introduce a point system that will permit Orange Tree owners to exchange points for experiences such as a hotel stay, airplane trip, or cruise.

The development's major selling point was its legendary golf course. Among Scottsdale courses, Orange Tree is distinguished by its mature cottonwoods and ponderosa pines that shade the course and provide relief from the desert sun. At most other area courses, participants play under the sun. In addition, Orange Tree is easy to play. Players lose few golf balls and are not severely penalized if they are caught in a trap or slice a drive. Moreover, while other golf courses are irrigated with treated effluent, the greens at Orange Tree are watered by a well that pumps 1,000 gallons of crystal-clear water per minute onto the resort's grounds and lakes. In 1993, Orange Tree spent nearly $1 million on golf-related improvements, including refurbishing the sand traps, rebuilding the paths, and enlarging the pro shop.

Consumer purchases were financed with loans that required 10 percent down, with no qualifying criteria and no credit checks. Only individuals with a previous bankruptcy were disqualified. FINOVA financed all units. Orange Tree borrowed funds at the prime rate plus two percentage points and lent at prime plus four. The developer took the risk that profits would decline or even plunge to zero if interest rates rose. When, however, interest rates fell, the project made more money than projected. Today, Orange Tree offers loans at variable rates. It does not operate an in-house resales program.

Shell's Interval Owners Association (IOA) charges a fee of approximately $350 per week per unit/week, which includes real estate taxes and other expenses. Exchange fees are additional. Orange Tree offers a rental program operated through Shell Vacations's management company, Shell Hospitality. Under that program, Shell can rent a suite for $240 per night during the peak winter season and $80 per night in the summer. The company retains 25 percent of the fee; the remainder goes to the owner.

Sales and Marketing

The selling of timeshare units at the Orange Tree Golf & Conference Resort was unusual in that families living within 20 miles of Scottsdale accounted for 95 percent of sales. Indeed, Shell decided to market Orange Tree as an urban timeshare rather than as a resort. It reasoned that, as a major resort destination, Phoenix is a sprawling metropolis that lacks the focal points where

visitors congregate. In Maui, for example, nearly all tourists at one time or another walk along Front Street in Lahaina. Not so in Phoenix, where visitors travel to a specific resort and remain there. In addition, the area hosts few public events that provide a stream of visitors who might be enticed to attend a timeshare presentation.

In selling the resort's intervals, Shell benefited from a number of unforeseen factors. For example, while the project is legally located in Phoenix, it has a Scottsdale address. Scottsdale is considered an upscale suburban community beyond the reach of metropolitan Phoenix. In addition, Shell's sales personnel sold the resort as a lower-price alternative to higher-end timeshare projects—such as projects in Hawaii—that could be exchanged for other destinations. Representatives sold the *concept* of timesharing rather than Orange Tree itself as a place to return each year. Four-fifths of the families who purchased unit/weeks said that they intended to use their weeks for exchange purposes.

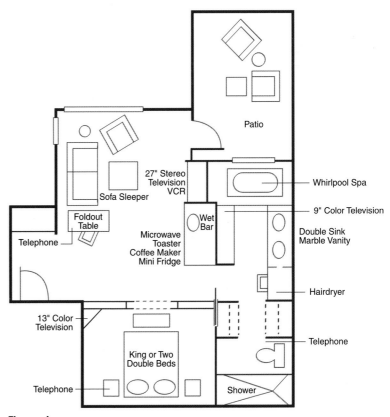

Floor plan.

Shell targeted sales to families with incomes of at least $40,000 whose heads were at least 28 years old. The company's marketing approach was simple and traditional and included telemarketing as well as selling in shopping malls and car washes and at events. Orange Tree personnel attended every major event in the state of Arizona and marketed at every major venue in Phoenix, including the America West Arena, which hosts the National Basketball Association's Phoenix Suns and concerts. Initially, Shell employed 50 telemarketers and, at its peak, made 1,600 presentations a month. To attract potential purchasers, Shell offered incentives ranging from rounds of golf at the resort to shopping and travel certificates.

When Shell started marketing Orange Tree, it found itself in the midst of a shortage of experienced timeshare sales and marketing personnel. In what proved to be a boon, the company did not have to offer salespersons the inflated salaries commanded by experienced marketing personnel in Orlando or Hawaii. Instead, Shell compensated sales personnel on the basis of a good wage for Phoenix rather than on the basis of a good wage for the timeshare industry, thereby lowering the project's projected sales and marketing costs. Accordingly, of total sales expenses, 45 cents of each dollar went to sales and marketing and 10 cents to administration. About 85 percent of the sales closed.

In the absence of competition, Shell could negotiate with outside suppliers who recruited potential clients for sales presentations. In the beginning, Orange Tree paid approximately $200 per tour; the average cost per tour has subsequently increased to over $300, with some competitors now paying over $450 per tour exclusive of premiums. At the same time, in the face of competition, the cost of gifts to prospective buyers has escalated from $40 to an average of $75.

In over 42 months, from February 1, 1993, to September 30, 1996, Shell sold 8,152 intervals at an average price of $7,240.

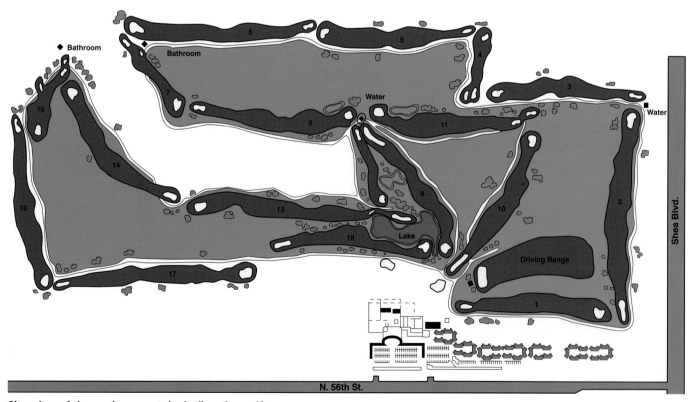

Site plan of the entire resort, including the golf course.

Currently, Orange Tree has about 40 intervals in inventory, primarily from foreclosures, that are for sale. The company initially budgeted its Orange Tree profit margin at under 15 percent, but actual profits achieved double that figure as a consequence of several factors, including high sales efficiency and the project's low cost. For instance, the average product cost in a five-star resort timeshare product is typically about 30 percent; the cost of the Orange Tree units was a mere 18 percent. In addition, given that Orange Tree sold out its intervals in less time than planned, Shell significantly reduced its financing expenditures.

Operations and Management

As noted, Shell Hospitality, a subsidiary of Shell Vacations, manages Orange Tree. Khedouri, regional vice president of Shell Vacations, LLC's western division, is responsible for the entire operation. He is the senior staff person on the property and serves as project director. The hospitality manager, marketing director, and sales director report to Khedouri.

One of the chief management challenges at Orange Tree was how to integrate the sales, marketing, and hotel staffs—all of which have different agendas. The marketing personnel are paid for producing sales prospects. The sales personnel are remunerated if a prospect purchases an interval. The hospitality staff wants to provide the best level of service possible and does not want sales personnel to pester guests. To resolve these issues, Shell instituted a system whereby each group coaches the other two to ensure that all three groups work together as a synergistic team.

Experience Gained

While an aggressive personality is often a positive attribute in the timeshare business, especially in sales, managing aggressive individuals in a way that allows for lati-

Courtesy of Shell Vacations, LLC

Units are clustered geometrically to take advantage of lake and golf course views and are interlaced with landscaped walkways.

tude while insisting on integrity can pose a major challenge. To ensure that salespersons did not make promises that they could not fulfill, Orange Tree placed great stress on honesty, with misrepresentation grounds for dismissal.

The Orange Tree experience illustrates that, if purchased at the right price, a timeshare development can generate a substantial profit. In fact, Shell could have earned an even greater profit by increasing its interval prices, but instead it decided in favor of providing customers with a good

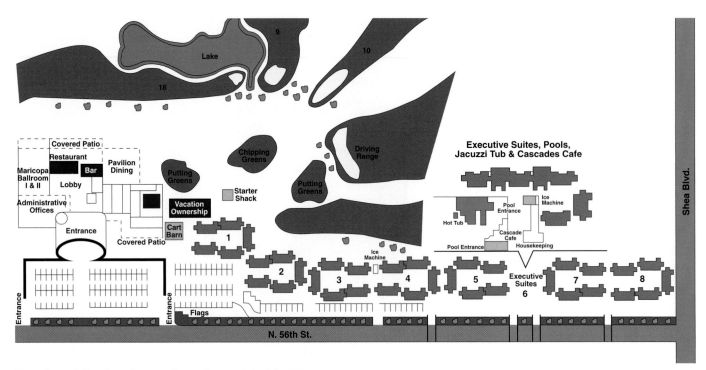

Site plan of the timeshare units and associated facilities.

deal, thereby selling out the project early. In a market with little competition, delivering superior value for the price is a strategy that leads to success.

Over the years, the timeshare industry has become more challenging. In most of today's markets, competition and escalating costs are formidable issues for timeshare developers. Many companies that are not earning profits on sales or that have seen their margins erode dramatically are surviving on financing alone. Tight labor pools also affect sales costs. In addition, customers have become more knowledgeable of timeshare and spend more time comparison shopping before making a purchase.

Another valuable lesson learned at Orange Tree is how to recover from a potential follow-up problem. Shell officials misjudged the length of time it would take to line up a new project after Orange Tree's sellout. The company believed that it had a contract with a developer to build a small timeshare project; at the last minute, however, the deal fell through. Thus, Shell found itself with one of the best sales forces in the country—but nothing to sell. The company decided to use Orange Tree as an off-site sales office for a Shell timeshare project in Hawaii—Paniolo Greens located on the Big Island of Hawaii between Waikolo and the Parker Ranch. As in the case with Orange Tree, Shell based its sales pitch on exchange and price value, with sales associates pointing out that comparable units on the beach seven miles away would cost twice as much. The strategy proved successful, and, according to Shell, the success of the Orange Tree off-site sales office exceeded that of Paniolo's on-site sales operation—a timeshare first.

◆ Project Data[1]

Development Schedule

Planning started	1992
Construction started	(not available)
Conversion completed	1993
Sales started	1993
Sales completed	1996

Land Use Information

Site area[2]	120 acres
Total number of timeshare units	160 on 8 acres
Gross density	20 units/acre

Unit Information

Unit type	one-bedroom, one-bath
Floor area	748 square feet
Average price/week (1996)	$7,240
Number of unit/weeks sold	8,160

Administrative, Recreation, and Commercial Facilities

	Square Feet
Reception building	1,428
Activities building	4,367
Restaurant/food service	12,400
Golf pro shop	1,860
Meeting and banquet space	13,500

Annual Assessments per Unit/Week (1997)

Operating costs	$314.70
Reserves	$45.67
Property tax	$26.63
Total—all fees	$387.00

Developer

Shell Vacations, LLC
Northbrook, Illinois
Orlando, Florida

Architect

Frizzell Hill Moorhouse Architects, Inc.
San Francisco, California

Interior Design

Resort Source
Chicago, Illinois

Merilee Elliott Interiors, Inc.
Chicago, Illinois

Notes

1. Project cost information is not available.
2. Including golf course.

Date of site visit: November 8, 1998
Author of case study: Mike Sheridan

Hilton Grand Vacations Club Flamingo Hilton

Las Vegas, Nevada

The Hilton Grand Vacations Club (HGVC) Flamingo Hilton is a 200-unit purpose-built vacation-ownership development constructed adjacent to the Flamingo Hilton Hotel on "the strip" in Las Vegas. As the first new timeshare resort developed by HGVC, the property opened on the south side of the Flamingo Hilton site. Sales of the timeshare units began in October 1993, and the project opened in October 1994. As of August 1998, the project was 95 percent sold, with full sellout expected by the end of 1998.

In 1996, HGVC opened its second new vacation club, adjacent to Sea World in Orlando, Florida. Two more HGVC timeshare facilities are now under construction and being sold in Las Vegas and Miami Beach.

Background

In 1992, Hilton Hotel Corporation followed the lead of other hotel chains and decided to enter the timeshare business. Timesharing had achieved consumer acceptance and appealed to a broad consumer base. Moreover, even though the hotel industry was in a downturn during the late 1980s and early 1990s, timeshares were experiencing reasonably strong sales. Lacking in-house expertise in the timeshare business, Hilton formed a joint venture partnership with Grand Vacations, Ltd., which had been created by American Resorts Development Co. and the Mariner Group. The resulting entity—HGVC—combined the established name recognition and financial strength of Hilton Hotels with the organizational experience, existing resort systems, and marketing opportunities represented by the existing owner base of Grand Vacations.

HGVC agreed to incorporate the 16 Grand Vacations resorts in south Florida into the HGVC system. Those resorts provided an instant owner base for the newly formed club. In addition, HGVC immediately affiliated with Resort Condominiums International to provide call-center and exchange services for HGVC members.

In deciding to build its first timeshare project in Las Vegas, Hilton took advantage of its single largest hotel concentration, which accounted for nearly 14,000 rooms in four properties. "One of the great challenges and expenses in the business is marketing," says Don Harrill, chief executive of HGVC. "We knew that by coming to Las Vegas, we'd have an existing nucleus of Hilton hotel customers to market to, thus minimizing our costs and risks." An additional draw was Las Vegas itself, which as one of the most popular tourist destinations in the country, offers a ready-made market of prospective timeshare customers.

In 1993, HGVC formed a homeowners' association (HOA), as required by Nevada law, that purchased the three-acre site at the Flamingo Hilton from Hilton Hotels Corporation. Under zoning that permitted additional density, Las Vegas rezoned the parcel for timeshare use. While several timeshare facilities are located in Las Vegas, the HGVC Flamingo Hilton is the city's first hotel-branded project.

HGVC self-finances its timeshare resorts and customer purchases of unit/weeks. Loans generally run for five to seven years with downpayments of 10 to 15 percent. Interest rates vary from 12 to 16 percent depending on the amount of the downpayment, the buyer's creditworthiness, and the choice of payment method. Loans are serviced in-house.

Resort Facilities and Design

One benefit of combining hotel and resort uses is the opportunity to leverage the hotel's existing amenity base. At the Flamingo Hilton Las Vegas HGVC, club members can share the hotel's tennis courts, restaurants, shops, wedding chapel, casino, health club, and pools with guests at the Flamingo Hilton. The hotel subsidizes these amenities, thereby permitting the homeowners' association to save money and enabling owners to obtain additional value for their investment. The hotel also benefits from the arrangement. For example, HGVC minivacation guests used 7,000 room nights at the Orlando Hilton in 1997. Likewise, the HGVC at the Flamingo Hilton keeps customers flowing through the hotel's stores, restaurants, and casino.

Even though the club and hotel share some amenities, the 16-story timeshare tower is a freestanding entity with its own front door and lobby. Club members have their own reception desk and check in separately from hotel guests; thus, they are spared the crowds and long waits sometimes endured by hotel guests. Club members enjoy exclusive use of the timeshare's private pool, along with a pool bar, workout room, small health club, and delicatessen. The separate facilities also make it possible for the HOA to be self-sustaining in the event that the hotel and HOA decide to operate independently—a consideration that is important to real estate regulators whose evaluations of long-term project feasibility are intended to protect the interests of purchasers.

Sixty percent of the timeshare units have two bedrooms; the rest, one. Hilton is developing a second Las Vegas timeshare club, which is slated to open in 1999, next to the Las Vegas Hilton. It will feature 232 one- and two-bedroom suites. The percent-

Photo on page 196:
The 200-unit HGVC Flamingo Hilton presents a dramatic appearance, looming majestically over the pools and palm trees below.

Fresh, bright colors illuminate unit interiors, which offer luxurious touches such as a spa tub in the master bath.

age of two-bedroom suites will be higher —80 percent.

Hilton finds that families spend more time in timeshare units than in hotel rooms and therefore expect all the amenities they enjoy in their private homes, such as telephones in every room, several televisions, and VCRs. The second-bedroom lockoff units, however, do not have kitchens but instead are equipped with a small refrigerator and a microwave oven. In response to owner demand, interactive television and safes will be incorporated into future timeshare units. Given the area's wide variety of nearby restaurants, HGVC members spend less time in the kitchen than at some other clubs' locations. Therefore, the kitchens in the new units at the Las Vegas Hilton timeshare will be 10 percent smaller and the living areas almost double in size. Overall, the new units will be smaller—1,220 square feet instead of 1,400 square feet—but the space is designed more efficiently to make the units appear larger. The new unit design also eliminates the entry hallway connecting the lockoff with the main unit. In addition, the simplified design features fewer architectural embellishments and corners, making the units easier to clean and less costly to maintain. Whereas the Flamingo units have whirlpool baths in both bedrooms, only the new units' master baths will feature whirlpools.

HGVC recently began creating full-scale models of all its timeshare units to provide representatives of various HGVC divisions with an opportunity to critique the products and their interior design and suggest refinements before the units are built. To the extent that individual sites permit, HGVC prefers to build standardized floor plans.

Purchase Arrangements And Pricing

HGVC offers purchasers a point-based system. When the vacation club first formed, it set forth a primary goal of achieving maximum flexibility. Thus, while club members purchase a secured deeded interest, the point-based reservations and exchange system enables members to select alternative ways to exercise their ownership.

For example, a purchaser usually buys a vacation week in a two-bedroom unit in a specific season. The purchase is equivalent to a designated number of vacation points. (The typical purchase averages $12,500 and is equivalent to 5,500 vacation points.) The purchaser must then select one of HGVC's resorts as a home base. That resort is listed on the deed, but members are free to use their points at any HGVC location or at certain other resorts with which HGVC has established an affiliation. As a result, although members technically hold a real estate property interest in a specific location, the location is not fixed; in practice, they own a bundle of vacation rights.

Members can use their points to maximize what is most important to them. For example, a member might decide to obtain more vacation time by traveling during a low-demand season or staying in a lockoff. A lockoff unit requires fewer points than a primary unit.

HGVC members can exchange or convert points in three ways.

◆ They may use points to vacation within the HGVC system of 23 resorts, including the resorts recently developed in Las Vegas and Florida and the 16 resorts in south Florida that were part of the original Grand Vacations portfolio. They may also use their points at resorts in Mexico and Hawaii that are available through HGVC's alliances with Fiesta Americana Hotels and Bay Club. A member who owns a week at HGVC-Las Vegas and wants to vacation at HGVC-Orlando can use HGVC points as currency to "purchase" a vacation in the second location at a designated time. If an owner selects a resort other than the home resort, he or she must pay a small transaction processing fee.

◆ Members may also convert their HGVC points into Hilton Honors points and redeem them for stays at Hilton Hotels, airline tickets, cruises, car rentals, casino chips, and so forth. All HGVC members automatically become members of the Hilton Honors program, which functions much like an airline frequent flyer program.

◆ Members may exchange points through RCI to vacation in more than 3,300 resort destinations around the world.

Although points expire at the end of the year, HGVC members are permitted to redeposit their points for up to one year. For example, in a given year, a couple might decide to save their points in order to rent several units for an extended-family get-together the following year. Members may also borrow points against the next year. "At my old company," says Dave Pontius, who heads HGVC owner services, "members were allowed to bank points longer and we saw people procrastinating and pushing their points out further and further. Our attitude at Hilton is if you buy with us, you're going on vacation." HGVC members who are not able to use their points for two years may exchange them for an equivalent amount of Hilton Honors points, which do not expire.

Following the national trend of shorter vacations, members may reserve split weeks. At the Las Vegas Flamingo Hilton club, more than half of members have used their points to vacation in three- or four-day increments. Some owners acquire points by placing their lockoffs in the RCI exchange pool and thus spend three or four vacations each year in Las Vegas.

The club reservation system is partly organized on a first-come, first-served basis; however, members who want to vacation in their "home unit" can reserve their unit up to 12 months in advance and enjoy first priority. By contrast, "open season" reservations are accepted right up to the day before arrival, and all members have access to whatever club inventory is left unreserved. Fewer than 20 percent of HGVC members reserve at their home resort during their priority period.

Marketing and Sales

People do not generally shop for timeshare products. Therefore, one of the industry's greatest challenges and expenses is attracting the attention of prospective customers. HGVC typically spends about 45 percent of the product's retail sales price on marketing, sales, and commissions (plus administrative costs). In Las Vegas, however, Hilton operates four large hotels, which provide a large marketing base. On the other hand, with no major presence in Orlando and Miami, the company must spend a considerable amount for direct mail to invite people to visit HGVC properties. Moreover, the company must negotiate with an outside hotel for the right to set up an OPC booth to meet with guests.

Most of the 80 to 100 couples that visit the Flamingo timeshare resort each day were referred by the OPC at the Flamingo Hilton Hotel. HGVC operates several OPC booths in each of its Las Vegas hotels. The OPCs offer incentives such as free show tickets, dinner coupons, or casino chips to visitors who agree to tour the timeshare resort. Hilton also sends out direct mail, offering subsidized minivacations in Las Vegas in exchange for participation in a sales presentation.

"The Hilton name is our most valuable asset," says Harrill. "It affects everything from our product design to marketing and operations. But having a brand name also creates special challenges. It means we have more at stake and have to treat Hilton customers with kid gloves. Therefore, our marketing style is deliberately low key. When a Hilton guest walks away from an OPC contact, for example, we want them to be happy with Hilton, whether or not they're interested in our timeshare product."

Three or four waves of couples tour the Flamingo Hilton timeshare each day. Tours last 90 minutes. The conversion rate is approximately 15 percent. While the rate was higher in past years, many buyers rescinded. Nevada state law mandates a five-day "cooling off" period. To protect the Hilton brand name and reputation, HGVC would often return purchasers' money well after the rescission cut-off date. One reason for the high rate of rescissions, according to Harrill, is that "we overpromised and the customers' expectations were unrealistic." As a result, Harrill instituted what he calls "a kinder, gentler" sales approach.

Harrill says it was necessary to exert more control over the sales force and retrain the staff to take a less aggressive approach—a major challenge in an industry where salespersons often work on commission. One control method Hilton uses is "shopping" its staff. HGVC employs "mystery firms" to send out prospects, typically a couple, who pretend to be interested timeshare customers. They check into the Flamingo Hilton Hotel, meet with the OPC, sign up for a tour, and then purchase a timeshare unit. The shoppers tape the entire process and prepare a transcript for HGVC executives. In this way, management keeps informed of staff practices and can better control the marketing/sales process. In some instances, a shopper report indicating that a particular salesperson (or counselor, as a salesperson is called) is "overselling"—for example, raising unrealistic expectations—might be the basis for firing that member of the sales force, even if he or she is a top seller. As a result, Hilton's sales rate is somewhat slower than in the past, but its rescission rate has decreased.

Harrill also improved control of the OPCs by staffing them with HGVC employees rather than with contractors. At the same time, Hilton increased the number of OPC booths.

Because Las Vegas draws vacationers and convention-goers from around the country, Hilton has made the Las Vegas sales center at the Flamingo Hilton timeshare into a distribution hub. The sales center features information about the Hilton timeshare resorts in Florida and the two resorts in Las Vegas. Prospective purchasers can also view photographs of other RCI resorts throughout the world.

Palm trees rise from within the club's freeform swimming pool, which is both a day- and night-time amenity.

Courtesy of Hilton Grand Vacations Club

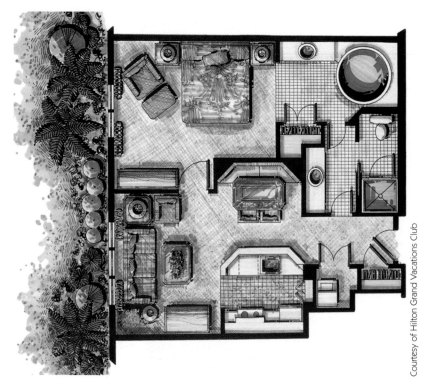

One-bedroom suite.

In 1999, Hilton will open a second major sales center in Las Vegas at the Las Vegas Hilton, where it is now building a new timeshare resort.

HGVC has sold 20,000 memberships since it started in 1993 and is adding approximately 6,000 to 7,000 members each year. In 1997, the Flamingo Hilton timeshare resort earned an award in recognition of its high sales rate—the highest single-site sales in one year for any timeshare facility. What the award did not mention is that "that same year we lost several million dollars," notes Harrill. "The volume was fine," says Harrill, "but we spent too much money achieving that volume." HGVC now spends about 40 to 45 percent of the purchase price amount on sales and marketing—a lower proportion today than in the past.

If, however, HGVC members follow the trend of other timeshare owners and purchase additional units, Hilton will probably save on future marketing costs. Pontius says that between 10 and 20 percent of HGVC members own timeshares in other resorts outside the club. Based on HGVC's

annual customer survey, he estimates that about 60 percent of HGVC owners aspire to purchase additional Hilton timeshare intervals. "This is where customer satisfaction, which we try so hard to achieve, can really pay off."

Most HGVC members are married couples between the ages of 45 and 65, college-educated, with household incomes greater than $70,000. More than 30 percent have incomes exceeding $130,000. Hilton does not make sales offers to persons with annual incomes less than $60,000. Most owners are from California and the Midwest. Hilton is developing new vacation products and experiences—such as bicycle trips, cruises, river rafting, sailboat trips, and so forth—that will appeal to the younger members of the baby boom generation.

Resales

When all the units at the Flamingo timeshare resort are sold, Hilton will offer owners a resales service. As at the other resorts managed by Hilton, sellout creates a resales market. The economics of resale are such, however, that it is too costly to provide the resales service from existing sales centers. Sales centers operate at 40 to 45 percent of retail sales costs. Therefore, to facilitate resales, HGVC has found that it must use less costly, slower, and less productive channels, such as the Internet —possibly in conjunction with independent broker networks—to achieve a satisfactory price for existing owners.

Management and Operations

Because it is a recognized brand name in the hotel industry, HGVC first operated the timeshare resort as a hotel, renting out units until they sold. With the hotel reservation systems already in place, HGVC used the systems to book the rooms. The rental income helped defray the project's carrying costs. As units sold, the hotel portion of the resort grew smaller and the homeowners' association took over more ownership of the building. In fall 1998, HGVC turned over operation of the resort to the board of directors of the homeowners' association. The company continues to manage the project under contract to the HOA.

Annual club fees amount to $82 a year, which includes RCI services. Members' annual homeowners' association assessments for 1999, which cover expenses such as real estate taxes, operating expenses, resort maintenance, and insurance, average $450 for a one-bedroom unit and $492 for a two-bedroom unit.

Managing the club system has posed specific challenges. One of Harrill's first actions when he joined HGVC was to establish an owner services department and set up in-house customer service-related operations. Previously, HGVC had contracted out services such as telemarketing, customer service, and telephone inquiries. For example, HGVC had used RCI to handle customer inquiries. The arrangement worked as long as club members knew exactly what they wanted, but most members did not fully understand the product they had purchased and all the intricacies of the complicated point system. The problem, according to Harrill, was that RCI did not have the knowledge base to respond adequately to owners' wide-ranging inquiries, which ran the gamut from loan payments and maintenance fees to reservations. Owners were frustrated because they could not get their questions answered quickly and easily. By consolidating owner services functions in-house, Hilton could train its staff to respond to the myriad of owner inquiries.

HGVC has also centralized its management functions wherever possible. For example, Hilton's corporate office in Orlando handles member services and computer operations, whereas day-to-day operations, such as housekeeping and programming social activities for club members, are

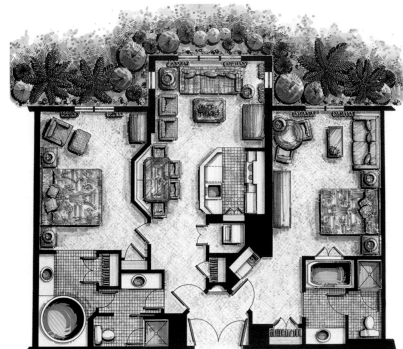

Two-bedroom suite.

Courtesy of Hilton Grand Vacations Club

handled on site. According to Pontius, the centralization of functions has enabled HGVC to achieve certain economies of scale that bring down costs. Hilton recently switched its straight cable service to a cable/on-command provider (both in its hotels and timeshares), which as a revenue-sharing program, is less expensive than cable. Pontius attributes 1999's slightly lower maintenance fees largely to increased efficiencies and centralization of functions.

After enduring frustrations with off-the-shelf computer software and contracted computer services, HGVC decided to develop and manage its own computer system. Pontius notes that HGVC's in-house computer system required a few years' investment that has paid off handsomely; the only significant expense is system maintenance. HGVC employs a staff of four who serve 500 computer users throughout the company. "Systems design," says Pontius, "is critical to providing comprehensive customer service, especially if you want to achieve the flexibility that our owners expect."

Site plan.

Experience Gained

"In developing a club product, one of the most important things is keep it simple," says Dave Pontius. In the beginning, HGVC had a long list of rules that often confused and frustrated customers who did not understand the vacation club concept. Moreover, the rules were too complicated to explain to prospective members in 90 minutes. Within two years, HGVC completely redesigned its club product, simplifying the point system and streamlining or eliminating many of the rules to make the club more consumer-friendly. Even so, the club system remains more complicated than an individual timeshare product and requires significant infrastruc-

ture to support its operations. This complexity poses a major barrier to entry for smaller operators.

Another significant challenge is securing sales staff knowledgeable of real estate and the timeshare business. Many persons in the industry are salespersons experienced in selling products, not real estate. However, many of the questions asked by prospective buyers revolve around real estate matters, such as deeds, mortgages, and resales. Thus, sales staff must undergo comprehensive training in real estate issues relating to the timeshare business.

One advantage of a mixed-use facility is the opportunity for efficient integration of some hotel and timeshare operations systems. Hilton, for example, inte-

◆ Project Data

Development Schedule (Phase I)

Number of units	200
Planning started	July 1992
Construction started	June 1993
Construction completed	October 1994
Sales started	October 1993
Sales completed	November 1998 (projected)

Land Use Information

Site area	3 acres
Total number of timeshare units planned	200
Total number of timeshare units completed	200

Unit Information

Unit Type	Square Feet	Number of Units Planned/ Number Completed
One-bedroom	900	60/60
Two-bedroom	1,325	140/140

Unit Prices (1997)	Average Price per Week	Weeks Sold
One-bedroom	$13,000	2,637
Two-bedroom	$16,000	6,892

Project Costs (1997)

Project Costs (1997)	Hard Costs	Soft Costs
Phase I—total	$46,000,000	$5,000,000
Phase I—per unit	$230,000	$25,000

Annual Operating Expenses (1997)—Phase I

Annual resort operations	$5,500,000
Annual sales center operations	$15,000,000

Developer

Hilton Grand Vacations Company
Orlando, Florida

Architect

Sandy & Babcock International
San Francisco, California

Date of site visit: October 6, 1998
Author of case study: Terry Jill Lassar

grated the telephone systems of the Flamingo Hotel and the timeshare. Timeshare owners can also use hotel restaurants and bill charges to their unit, just the way hotel guests can bill expenses to their hotel room.

Harrill has found the Hilton name to be a mixed blessing in timeshare development. "When we started, there was a feeling that the brand association would immediately improve the pace of sales. In reality, sales slowed as 'brand representation require-ments' were applied." Learning to improve performance while still protecting the brand took time, during which Hilton deferred initial plans for rapid expansion. Central to the long-term commitment of the Hilton brand was ensuring that salespersons made accurate representations, Harrill explained. "At the same time, we focused on building a strong customer service support team dedicated to meeting owners' expectations and delivering quality products."

The Bay Club at Waikoloa

Waikoloa, Hawaii

The Bay Club is a 125-unit vacation-ownership property located in the destination resort community of Waikoloa on the Big Island of Hawaii. The property was purchased in 1991 while under construction with the intent of selling the units as condominiums. The Bay Club is an example of how vacation ownership can be implemented successfully when a troubled economy halts a condominium sales strategy. Since sales began in 1995, The Bay Club has proven itself one of the top-selling vacation-ownership projects in the world.

The Bay Club includes 18 one-bedroom/ one-bath units, 36 one-bedroom/one-and-one-half-bath units, 90 two-bedroom/two-bath units, and 28 two-bedroom/two-and-one-half-bath units. Situated on a 15.5-acre site, the project consists of 172 units housed in six three-story buildings with elevators and seven two-story fourplex buildings. Units are fully furnished and feature gourmet kitchens, private lanais, and mid-week maid service. Outdoor amenities include two swimming pools with hydro spas, men's and women's saunas, two plexipaved tennis courts, a fitness center, and barbecue and picnic areas. A full-service activities desk is located on site to help residents schedule activities during their stay.

The Bay Club is a member of the Waikoloa Beach Resort, which owns and manages all of the master-planned community's recreational facilities. Owners and residents of The Bay Club are offered reduced rates for use of the community's two golf courses —$55 per play compared with $85 for nonowner residents of Waikoloa. Bay Club owners are also entitled to reduced rates on other recreational activities within Waikoloa, such as snorkeling, scuba diving, deep-sea fishing, sunset cruises, and helicopter tours.

Although the property contains 172 units in total, only 125 are included within the vacation-ownership program. Thirteen units are part of a long-term lease to a separate operator that, in turn, markets the units as short-term vacation rentals. Seven of the remaining units are privately owned, and the remaining 27 are used for offices and sales support functions. (Over time, the owners intend to include 40 more units in the timeshare program, for a total of 165 timeshare units.)

Location and Site

Waikoloa is a full-service resort community located on the Big Island's Kohala Coast, approximately 18 miles north of Kona International Airport and 25 miles north of Kona, the island's second largest town. Part of a 31,000-acre landholding under development by the Waikola Land Company, the resort community offers visitors a wide range of recreational activities and housing options. Popular with both U.S. and international tourists, Waikoloa features two 18-hole championship golf courses; two large resort hotels—the Hilton Waikoloa and the Royal Waikoloan; a shopping village with over 35 stores and restaurants; a mix of condominium housing units; and a broad array of land- and water-oriented recreational offerings. Like other large resort communities, Waikoloa is intended to provide visitors with everything they need within the confines of the community. The Bay Club is the only vacation-ownership property within Waikoloa and along the Kohala coasts.

Located near the Hilton Waikoloa Village Resort Hotel, The Bay Club's buildings are situated to allow most units to enjoy a golf course view. Before development, the site—like most of the Kona and Kohala Coast area—was a lava field devoid of vegetation.

As part of the routine development process for this area of Hawaii, the lava was pulverized and covered with a layer of topsoil mined from another area of the Big Island. The underlying crushed lava rock provides excellent drainage and good opportunities for plant growth. Natural lava formations have been preserved and incorporated into the landscape design.

All 172 units and the supporting amenities at The Bay Club were developed in a single phase. A second phase of ten acres and 120 units has been approved, but development scheduling is pending.

Development Process

In 1990, Wisconsin-based Town Realty began construction of The Bay Club but in 1991 sold the project, while still under construction, to Tokyo-based Nichiei Construction Co., Ltd. Nichiei, whose name was later changed to the AZEL Corporation, Limited, is the parent owner of The Bay Club Ownership Resort. AZEL is listed on both the Tokyo and Osaka stock markets and is involved in real estate ventures throughout Japan, primarily the development of residential condominiums. AZEL's annual sales exceed $50 million and its marketing strategy for The Bay Club called for selling the units as condominiums. Shortly after the purchase, however, Hawaii—like all of the United States—fell into a major recession. The condominium market largely evaporated.

The original marketing strategy priced the units at $350,000 for a one-bedroom unit and $850,000 for a two-bedroom villa with golf course view. By 1994, only nine of the 172 units had sold as Hawaii continued to suffer economically from sharply decreased domestic and international tourism. By this time, AZEL realized that a revamped marketing strategy was necessary in order to reposition the project in the market.

AZEL's new strategy involved a conversion from condominium sales to sales of

Photo on page 206:
The Bay Club, a once-troubled condominium development located on the Big Island of Hawaii, found economic success when it was converted in 1995 to vacation ownership.

The Bay Club consists of 172 units housed in 13 two- and three-story buildings. As of the end of 1998, 125 units were in the vacation-ownership pool; the remainder were leased for short-term vacation rentals, privately owned, or being used for marketing purposes.

vacation ownership. The owner applied to the state of Hawaii for a timeshare conversion and received approval in July 1995. Concurrently, AZEL formed a new Hawaii-based corporation called Nikken Corporation, of which The Bay Club Ownership Resort, Inc., is today a subsidiary. During the period of conversion, AZEL generated income by offering the units as short-term vacation rentals. Two of the nine units that originally sold were purchased back by Nikken and put into the vacation-ownership marketing pool. The Bay Club at Waikoloa is the owner's only timeshare property.

Purchase Arrangements, Pricing, and Financing

Vacation ownerships at The Bay Club sell on the basis of one week per year or one week per every other year. Each unit has a potential 51 intervals, or weeks, for sale, with one week per year reserved for maintenance. Although buyers see their purchase applied to the deed of a particular unit, they might never occupy that unit. Purchasers may, however, buy into a plan that guarantees their use of a particular

unit for a fixed week each year. Alternatively, for a lower price, purchasers can let their unit location and week float. Under the more flexible plan, The Bay Club ensures that the purchaser occupies the particular "type" of unit purchased (e.g., two bedroom) but not in a particular building or on a particular floor.

The total number of weekly intervals that will ultimately sell at The Bay Club is estimated at 8,415, which is calculated by multiplying 51 intervals per unit by the total number of units that are eventually placed in the pool (172 total units minus seven that are privately owned).

Pricing at The Bay Club, as with most timeshare properties, is somewhat complicated. Base prices for a one-bedroom unit range from $14,990 to $15,990 for one week per year; on an alternate-year basis, the same unit sells for $9,490 to $9,890. At the top end of the spectrum, a two-bedroom/two-and-one-half-bath unit sells for $22,990 for one week per year and $13,590 for one week per every other year.

In addition to these base charges, a $2,000 to $3,000 per week premium is assessed on the sale of units specified for premium weeks during the Christmas holiday season and peak summer vacation months. The guarantee that a unit will be available during Christmas week adds $3,000 to the price of a unit.

The Bay Club Ownership Resort and its parent companies finance purchases and require a standard downpayment of 10 percent of the purchase price. Payments can be scheduled in equal annual payments spread over five, seven, or ten years.

Marketing and Sales

Before conversion of the property, The Bay Club Ownership Resort and its parent companies had no experience in the development and marketing of vacation-ownership projects. To develop a marketing strategy, company management retained the consulting services of Mark Wang, who had demonstrated experience in selling time-shares at locations elsewhere on Kauai and on Maui.

As with most vacation-ownership developments, the first step to a successful marketing strategy is to generate visits to the property. Marketing offices were located in Kona, which is approximately a 30-minute drive from Waikoloa and accounts for the greatest number of hotel rooms and visitor accommodations on the Big Island. Marketing offices were also opened on the nearby island of Maui to capture potential buyers who might not otherwise visit the Big Island during their Hawaii vacation. The Maui office was closed in 1997 after demonstrating only mixed success. Another marketing office was opened in the Kings' Shops Shopping Village in Waikoloa. It is located less than a mile from The Bay Club and targets vacationers staying at the community's resort hotels and rental properties.

Units range in size from 822 square feet for a one-bedroom/one-bath floor plan to 1,484-square feet for a two-bedroom/two-and-one-half-bath floor plan; all feature gourmet kitchens and elaborate furnishings.

As an enticement for visiting The Bay Club, potential buyers are offered discounts on leisure and recreational activities such as helicopter tours and snorkeling trips. Once on the property, customers view a brief audiovisual presentation on The Bay Club and tour fully furnished model units. A sales representative then explains the intricacies of vacation ownership, including pricing and exchange options.

Another important component of the marketing and sales strategy involves referrals by owners. The Ohana (family) Awards Program provides owners with award points for each potential buyer they refer to The Bay Club. Prospective buyers receive discounted rates as an inducement to vacation at the property. During their stay, they are asked to spend 90 minutes touring The Bay Club and meeting with sales agents. Owners who refer potential buyers

may redeem their award points for bonus nights to extend their own vacations, to use as a credit toward maintenance fees, or to receive discounts on nearby recreational activities or retail purchases.

Generally consistent with other real estate ventures in Hawaii, the primary geographic market for The Bay Club has proven to be the West Coast and Midwest regions of the United States. Interestingly, of the approximately 4,500 Bay Club owners to date, only 420 are Japanese. The Bay Club Ownership Resort has made no special efforts to market the property in Japan despite the company's base there. Japanese tourism to Hawaii is down by 15 to 20 percent since its peak in the late 1980s; the effect on the state's economy has been significant. The Kona and Kohala coasts of the Big Island are now faring better than other parts of Hawaii due to

Buildings are situated so that most units have views of the golf course. As part of the development process, the lava that once covered the entire area was pulverized and covered with imported top soil.

Japan Air Lines's introduction of daily non-stop flights between Kona and Tokyo. Still, the U.S. market for purchasing vacation-ownership properties far exceeds that of Japan.

The typical buyer at The Bay Club is over age 50. The minimum household income to qualify for purchase is $75,000; however, the typical purchaser has an income well in excess of $100,000. Given the current and projected sales pace, the property is expected to sell out in late 2001 or early 2002.

Operations and Management

The Bay Club is managed by Quality Resort Management, another subsidiary of Tokyo-based Nikken. The management company is responsible for all landscaping, building, and housekeeping services. Owners pay an annual maintenance fee that in 1999 ranges from $499 for a one-bedroom unit to $690.75 for a two-bedroom/two-and-one-half-bath unit.

Following a competitive bidding process, The Bay Club Ownership Resort selected Resort Condominiums International (RCI) to manage timeshare trades with other properties and locations. The decision was based in part on RCI's presence in Japan's vacation-ownership market and the expected growth in Japanese tourism in Hawaii. RCI has conferred its most prestigious ranking—Gold Crown Resort—on The Bay Club.

Experience Gained

When a conventional condominium sales approach proves unsuccessful, converting to vacation ownership can offer a feasible alternative for certain properties. Conversions, however, require time, a long-term financial commitment to the project, and

A typical two-bedroom/two-bath unit offers 1,283 square feet and generous outdoor lanai space with wet bar.

an aggressive sales strategy. The conversion of The Bay Club to timeshare succeeded in large part because of the financial commitment and strength of the owner's parent company, AZEL Corporation, and the property's attractive location in one of Hawaii's top resort destinations. The lack of any nearby competition has been a major boon to sales.

Because The Bay Club was (and remains) the owner's only timeshare property, the learning curve was steep. Engaging an experienced consultant helped the owner make a relatively smooth transition. Still, the owner initiated vacation-ownership sales as quickly as possible—even before a tested accounting system was fully in place—to generate needed income. The luxury of time and experience would have allowed the owner to have all financial and accounting systems up and running before the first sale.

Site plan.

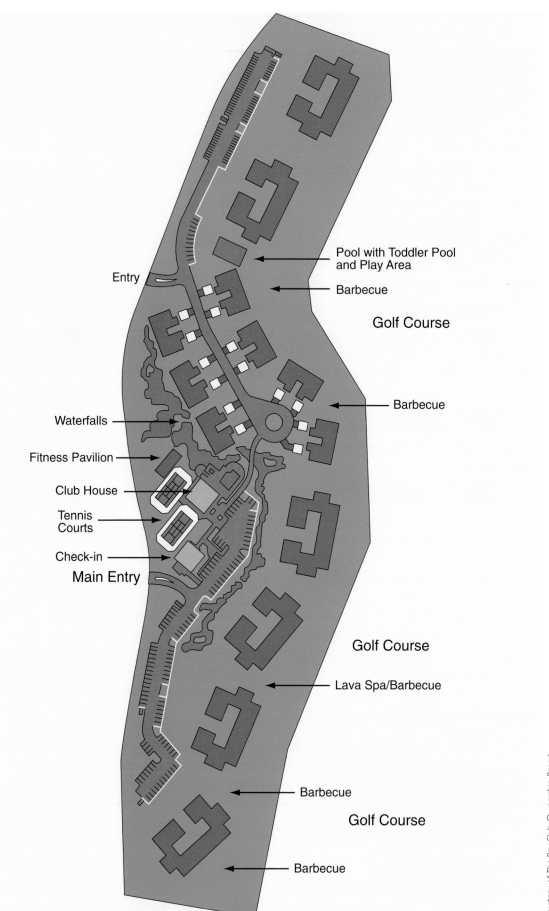

Entry

Pool with Toddler Pool
and Play Area

Barbecue

Golf Course

Barbecue

Waterfalls

Fitness Pavilion

Club House

Tennis
Courts

Check-in

Main Entry

Golf Course

Lava Spa/Barbecue

Barbecue

Golf Course

Barbecue

◆ Project Data

Land Use Information

Site area	15.5 acres
Total number of units	172
Total number of units in vacation-ownership pool (1998)	125
Individually owned units	7
Units in long-term rental progam	13
Units used for sales and marketing purposes (1998)	27
Total number of parking spaces	230
Gross density	11.1 units per acre

Property Purchase Price

Purchase price in 1991	$60 million

Unit Information

Plan Type	Number of Units	Number of Bedrooms	Number of Baths	Square Feet (indoor/outdoor)
Plan A	54	2	2	1,283/648
Plan B	36	2	2	1,118/456
Plan C	18	1	1	878/324
Plan D	36	1	1½	822/337
Plans E and F	28	2	2½	1,484/562

Pricing Information

	Every Year	Every Other Year
One-bedroom	$14,990–$15,990	$9,490–$9,890
Two-bedroom	$19,490–$22,990	$11,390–$13,590

Note: Additional charges apply to the above prices for certain peak weeks such as Christmas, the weeks during the Christmas holiday season, and peak summer weeks. Charges range from $2,000 to $3,000 per unit. For "fixing" use during any particular week, $1,000 is added to the purchase price.

Maintenance Fees (1999)

Typical one-bedroom unit	$499 per year
Two-bedroom unit	$594.50–$690.75 per year

Date of site visit: December 1998
Author of case study: Lloyd Bookout

Shore Crest Vacation Villas

Myrtle Beach, South Carolina

Shore Crest Vacation Villas is a purpose-built regional timeshare resort located on the ocean in Myrtle Beach, South Carolina. Developed by Bluegreen Corporation, the project capitalizes on a high-demand feature—the beach—within a popular destination market. Myrtle Beach is renowned as a golfer's paradise, but it is also a family-oriented beach resort offering a wealth of recreational, shopping, and dining opportunities. Bluegreen is developing another timeshare property, Harbour Lights, on the Intracoastal Waterway near the Fantasy Harbor shopping and entertainment complex, and it plans to continue to develop in the Myrtle Beach area.

Bluegreen Corporation is a Boca Raton, Florida-based publicly traded developer of residential land, golf course communities, and vacation-ownership properties. Its timeshare resorts are located in Daytona Beach, Orlando, Ft. Myers Beach, and Panama City Beach, Florida; the Wisconsin Dells; Myrtle Beach, South Carolina; Virginia; Branson, Missouri; the Great Smoky Mountains of Tennessee; and Aruba. Interval International has awarded its five-star rating to five of Bluegreen's timeshare resorts, including Shore Crest Vacation Villas.

History and Location

In early 1995, George Donovan, president and CEO of Bluegreen Corporation, identified Myrtle Beach as a desirable location for the company's timeshare activities. He subsequently located an appropriate site —a two-acre parcel with an old, rundown motel that had been inundated by Hurricane Hugo in 1989. After the property's owners cleaned up the hurricane damage, the motel enjoyed high occupancy during the three summer months but was little used during the rest of the year. In 1995, the owners divorced and the property went into debt.

According to Michael Cousins, Bluegreen's regional vice president for South Carolina, when Donovan purchased the motel site in September 1995 for $3.4 million, the parcel contained 84 motel units, two swimming pools, a "lazy river" water feature, a video room, and a front desk reception area. Bluegreen demolished all existing structures and facilities and cleared the site before undertaking construction of the first phase of Shore Crest Vacation Villas.

The site is located about 15 miles from the central core of Myrtle Beach, near the Windy Hill section of the city. Windy Hill is a largely upscale residential area that encompasses a popular shopping and entertainment complex called Barefoot Landing. The area surrounding the site is generally a single-family neighborhood in which modern homes have replaced some older cottages. The most intense development has taken place along the ocean. To the immediate north of the site are whole-owner condominiums in good condition; across the street is a small motel. These properties remain today.

Project Development

Shore Crest Vacation Villas is undergoing development in two phases. Phase I, which has been completed, consists of 114 units on 0.75 acre on the oceanfront. As of September 1998, it was 70 percent sold.

The first two floors of the 11-story Phase I building provide surface and deck parking. The third floor includes a lobby, a 20-foot-by-40-foot indoor pool situated within a greenhouse structure, an adjacent open garden terrace with tables and chairs for gatherings, an owners' lounge facing the ocean, offices, the VIP sales operations office, an activities desk, a video game room, housekeeping headquarters, and an employees' lunch room. (VIP sales refers to sales of timeshare intervals to prospects staying at the resort—both renters and owners.) The third floor also houses some villas. An exercise room on the mezzanine level overlooks the indoor pool. The remaining eight floors are dedicated exclusively to the villas. In total, the building counts 17 one-bedroom units and 97 two-bedroom units. One-bedroom units sleep four; two bedrooms sleep six.

Phase I also features a large, freeform outdoor pool (approximately 30 feet by 75 feet), a 160-foot-long, six-foot-wide "lazy river" current pool, and a hot tub for 12, all situated within a lighted garden between the building and the ocean. A year-round program of activities and guest services enhances the physical facilities.

The Phase II building, now under construction on the "back row" across the street, will include 126 units on 1.25 acres as well as three structured parking decks

Photo on page 214:
The single building that constitutes Phase I of Shore Crest Vacation Villas sits right on the beach in Myrtle Beach, a destination resort that is one of the country's great golf and seaside playgrounds.

and nine floors of villas, for a total of 12 floors. The second phase will also feature another outdoor swimming pool, a second lazy river, and an indoor spa (on the fourth floor). Cousins expects Phase II to be ready for occupancy by July 1999.

None of the units offers lockoffs; lockoffs consume density and require additional parking. Bluegreen has decided that it cannot sell units with lockoffs at a sufficiently high price to justify the cost and space requirements.

Villas are distinguished by large windows with panoramic views of the ocean; balconies with a table and chairs; sleeper-sofas; entertainment centers with a large-screen television, VCR, video game systems, and compact disc stereo system; washer-dryers; and modern, fully equipped kitchens. Interior decoration is "beach casual" style, with simple, clean-line furniture in light, bright, cheerful colors. The lobby, guest lounge, and sales rooms overlook the ocean and recreational water features.

Development Challenges

The major challenges during the development process have included floodplain restrictions, beachfront restrictions, and parking issues. With the site located in a floodplain, living areas are not permitted to be sited below 19 feet above sea level, thus forcing the front desk to a location on the third floor. This arrangement has proved inconvenient for owners and guests arriving with a carload of luggage. The buildings themselves are constructed on reinforced concrete pilings sunk 30 feet below ground. Additional environmental concerns related to the project's beachfront location have imposed other requirements and costs, such as setbacks and limits on the type of lighting that can be used (the site is a nesting area for loggerhead turtles).

Moreover, the site's small size has made it difficult to provide parking economically. Virtually all owners drive to the resort. Parking requirements call for 1.5 spaces for each two-bedroom unit, one space for each one-bedroom unit, and one space for every three employees. This formula generally results in sufficient parking for all but peak-load periods. To ensure adequate parking, Bluegreen acquired three additional lots on the third row back from the ocean and created 85 parking spaces to accommodate employees and overflow guest parking.

In addition, the small site leaves little room to maneuver. During Phase I, the project's neighbors objected to noise and construction amid a vacation environment. Tower cranes swung over adjacent properties and necessitated Bluegreen's purchase or rental of the properties' air rights. Working on a small, confined site also poses challenges for stockpiling construction materials.

As a result of lessons learned in Phase I, Bluegreen introduced several design changes during Phase II. For example, with little demand for one-bedroom units in Phase I, all Phase II villas will be two-bedroom units with two baths. Similarly, the developer found that Phase I included more handicapped units than were needed; market demand for these units is limited, making them slow to sell. Finally, Phase II will include an auxiliary lobby on the third-floor parking level to permit arriving owners and guests to unload baggage directly from their cars.

Management

Bluegreen rents unsold time and, for a fee, owners' unused time. Rentals provide the company with a double benefit: the income offsets the developer's keep-well subsidy (the portion of the property's operations costs guaranteed by the developer based on unsold weeks) while the pool of potential buyers who will have experienced the resort as renters may prove receptive to the overtures of the sales team.

According to Cousins, the timeshare resort is operated in much the same man-

Within view of a villa's balcony, vacationers can float along a "lazy river," soak in the whirlpool spa, swim in a freeform pool, make tie-dye shirts on the lawn, and swim or play volleyball on the beach.

ner as a hotel resort except that it provides no food and beverage service and offers only weekly maid service (with a mid-week tidy service). In addition, unlike a hotel, a timeshare's turnover time is more concentrated and difficult to manage. At Shore Crest, check-in time is spread over three days, alleviating the problem of delays at check-in but creating challenges in inventory management.

The developer will control the management of Phase I until the project is 90 to 95 percent sold. At that point, active sales will cease for lack of inventory except for resales or the passive sale of remaining unit/times. Annual maintenance fees as of October 1998 were $345 per unit/week for a two-bedroom unit, including taxes and insurance. The only other charge to residents, which is optional, is an extra fee

for a full mid-week cleaning (as opposed to a mid-week freshen-up) or daily cleaning.

Purchase Arrangements And Pricing

Bluegreen Corporation is in the midst of converting its timeshare purchase arrangements from a traditional fixed-time/fixed-week purchase with a float option to the sale of points within a vacation club. As of September 1998, Bluegreen was still selling Shore Crest Vacation Villas as a traditional timeshare product, but it planned to shift to point-based sales in November 1998.

Buyers who have purchased a fixed week with a float option can use their unit for their designated week or exchange it for a different week at the same resort. Within a certain time frame, owners can even

Bluegreen's storefront OPC in a local shopping mall attracts visitors with its souvenirs and promotions and provides information about Bluegreen's Myrtle Beach resorts.

deposit the week they purchased (week A) and simultaneously request an alternative week (week B). When the owner of week B deposits that week into the pool for exchange, the owner of week A can make the exchange for week B on a first-come, first-served basis.

Prices are demand-driven and periodically adjusted to correspond with the market. As of September 1998, prices for a unit/week at Shore Crest Vacation Villas were as follows: $8,900 to $17,400 for two-bedroom oceanfront villas depending on the season; $7,900 to $12,900 for two-bedroom oceanview units; and $5,900 to $10,400 for one-bedroom oceanview units. Members pay annual membership dues that include maintenance fees.

By contrast, a vacation club, as Cousins explained, is an enhanced internal exchange system that includes all of Bluegreen's timeshare resorts. Owners can use their points to exchange within the Bluegreen system at no fee, or they can go outside the system through one of the fee-based exchange companies.

The shift to a vacation club point system is strictly voluntary and will give participating owners increased flexibility by enabling them to redeem points on a nightly basis. Current owners can retain their existing ownership status (fixed week, floating time), convert to the club system, or retain their existing status and buy a package of points in addition to what they already own. As Cousins explained, "The current owners are in control."

The number of points offered by Bluegreen will be based on the size of the club inventory (number of units times 52 weeks times the value of each point equals the total number of points). According to Cousins, point values will range from 5,000 to 8,000 for a one-bedroom unit depending on the season and from 7,000 to 13,000 for a two-bedroom unit. Points will be priced at a certain dollar amount per point to reflect current market conditions and the actual construction value of each villa. (As is standard for the timeshare industry, 25 percent of the yield is the maximum amount allocated to product cost.) Bluegreen's primary challenge in operating the club is to keep the inventory and reservations system in balance.

Bluegreen is now in the process of retraining its sales force to ensure that all salespersons understand the transition and the benefits it provides to the company's customers.

Marketing

As explained by Martin "Marty" Yancy, director of marketing, Shore Crest Vacation Villas, like other Bluegreen resorts, is marketed through five programs that include the following:

- Direct mail that uses the offer of a mini-vacation. Direct mail advertising is targeted to married, college-educated home-owners with household incomes of $40,000 and above who live within five hours' driving time of the resort;
- Local tourists whose presence indicates their interest in visiting the Myrtle Beach area. Outreach programs in high-traffic areas such as shopping malls target these visitors. For example, Bluegreen maintains guest information booths at a nearby factory outlet mall, where a uniformed marketing representative engages passers-by in conversation amid a display of premiums—tickets, coupons, gift certificates—that can be exchanged for a tour of the property;
- Telemarketing, which is used to sell discounted three- to four-day vacations at Shore Crest. Despite no sales pressure, purchasers of the vacations are

offered an upgrade to an oceanfront unit in exchange for taking a tour;
- In-house sales, which include reloads, upgrades, conversions from renters, conversions from exit programs, walk-ins, and people vacationing at Shore Crest through one of the exchange company programs; and
- Owner referrals generated at the point of sale. The telemarketing group pursues the referrals and sets appointments for tours and visits.

Each marketing method imposes different costs, generates a different number of tours, offers a different degree of predictability, and results in a different average percentage of sales. It is the careful blend of all five methods that yields a workable marketing program.

Cross-marketing with Bluegreen's nearby Harbour Lights development is minimal and generally opportunistic. The two properties are located, designed, and priced differently. Harbour Lights is a low-rise development located on the Intracoastal

A glass-enclosed indoor pool offers opportunities for fun and exercise on rainy days.

Diane R. Suchman

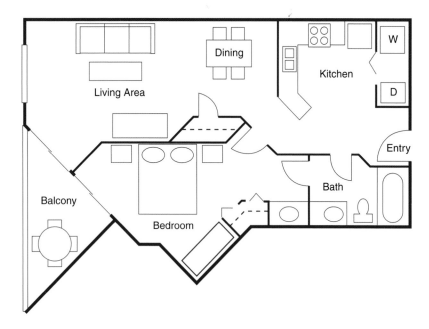

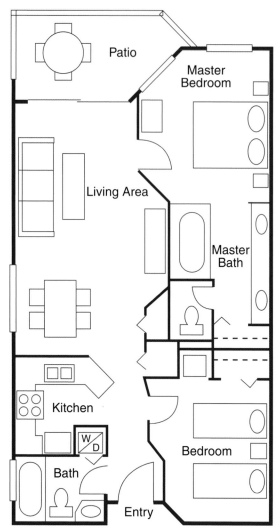

Floor plans.

Waterway rather than on the beach, and its prices are somewhat lower.

Bluegreen Corporation maintains offices in a nearby high-profile shopping center four miles from Shore Crest Vacation Villas. Within this office complex, the company operates an active sales program. The sales staff ranges from 26 to 48 persons depending on the season. Parents interested in attending a sales presentation can leave small children in the company's supervised playroom. First-day purchasers are offered premiums such as coupons for shows or golf. The marketing department fields calls from telemarketing and direct-mail respondents as visitors check in at the office lobby for their tours and mini-vacations. Office hallways showcase photographs of satisfied purchasers. And a

quality assurance officer (who does not report to the sales director) talks with buyers after their purchase to ensure that they understand and are satisfied with their purchase and that ethical standards were honored during the sales process.

◆ Project Data

Development Schedule

	Phase I	Phase II
Number of units	114	126
Planning started	November 1995	May 1998
Construction started	May 1996	July 1998
Construction completed	May 1997	(July 1999)
Sales started	May 1996	December 1998

Land Use Information

Site area	2 acres
Total number of timeshare units planned	240
Total number of timeshare units completed	114
Off-street parking spaces	226

Unit Information[1]

Unit Type	Square Feet	Number of Units
One-bedroom	700	17
Two-bedroom	1,000	97

Unit Prices (1997)

Unit Type	Average Price per Week
One-bedroom	$8,000
Two-bedroom	$11,000

Project Development Costs (per unit)

	Phase I	Phase II
Construction	$91,500	$104,000
FF&E	$15,100	$15,300
Soft costs	$48,200	$25,800
Total	$154,800	$145,100

Annual Operating Expenses (1997)

Phase I total	$1,300,000

Developer

Bluegreen Corporation
Boca Raton, Florida

Architect

Thomas Pegram, AIA
Pegram Associates
Myrtle Beach, South Carolina

Note

1. Phase I.

Date of site visit: September 22, 1998
Author of case study: Diane R. Suchman

Pacific Shores Nature Resort*

Vancouver Island, British Columbia

Pacific Shores Nature Resort is a 76-unit family-owned and -managed mixed timeshare and condominium resort on Craig Bay in Vancouver Island, British Columbia. Featuring luxurious accommodations nestled in a gorgeous ecologically sensitive and horticulturally enhanced natural environment, the resort also includes a resort center, swimming pool, health club, and small convenience store. Pacific Shores Nature Resort is affiliated with RCI, which has designated it a "Gold Crown" Resort.

Since 1964, developers Andrew and Susan Pearson had been developing residential subdivisions on Vancouver Island, including five resort condominium projects on Craig Bay. Although some resort locations such as Whistler had already seen the development of resort condominiums, both resort condominiums and the timeshare concept were new to Vancouver Island.

Location

Located 100 miles northwest of Victoria, the capital of British Columbia, Canada, and 30 miles west of the province's largest city, Vancouver, on the mainland, Pacific Shores Nature Resort is the only vacation-ownership resort on Vancouver Island. It is situated on a peninsula that juts into Craig Bay on the island's sunnier, more temperate eastern shore, an area that is a popular retirement and year-round vacation destination. The closest cities are Nanaimo, 20 miles southwest of Pacific Shores, and

*Dollar amounts in this case study are in Canadian dollars, unless otherwise noted.

Parksville, approximately four miles north-west on Vancouver Island.

More than a 100 years ago, Craig Bay had been an anchorage for supply ships and a log-dumping ground for timber companies. As the area grew more popular as a tourist destination, logging practices gradually subsided while the ocean tides eventually cleared away the wood debris. In the mid-1960s, a camping club operated a campground and trailer park on the 15-acre site where Pacific Shores was later built.

Project Planning and Development

Pacific Shores was initially planned as a resort condominium project targeted to tourists. The first phase, built in 1990, consisted of large, luxurious fee-simple condominium units. Though offered the opportunity to participate in a rental pool, many early owners were retirees who wanted to occupy their units year-round as retirement homes. The owners' desire for full-time occupancy conflicted with the Pearsons' hope of establishing a regional tourist resort. The Pearsons also found that the cost to construct Pacific Shores's large units made it difficult to sell the condominiums profitably as whole units.

At about the same time, a downturn in the Canadian economy prompted the Pearsons to revamp their development strategy. Their initial plans had called for the eventual development of a timeshare component, but certainly not immediately. The economic downturn, however, made the timeshare component financially feasible. In 1991, the Pearsons decided to transform the remainder of the development into timeshare units.

For the first eight years, the Pearsons followed a deliberately cautious development schedule, building no more than a dozen townhouses at a time. In the early phases, they developed 39 timeshare units and 13 wholly owned units. In 1998, they added a 24-unit apartment complex with underground parking. At buildout (in or about 2005), the resort will count 127 units (including both timeshare and wholly owned units).

Design

The site plan and building configuration take advantage of the dramatic, irregular contours of a site surrounded by water on three sides. The 52 townhouse units are single-loaded to provide views of the water or of a central open space that is interspersed with walkways and gardens. The developers opted to build at a low density of 8.5 units per acre and to cluster the units to maximize open space and wildlife habitat. The mix of one- and two-story townhouses creates a low profile that blends into the landscape.

The two-bedroom units (one is a lockoff) range in size from 1,285 to 1,500 square feet and sleep six to ten guests. Owners enjoy views of either the bay or a creek estuary. In most units, the master bedroom includes a double-sided gas fireplace that also warms the master bathroom, which features a whirlpool bath and heated tile floors.

High-quality, durable, natural products such as wood fixtures and ceramic tile floors, which do not require frequent replacement, are used throughout the units wherever possible. The cedar-shake roofs are expensive but last twice as long as conventional roofs. Energy-saving features, such as low-flush toilets and timers on the gas fireplaces, contribute to lower maintenance fees. Many decisions (for example, the decision to forgo garbage disposals, which use great quantities of tap water) grew out of ecological concerns and energy conservation goals. In the same spirit, each unit has a compost cone for table scraps; the compost is used to fertilize the gardens.

The 24 recently constructed units are smaller than the older units, averaging 1,060 square feet instead of 1,400 square

Photo on page 222:
Buildings were deliberately clustered to leave more room for gardens and landscaping. High-quality natural products that are renewable and often biodegradable were used wherever possible. Roofs are made of cedar shakes, which are expensive but last twice as long as conventional roofing materials.

feet. The units are located in a three-story elevator building with underground parking for 48 cars. Both the master bedroom and second bedroom face the bay. Whereas the older units are equipped with whirlpool baths in only the master bathroom, both bedrooms in the newer units feature full bathrooms with whirlpools. The color palette for the new units—rich, dark sage greens, beiges, and grays—is more soil-resistant and thus more practical than the pastels in some of the earlier units.

Pacific Shores Nature Resort offers amenities such as an indoor pool and hot tub, a sauna, a fitness center, and a small grocery store with a delicatessen. The resort

center will be expanded in the summer of 1999, doubling the existing 14,000 square feet with the addition of a new restaurant, shops, and health spa. An outdoor hot tub complex and tennis courts will also be constructed. The grocery store and pool are owned and operated by the developer as profit centers. The pool and fitness center operate on a fee-for-service basis. Each year, the Pacific Shores homeowners' association votes on the fee for these two facilities. To generate additional income, Pacific Shores permits local residents to purchase memberships in the resort swimming pool. The resort plans to invite these nonmembers to purchase memberships in the new hot tub complex.

The resort is located near many sports opportunities and outdoor activities, including eight golf courses, freshwater and saltwater fishing, scuba diving, windsurfing, and boating. Snow skiing is available during the winter months at Mount Washington, 50 miles from the resort.

Environmental Appeal

Pacific Shores's signature amenity is its landscaping. Andrew Pearson is just as comfortable crawling on the ground with pruning shears in hand as he is manipulating spread sheets on his computer, and his passion for horticulture is manifest throughout the resort property. Pearson was willing to incur the significant expense of building underground parking for the new three-story structure in order to save space for additional gardens.

Pearson is especially interested in creating diverse landscapes—from a "manicured" high-maintenance, domesticated zone near the buildings to an intermediate zone where natural flora, such as wild berry bushes, are planted to attract wildlife to the natural zone along the seashore and creek estuary. Although native plant species predominate, exotic plants, including Japanese bananas, figs, and kiwis, abound. The resort also features a series

Pacific Shores Nature Resort is located on a peninsula that juts into Craig Bay.

Courtesy of Pacific Shores Nature Resort

During summers, an on-site naturalist leads wildlife walks on the resort grounds several times a week.

of minigardens that showcase plants that originate in South Africa, China, and Italy. Eventually, Pearson will develop many more gardens representative of areas from around the world. Pacific Shores employs two and one-half full-time gardeners. Plans call for a resort garden club that will encourage neighborhood residents, owners, and guests to work alongside Pacific Shores gardeners.

The resort also maintains a nursery known for its more than 750 perennial species. The Pearsons operate the nursery as a profit center and sell a wide variety of plants to resort visitors and island residents. While it does not yet generate significant income, the nursery does break even. Pearson plans to replace the temporary nursery structure with a greenhouse that will house botanical displays.

The Pearsons' two primary, interrelated goals at Pacific Shores are to offer owners and guests memorable vacations while educating them about the long-term preservation of wildlife habitat. To those ends, all plants are scrupulously identified and marked. In addition, the nature-friendly resort offers a comprehensive schedule

of environmental appreciation programs, including garden tours, wildlife photography classes, bird watches, and wildlife walks. During the summers, an on-site naturalist leads wildlife walks and conducts boat cruises to view marine wildlife on local islands. The island's temperate coastal climate draws many types of wildlife, especially birds; more than 250 species of birds have been sighted at the adjacent bird sanctuary. In conjunction with the Canadian government and a local fly fishing club, Pearson has embarked on a stream rehabilitation project aimed at establishing a coho and chum salmon hatchery on Craig Creek. He is also applying for permits to develop a tidal pool on the foreshore to act as a natural aquarium for starfish, sea anemones, and other marine organisms.

Pacific Shores's gardens and "ecotourism" amenities have been valuable marketing tools. Several owners have told Andrew Pearson that they were drawn to Pacific Shores specifically by the resort's gardens. One visitor, who decided to purchase after completing the garden tour, remarked that it was the most expensive garden tour he had ever taken.

Purchase Arrangements And Pricing

Timeshare owners at Pacific Shores purchase a fee-simple interest for a fixed week. While the resort initially sold floating weeks, the Pearsons found that the arrangement tended to confuse purchasers. Prices range between $11,000 and $20,000 per week. The average sales price is $15,000.

Andrew Pearson plans to convert to a point-based system in 1999 and is in the process of creating his own vacation club. He expects to develop two additional timeshare projects—both of which are in the approval stage—in Victoria. In addition, he is evaluating the possibility of developing several other timeshare resorts in Vancouver and Whistler and is considering a strategic alliance with another vacation club in a different geographic market (one with resorts in California or Arizona), thereby providing Pacific Shores owners with reciprocal exchange privileges.

According to Pearson, the primary attraction of a point system over fee-simple ownership is increased flexibility. A point system enables the developer to sell less than the equivalent of a week's time. Pearson has found that many people prefer to vacation in three- to four-day increments rather than for a full week. He has also learned that a significant segment of potential purchasers cannot afford the $15,000 price of a unit/week that is required to participate in the present system. Use of a point system would make it possible to reduce the initial purchase price to around $11,000 or $12,000—a price that would make ownership accessible to a broader, younger segment of the market.

A point system would also be more attractive for existing owners by making it possible for them to purchase additional product in one- or two-day increments instead of for a full week. Nearly 20 percent of Pacific Shores owners have purchased two or more weeks. Pearson expects that an even greater percentage of owners will purchase additional vacation time once Pacific Shores adopts a point system. Increasing the incidence of multiple sales to existing owners lowers marketing costs. It is far less expensive to market to existing owners than to new prospects.

Financing

Pacific Shores Nature Resort was initiated with investments from six corporate shareholders. The Pearsons subsequently bought out five of the investors and brought in a new partner—the Hill family; the Pearsons had partnered with the Hills on other developments. The two families own equal shares in Pacific Shores. The Royal Bank of Canada financed the development.

Financing fee-simple timeshare purchases has posed a challenge to the owners of Pacific Shores. To qualify for financing, purchasers must obtain a mortgage secured by a deed and title. Most owners obtain financing through the Royal Bank of Canada. However, the Royal Bank imposes fairly stringent underwriting criteria. For example, it will not finance self-employed persons or persons with incomes less than $40,000. In addition, it will not provide mortgage financing to U.S. citizens, effectively eliminating an important market for the resort.

Pacific Shores currently provides some in-house financing on an ad hoc basis but is seeking an arrangement with a timeshare lender that will enable the resort to offer consumer financing to all qualified purchasers. Andrew Pearson predicts that the availability of in-house consumer financing will play an enormous role in bringing down the resort's high rescission rate, which now totals about one-third of all sales. Another reason for the rescission rate is that the resort does not pressure reluctant buyers and rarely retains a deposit from a purchaser who wants to back out of a sale. (The rate also appears high because purchasers who do not qualify for loans are counted as rescissions.) The cooling-off period in British Columbia is seven days.

Marketing and Sales

Selling timeshare units at Pacific Shores means that prospects must be attracted to the resort for a visit. "In the case of multiple properties, where you're really selling a concept," says Jim Pearson (Andrew Pearson's son), "people are more willing to purchase sight unseen. But when you're selling only one resort product, people want to see the actual property." For Pacific Shores, generating leads has proved challenging.

Initially, Pacific Shores operated a sales office in downtown Vancouver. After less than a year, however, the office closed. One reason, according to Jim Pearson, who runs the marketing and sales department, was the language barrier. In recent years, a large influx of immigrants has transformed mainland Vancouver into a cosmopolitan city. Among the many persons who visited the Vancouver sales office, a large share did not speak English as a first language. As a result, visitors had difficulty understanding the complicated details of the timeshare arrangement.

When Pacific Shores Nature Resort first opened, Canada claimed fewer than 40 timeshare resorts. Today, there are about 80 timeshare resorts, but Pacific Shores is still the only timeshare on Vancouver Island. Jim Pearson notes that the dozen or so Canadian timeshare resorts that operated off-site offices in Vancouver have all closed their city offices.

For a time, the Pearsons mounted a variety of promotional events to help market the resort, including champagne cruises and dinner presentations at upscale hotels. However, the number of sales generated by the cruises did not justify the expense and put an end to them.

The resort employs a sales staff of 12 as well as 30 telemarketers who operate out of Nanaimo. The resort's relatively secluded island location works against the recruitment and retention of experienced sales staff, who tend to prefer more cosmopolitan locations.

Ultimately, Pacific Shores concentrated on on-site selling targeted largely to area residents who can visit for a day without staying overnight. The primary market area includes Vancouver, which is a pleasant two-hour ferry ride from Nanaimo, but not Seattle (the next largest population center), which is four or more hours away and thus too distant for a day trip. To market to local residents, Pacific Shores relies on targeted direct mail and telemarketing. The resort placed more than 500 draw boxes with Vancouver Island businesses. To win a prize, respondents completed a questionnaire. The resort used the ques-

Courtesy of Pacific Shores Nature Resort

The lobby in the resort center is designed with a palette of earth tones —rich sages, beiges, and grays—and features comfortable Craftsman-style furniture.

tionnaires to create lists for targeted direct mail.

To encourage prospects' visits, Pacific Shores offers visitors dinner certificates for use at nearby restaurants during their day trip to the resort. (The resort previously offered travel certificate incentives, but visitors complained that the certificate programs were too inflexible and complicated. Prospects prefer more tangible incentives such as restaurant certificates or ski passes.) Only two or three units are released on the market at any given time, and most of the unsold units are either rented to the public or reserved by RCI members. As a result, the resort has scarce facilities to offer for minivacations. Because of distance, marketing costs, and difficulties in providing end-loan financing, the Pear-

The resort offers hiking and biking trails and is located close to many outdoor activity venues, including five golf courses, freshwater and saltwater fishing, scuba diving, windsurfing, and boating.

Courtesy of Pacific Shores Nature Resort

sons have not actively marketed Pacific Shores to residents of the United States.

More recently, however, the addition of the 24 mulitfamily units at Pacific Shores and the planned development of several new resorts will mean significantly more inventory for accommodating prospective purchasers on minivacations. It will also mean a marketing effort—targeted direct mail and telemarketing—pitched to the United States. In addition, a new and faster ferry will start service in 1999, making the resort more accessible to mainlanders and permitting Seattle-area residents to make day visits.

Among RCI members, Pacific Shores is one of the most sought-after resorts. It is occupied 92 to 96 percent of the year with approximately 1,000 exchanges. The closing rate among Americans who visit as guests and then tour Pacific Shores is high —nearly 20 percent. In addition, the favorable exchange rate gives Americans better value for purchases made in Canada.

Sales prices average $15,000. The construction of smaller units in the most recent phase of development makes it possible to lower the selling price of a unit/ week to around $11,000 to $12,000, thus broadening the market of potential purchasers. Smaller units are also less costly to maintain. The net closing ratio is around 10 percent, which is expected to nearly double when Pacific Shores brings in a larger base of potential purchasers on minivacations.

Most owners are married couples; the median age is 56. More than half have earned college degrees; many are teachers and many are government workers from Victoria. Teachers and health care professionals make up 25 percent of purchasers. Ninety-five percent of owners hail from Vancouver Island and nearly 45 percent from Victoria. Once Pacific Shores affiliates with a vacation club and starts marketing to the United States, the resort's owner demographics are projected to grow far more diverse. In addition, the Pearsons

Floor plans.

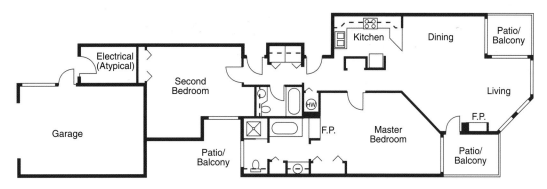

A (Ground Floor)—**Harlequin**—1,265 Sq. Ft. **A** (Upper Level)—**Heron**—1,265 Sq. Ft.

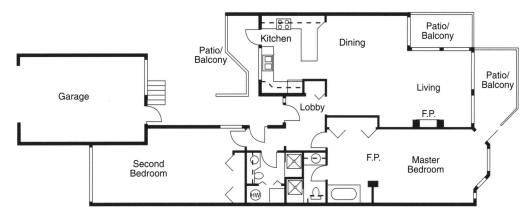

B (Ground Floor)—**Kestrel**—1,432 Sq. Ft. **B** (Upper Level)—**Kingfisher**—1,432 Sq. Ft.

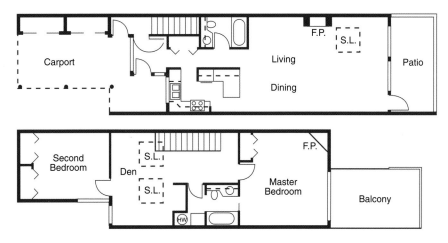

C—**Merlin**—1,500 Sq. Ft.

expect that the addition of amenities such as the restaurant and tennis courts will draw younger guests and reduce the median age of owners to around 46.

When Pacific Shores first opened, the resort occasionally offered a buyback program as an incentive to close a sale. The resort terminated the program when the British Columbia government authority instituted a bonding requirement to secure the buyback guarantee. Nonetheless, Pacific Shores owners are free to sell unit/weeks through the owners' association website. In addition, they can bank weeks with RCI or rent out unused time through Pacific Shores's rental management company. In

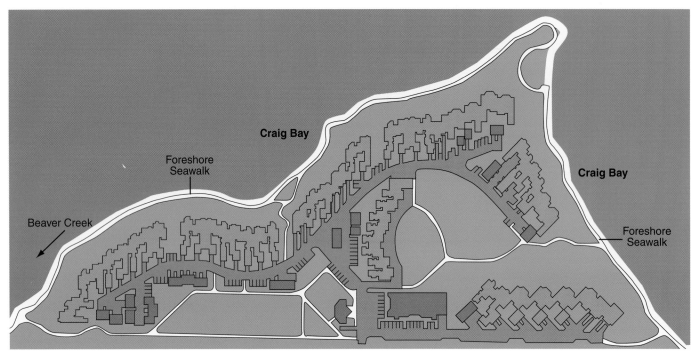

Site plan.

August 1998, out of a total 1,800 weeks, only 60 weeks were available for resale.

Management and Operations

As the homeowners' association, the Strata Council is responsible for making decisions about the resort's common facilities and exterior maintenance, especially with respect to garbage collection, landscaping, lighting, and so forth. All units (both condominiums and timeshare) elect members of the Strata Council. In addition, timeshare owners belong to a separate homeowners' association whose board of directors makes decisions relating to interior maintenance of the timeshare units.

Timeshare owners pay a maintenance fee that covers operations costs, taxes, a contingency reserve, furniture replacement, and their portion of the common-area strata fees. Because the resort is a family-operated business, the Pearsons are able to keep owners' costs in check by not charging for management services. As a result, owners pay an unusually low annual maintenance fee of $376 for a two-bedroom unit—an amount that has remained about the same for the last three years. Energy-saving features such as low-flush toilets and timers on the gas fireplaces also contribute to lower maintenance fees.

As at other resorts, timeshare owners at Pacific Shores would like more services for less money. At the same time, though, they believe that it is important to retain the RCI "Gold Crown" designation, which translates into excellent exchange power.

Experience Gained

Andrew Pearson emphasizes the importance of phasing development, particularly in the case of a small resort operation with limited resources. First, developers find it easier to obtain financing for a single phase than for an entire project, especially in Canada, where banks tend to be more conservative. Second, phasing helps minimize operations costs during the development period.

Pearson also recommends an incremental marketing strategy. "Some developers make the mistake of selling too many units at one time. We made a strategic decision not to sell more than two to four units at once." He added, "It's best to limit choices. If purchasers have too many selections to choose from, they can grow confused and find it difficult to make a decision." If shares in a particular unit are moving slowly, Pearson offers various incentives to boost sales.

Pearson notes that timeshare differs dramatically from traditional residential products. For example, residential developers generally want to get in and sell out before the economy changes. In his earlier residential developments, Pearson typically sold all units within two years of obtaining the required approvals. By contrast, timeshare development takes much longer. Adds Andrew Pearson, "You'll need patience and fairly deep pockets."

Most developers have no idea how much it costs to market and sell timeshare units. What makes the timeshare product more valuable is marketing and sales rather than the quality of the buildings or the location.

"In the timeshare business, you're not selling real estate primarily as an investment," Pearson observed. "You're selling a product that people can enjoy, which eventually may become an investment. However, timeshare enables the public to obtain better-quality vacations for less cost in the long run, and in this sense, it's an investment in one's family future."

◆ Project Data[1]

Development Schedule

Planning started	November 1989
Construction started	April 1990
Timeshare sales started	April 1991
Sales completed	2005 (projected)

Land Use Information

Site area	15 acres
Total number of units planned (Phases I–XII)	127
Total number of units constructed (Phases I–VIII)	76
Total number of timeshare units constructed	63
Total number of timeshare unit/years sold	39
Total number of whole units sold	13

Unit Information

Unit Type	Square Feet	Number of Units Planned/ Completed
One-bedroom	800	1/1
Two-bedroom	1,060–1430	113/63

	Average Price per Unit/Week	Weeks Sold
One-bedroom	(not available)	none
Two-bedroom	$15,000	1,980

Project Costs

	Hard Costs	Soft Costs	Total Costs
Project total to date	$11,300,000	$1,900,000	$13,200,000
Per unit	$180,000	$30,000	$210,000

Annual Operating Expenses (1997)

Annual resort operations	$1,200,000
Annual sales center operations	$2,000,000

Developer

Pacific Shores Nature Resort, Ltd.
Nanoose Bay, British Columbia, Canada

Architect

Zoltan Kitka
Nanoose Bay, Vancouver Island, British Columbia

Date of site visit: September 10, 1998
Author of case study: Terry Jill Lassar

Note

1. Unless otherwise noted, all dollar amounts in this case study are in Canadian dollars. The conversion rate at the time the case study was written was Can$1.54 = US$1; Can$1 = US$.65.

Chapter 10
Trends

Mike Sheridan

Since it originated in the French Alps three and a half decades ago, timeshare has matured and expanded into what is now an estimated $6 billion industry poised for multibillion dollar growth. With its huckster image and high-pressure sales tactics now largely a thing of the past, timeshare has attracted legions of satisfied customers around the world. A confluence of events—some social, some political, some economic—is expected to boost the industry even further in the years ahead.

A Growing Industry

As noted in chapter 2, the industry's low penetration rate world-wide, the extremely high proportion of satisfied customers, and the growing number of companies—particularly hospitality companies—that are entering the timeshare business all point to a continued upward trend for the timeshare industry. In the final analysis, many believe that the future of timeshare will be shaped by the number of potential buyers. Developers, builders, and hoteliers are salivating at the demographics as the global population ages. In a world where every seven seconds a U.S. citizen turns 50 years old, an age when people begin to look for a place to vacation with their grandchildren, vacation ownership becomes a reasonable option.

Given that the industry is heavily dependent on periodic infusions of funds for development, expansion, and sales and marketing, the availability of capital has become a crucial concern. As a capital-intensive industry, timeshare requires access to financing to ensure future growth. William E. Ward, Jr., vice president of Ward Financial in Pittsburgh, one of the nation's leading brokers for timeshare financing, notes that obtaining financing is easier now than three years ago. "When more of the consuming public becomes enamored of timeshare, it will open the eyes of more lending institutions," he adds.

Industry Consolidation

With its increasingly visible record of success and clear growth potential, the timeshare industry will continue to attract more players in the next millennium. At the same time, the industry will see more consolidation and greater horizontal and vertical integration within individual companies.

Ed McMullen, Sr., chair of Shell Vacations, LLC, of Orlando, Florida, and the 1997–1999 chair of the American Resort Development Association, notes that three key trends have driven the timeshare business over the past few years: consolidation, segmentation, and internationalization. These three factors will continue to play a major role in the industry in the years ahead. According to McMullen, consolidation is a natural trend for any business as it matures. "You have to have a certain amount of consolidated activities to obtain efficiencies in almost all areas, particularly something as complicated as timeshare."

Many larger companies have already followed the consolidation route by acquiring small firms. Several companies have benefited from creating the critical mass needed for efficient operations. Growing through acquisition has been a major driving force at Sunterra Corporation, formerly known as Signature Resorts. At the end of 1996, Sunterra, which is based in San Mateo, California, owned nine properties. Two years later, it boasted 84 properties, nearly all of them associated with acquisitions.

Industry leaders expect that the trend toward consolidation will probably slow in the future. One reason is that many timeshare companies already have been purchased. Not only that, but the stock prices of vacation-ownership acquirers are not as high as they once were. Given that most companies use their stock to pay for acquisitions, they are finding it increasingly difficult to undertake stock-based transactions.

But even as the timeshare industry enters a maturing stage in which sophistication, specialization, and economies of scale are important, consolidation will continue. A major reason is that, today, less than 10 percent of sales volume worldwide involves branded companies. That percentage is bound to increase in the years ahead, making consolidation an industry phenomenon for some time to come.

Citing the hotel sector as an example, McMullen suggests that an industry tends to segment during consolidation. "In timeshare, we're seeing various products and price levels to meet market demand. And, generally, those businesses that are highly profitable soon go international. We're seeing more of that, too."

Economic changes, lifestyle demands, and other factors will further fuel the timeshare boom. The new tax laws governing capital gains associated with real estate downsizing will spur the industry as families discover that they can use their profits to buy another home, make a variety of investments, and even purchase a timeshare interval—or two. Moreover, many families find themselves with high levels of disposable income as they move through the life cycle. They often inherit estates later in life and, in many cases, complete the children's college tuition payments just as they retire the mortgage. Savvy marketers are already targeting the early years of the next millennium as a period when timeshare will experience a surge. More and more people are expected to start spending money from their investments and pensions.

Photo on page 232:

Brand-name hospitality companies continue to enter and change the timeshare industry. Shown here is an Embassy Vacation Resort by Embassy Suites.

Aerial view of the marina at Marina El Cid Hotel & Yacht Club, part of the El Cid Mega Resort complex in Mazatlan, Mexico, a privately owned, mixed-use resort complex that includes hotels, timeshare projects, single-family and multifamily homes, restaurants, a multifloor discothèque, spa, and extensive recreational facilities.

In addition, many of today's baby boomers and successful Generation X-ers are cash-rich but time poor. Peter Yesawich of Yesawich, Pepperdine & Brown in Orlando, Florida, a firm that tracks recreational trends, notes that time has become the new currency of the millennium and that many complain there is not enough of it. For that reason, consumers find it difficult to schedule vacations. Only one in five adults took a vacation of five nights or more last year, researchers say. Many households have dual incomes but suffer from "time poverty." According to John Russell, president and CEO of RCI's global operations, the dearth of free time means that dual-income households often do not take vacations of a week or two's duration but instead opt for shorter, more frequent, and more varied trips, some within 300 miles of home. The more flexible nature of today's timeshare products accommodates contemporary leisure patterns. Russell adds, "All these trends play to our industry."

Brands' Participation and Influence

While today's savvy consumers are short on time, they are long on labels. They can afford the best—and they frequently treat themselves to it. Thus, branding will play an increasingly larger role in the timeshare industry. Consumers look to brands as a way to make safe choices. Many, especially those skeptical of timesharing and sensitive to its former image, would rather choose a brand name than take a chance on a less well-known product. Today, McMullen estimates that brands represent

The architectural style at Sunterra Corporation's Sedona Summit Resort in Sedona, Arizona, reflects the Southwest's physical and cultural landscape.

10 percent of the timeshare inventory, but that figure is expected to increase dramatically. The transformation will be similar to that experienced by the hotel industry 20 years ago. At that time, only a few hotels were branded; today, more than 75 percent of hotels are brands.

Realizing it had strong brand-name recognition, the Toronto-based Four Seasons Hotels and Resorts entered the timeshare business several years ago. Anthony Sharp, executive vice president, notes that the Four Seasons moniker definitely enhances the status of a vacation-ownership development. He explains, "People know our name and like our product. We have very high standards and people recognize that."

Four Seasons began selling timeshare at the Four Seasons Aviara Resort Club in Carlsbad, California, near San Diego, where it is planning 240 villas in three separate communities. At Aviara, which is adjacent to a 330-room Four Seasons Resort, two-bedroom units total 1,670 square feet compared with the more typical 1,300 square feet. In keeping with the image of the Four Seasons brand, the furnishings are the same as or at a comparable level with those in the company's one-bedroom suites at Four Seasons Hotels—which, Sharp says, is a major selling point. The brand strategy is working: sales have been so strong that prices have increased by 45 percent to the range of $23,000 to $29,000.

Timeshare companies themselves can create their own brand identifications, provided that they attain sufficient critical mass, adds Jeffrey A. Adler, president and cochief executive officer of Vistana Development. He adds, "Our belief today is that, in the future, timeshare is going to be a lot like the hotel business, with three to five large branded players and plenty of room for independent players." In addition to providing credibility and ensuring consumer comfort with the timeshare concept, brands in the timeshare business build customer loyalty and gain opportunities for cross-marketing with the brands' other products.

Market and Product Segmentation

In timeshare, as with so many other products, one size does not fit all. Therefore, in the years ahead, timeshare companies will become increasingly segmented, offering multiple product and price levels. Each level may involve more than the physical lodging product. For example, products may be segmented around different levels of service.

Segmentation will bring on different products, at different levels, with fewer or more amenities, lower marketing and sales costs, and other benefits. Timeshare developers will eventually resemble hospitality companies that offer different types of hotels for different types of travelers. (The accompanying feature box discusses trends in timeshare product offerings.)

For example, Vistana Development built its first Hampton Vacation Resort in Orlando, where it operates a major timeshare project. It has also completed an Embassy Vacation Resort in Myrtle Beach, South Carolina. "Embassy and Hampton are good-quality products," says Adler. "Embassy is a three-star plus while Hampton is two-star plus." He explains that an interval at Embassy costs $12,000 to $18,000 depending on location while an interval at Hampton falls in the $7,500 range. "We feel the combination of Embassy and Hampton is an exciting opportunity to deliver a product across a broad income spectrum."

Timeshare companies can be expected to appeal to different buyer profiles. For example, Dallas-based Silverleaf Resorts, a public company that vows to become

the Wal-Mart of the timeshare industry, is targeting the value-conscious buyer. Silverleaf's philosophy is to provide high-value and -quality timeshare at an affordable price. The company's average timeshare unit costs about a third less than the industry average. Silverleaf also locates resorts close to major population centers, enabling buyers to drive rather than fly to their timeshare.

The industry will also place greater emphasis on responding to the specific desires of the aging baby boom genera-

Courtesy of The Criterion Group

While San Francisco entered the timeshare business slowly, recent ventures include the Inn at the Opera, a 48-unit urban timeshare.

◆ New Directions

High-end hotel owners and operators are beginning to develop upscale ownership "villas" at their new and existing resorts. At Carmel Valley Ranch, outside Carmel, California, Patriot American Hospitality has designed units that will be sold for month-long rather than week-long intervals. Longer intervals generate a far smaller pool of owners but cater to the highest end of the timeshare market. Orient Express Hotels plans to renovate its La Samanna resort in the French West Indies to include at least ten three- and four-bedroom villas. Designed (complete with kitchens and gourmet chefs) to attract the hotel's highest-end rentals, the villas as a product type will easily accommodate fractional-ownership arrangements.

Resort community developers are increasingly integrating fractional vacation-ownership products into their new mixed-use projects. Intrawest, known for the development of ski-oriented villa resorts such as Whistler-Blackcomb in British Columbia and Tremblant near Montreal, sees vacation ownership as an integral part of the village concept. Through its vacation-ownership division called Intrawest Resort Ownership Company (IROC), Intrawest has incorporated Club Intrawest—a point-based system—into a growing number of the company's locations.

"There are several reasons that vacation ownership works so well within the resort village," says Jim Gibbons, president of IROC. "There is tremendous opportunity for joint marketing—potential customers who do not purchase vacation ownership may well be interested in purchasing our other real estate products or simply vacationing at the resort. Vacation ownership also expands the market for high-end locations by providing a more affordable alternative, and it encourages year-round occupancy in more seasonal locations." He continues, "We definitely see a demand for vacation ownership within the resort village, and I believe that demand will follow as we expand into new desert and golf-oriented locations."

In keeping with a fast-paced corporate world, travelers and timeshare consumers are looking for flexibility and convenience in their short-term vacations as well as a spectrum of options and amenities, including technology linking them with the corporate office, that permits long-term vacations. As a result, timeshare is evolving along several dimensions in response to expanding markets.

Companies such as Seattle-based Trendwest are focusing primarily on a single region and targeting drive-to, flexible resorts for quick, convenient getaways. Other timeshare properties are undergoing development as true destination resorts that offer more and better amenities such as pools, tennis, water parks, health clubs, spas, and golf. Signifi-

tion. Randy Nakagawa, marketing director at Grand Pacific Resorts, which has developed seven resorts in California and Nevada, notes that many baby boomers began their families later in life. Now, when boomers take a vacation, they want to bring along their children. "So we're offering two-bedroom units to accommodate them," he explains. "Our new resort in Carlsbad has more two-bedroom units —about a 60-to-40 mix—compared with our resorts of several years ago, when we had more one-bedrooms."

Colocating with Hotel Operations

After more than two decades in the business, timeshare developers will become more attuned to the fact that consumers are buying a lifetime of vacation experiences —not merely one week. Accordingly, developers will devote greater effort to making the vacation experience more memorable regardless of market segment.

In keeping with the understanding that consumers are buying a vacation experience, analysts predict more cooperation between hospitality companies and timeshare developers—both to ensure a consistent-quality product and to take advantage of the synergies possible between the two industries (as described in chapter 3). A colocated hotel and timeshare project permits both facilities to share amenities such as a golf course and health spa, to say nothing of support services, including laundry. Food and beverage operations would also benefit in that one kitchen could serve both hotel and time-

cantly, the trend in upgraded amenities also extends to the units themselves. New technology (such as telephone/fax/Internet access) and office space within units as well as on-call secretarial support cater to longer stays and professional-level customers. Some amenities reflect the expansion of the market's upper end, such as second bedrooms designed as dedicated guest or nanny suites (not as lockoffs), separate his-and-hers dressing areas, stocked wine racks and libraries, and private splash pools.

Timeshare consumers, as with all hospitality consumers, are looking for cultural and geographic diversity in their vacations. While waterfront and ski locations will likely continue to be the most popular destinations, the next decade should see demand for new and varied locations around the world along with demand for resorts designed and operated with the needs of the environment in mind. Ecotourism, virtually unknown a decade ago, is one of the fastest-growing segments of the resort market. This trend opens up possibilities in areas around the world with proximity to significant cultural and natural resources. Locations in Central and South America are the most logical starting point for U.S.-based companies.

With self-improvement high on most consumers' lists of priorities, spa and wellness-focused resorts may see strong growth. And golf seems to have a never-ending appeal for consumers worldwide; as a result, resorts that cater to golfers should also see continued development. Several companies are exploring the possibility of adding luxury villas to existing golf clubhouse facilities both to respond to demand for short-term stays and to help sell high-end memberships. This trend might easily extend to timeshare in the near future. Resorts linked to golf or tennis academies—such as MVCI's Faldo Golf Institute in Orlando—are another significant new product type.

There is also a growing focus on the expanded, multiuse resort in which timeshare plays a role in a village, town center, or urban entertainment complex. Some resort communities, such as Amelia Island in Florida, are pursuing plans to combine timeshare and traditionally owned condominiums.

As resort developers amass capital and gain ever-deepening expertise through consolidations in the hospitality and timeshare industries, they can be expected to develop destination resorts worldwide that provide something for everyone. Without question, the timeshare industry will continue to grow.

Source: John F. Eller, "New Directions for Today's Timeshare Resorts," in *Urban Land* Timeshare Supplement, August 1998, p. 11.

---

share guests—an appealing possibility given that most hotel room service operations typically lose money. At the same time, thanks to promotions such as frequent guest awards and high-tech flourishes such as international reservations systems, the hospitality industry is expected to contribute significantly to the sales and marketing efforts of timeshare developments.

Not surprisingly, many traditional hotel developers are eyeing timeshare as either an addition to a traditional hotel or a stand-alone project, with 50 or 60 units in regional resort areas.

Increasing Flexibility

One of the reasons for the explosion in timeshare over the past several years is the product's increasing flexibility, a char-acteristic highly valued by the marketplace. More and more, timeshare operators encourage customers to purchase time that fits their specific vacation needs. Moreover, as national trends point to a preference for shorter, more frequent vacations, visionaries are allowing owners to make innovative use of the core week interval that has been an industry mainstay since the 1970s. Timeshare companies such as Fairfield Communities, Inc., and the Disney Vacation Club (DVC) have led the way in developing the highly flexible point systems and vacation clubs described in chapter 3.

No Tech to High Tech

As noted in chapter 6, the expense, inefficiency, and frequent consumer suspicion associated with the traditional methods of selling timeshare intervals have spurred the industry to explore new and less expensive marketing approaches. Experts predict that well-targeted relationship marketing and data-based marketing will offer developers more bang for their buck and thus supplant the high-pressure sales tactics that tainted the industry in its early years.

As for specific markets, when most people in the timesharing industry are asked to describe their target market, they say "families." Researchers, however, respond otherwise. In fact, an analysis by RCI Consulting indicates that 60 percent of timeshare owners are empty nesters. Statistics show that the average age of a timeshare buyer is 54 years old, eight years older than the buyer of two decades ago. Armed with such information, timeshare marketers and developers must necessarily create the tools for more precisely targeting their markets.

New sales approaches are aimed at increasing closing rates and reducing the percentage of rescissions. In the past, most companies simply bid farewell to prospects who declined to purchase a vacation-ownership interval. Today, many in the industry are engaging in more follow-up with the hope of making buyers out of prospects who have seen the sales presentation.

Finally, as discussed in chapter 4, the Internet will play an increasingly important role in timeshare marketing and re-sales by providing busy people with a convenient way to browse timeshare offerings.

Capitalizing on the "Urban Experience"

In the future, timeshare will no longer be confined to resort areas—or a few selected major cities. As discussed in chapter 3, after limiting itself to exotic locales, the industry has begun to recognize the market appeal of some of the nation's and the world's great cities, such as Chicago, Boston, New York City, and San Francisco.

The move to urban timeshare is another attempt to appeal to a different clientele—individuals or couples that use the product for special treks to the city for a night out with friends, an evening at the symphony, or several days of shopping. "The urban setting allows us to target a different owner profile than, say, a resort in Orlando," says Michael Kosmin, project director for the Suites at Fisherman's Wharf in San Francisco, an urban timeshare project. "Most of our owners will

Courtesy of Club Asia International

Exotic settings, such as that distinguishing the Holiday Inn Resort at Damai Lagoon in Indonesia, appeal to the adventure traveler.

Bicycling is one of the many activities enjoyed by vacationers looking for an active holiday at Pacific Shores Nature Resort on Vancouver Island, British Columbia.

Courtesy of Pacific Shores Nature Resort

be those who love the city life, but live in the suburbs."

Preliminary results from several urban timeshare products indicate tremendous success. In Boston, Marriott's Vacation Club International (MVCI) spent $25 million renovating the 150-year-old Custom House Tower, turning the property into 80 one-bedroom units initially offered for $12,000 to $16,000 per interval. Within weeks of launching its sales effort, Marriott discovered that many of the buyers —several of whom purchased multiple timeshares—were corporations dissatisfied with paying $250 to $275 a night at Boston hotels—if they could even get a room. In New York's Manhattan Club, a 250-unit urban timeshare project in the former Park Central Hotel near Carnegie Hall, buyers come from all over the world as well as from within 90 miles of New York City—despite prices of $35,000 per week for 1,100 square feet. Such success has spurred timeshare developers to scour more metropolitan areas for more urban timeshare locations.

International Expansion

"Globalization is a big story, with companies doing projects in new areas and the larger companies going offshore," says Jan Wyatt, vice president/marketing at Interval International. "Many more buyers are buying in markets where they don't necessarily reside." The United States and Europe have been the traditional areas of development, accounting for about 70 percent of today's timeshare properties. Observers say, however, that the industry will shift its focus to Asia, South America, India, Canada, Mexico, the Middle East, and the Caribbean.

Shell Vacations, for instance, is eyeing India, Asia, and other locations for possible development. Marriott Vacation Club has opened its first international site in Marbella, Spain; it plans others worldwide. Westgate Resorts of Orlando is cultivating clients in Brazil, Chile, Argentina, and most Latin American nations.

Westgate is an excellent example of a timeshare company that is thinking globally. The firm has established a network of brokers in almost every Latin American country to serve current owners and to prospect for new ones. "Servicing them has a direct correlation to future sales," notes Tim McLaughlin, director of sales and marketing at Westgate Resorts. "Once you've sold them, you have to take care of them. Our offices in Latin America work

Club La Costa at Marina del Rey, Spain.

like a referral base. We find out who would like what type of product and we can talk with them in their own language in their own country." Westgate is planning an additional 2,300 villas, many of which are geared toward Latin American clientele. "We're building three- and four-bedroom units because Latin Americans travel with extended families—their mothers and fathers, people to watch kids, aunts and uncles, and so forth."

Financing

While flexibility has been pivotal to many aspects of timesharing, it has not extended to one of the industry's central concerns: financing. During the mid-1990s, the timeshare industry was the darling of Wall Street. Companies such as Vistana and Silverlake went public; other firms used the financial wizards to raise money for the purpose of paring down company debt while still others tapped the money spigot for funds.

But Wall Street financing, like real estate, runs in cycles, and the short-lived love affair with the fundamentals of the timeshare industry came to an end by late fall 1998. At that time, the capital markets —roiled by problems with global currencies, concerned about the economies of some third-world countries, and worried that the real estate industry was overbuilding— pulled back from their aggressive financing stance. At about the same time, the stocks of timeshare companies, which had also won Wall Street approval, lost favor, making it difficult for companies to use their stock for further industry consolidations. Several larger industry players exited entirely from the timeshare finance business. While it remains to be seen if market conditions will return to the timeshare bonanza of the mid-1990s, many in the industry expect that Wall Street will soon reexamine its thinking.

Because timeshare is part development, part marketing, and part finance, many financial institutions simply do not understand the timeshare business. Until several years ago, timeshare financing was fairly standard. As the industry has expanded, however, financing has grown more refined —and will continue to do so in the years ahead. The traditional pricing formerly employed for timeshare financing is not necessarily appropriate for all players and financial tiers, and the larger, stronger players have enjoyed easier access to more attractive financing.

Meanwhile, traditional lenders, who are more expensive though more flexible than Wall Street, continue to provide funding to timeshare companies. Yet, timeshare financing is still considered a specialty area. A limited number of active lenders work with the timeshare industry. "If you wanted to finance a timeshare project and walked into a major bank right now, you couldn't get a loan," says Ward of Ward Financial. "Most banks don't have a department that understands the timeshare industry." According to Ward, if more lenders were involved and competing for the timeshare industry's business, the cost of funds would come down.